CW00684610

# DRAMATISTS OF THE RESTORATION.

## D'AVENANT.

### III.

# THE DRAMATIC

## WORKS OF SIR WILLIAM D'AVENANT.

### WITH PREFATORY MEMOIR AND NOTES.

#### VOLUME THE THIRD.

MDCCCLXXIII.

EDINBURGH: WILLIAM PATERSON.
LONDON: H. SOTHERAN & CO.

# CONTENTS.

# THE UNFORTUNATE LOVERS.

*The Vnfortunate Lovers: a Tragedie ; as it was lately acted with great applause at the private House in Black-Fryers ; By His Majesties Servants.*
*The Author Sir William Davenant,*
*Servant to her Majestie*
*London, Printed by R. H. and are to be sold by Francis Coles at his Shop in the Old Bayley, Anno Dom. 1643. 4to.*

*The Vnfortunate Lovers. London Printed for Humphrey Moxely, and are to be sold at his Shop at the Princes armes in St. Paul's Churchyard, 1649. 4to.*

*The Unfortunate Lovers.—In the folio edition of D'avenant's works, 1673.*

"This tragedy," says the *Biographia Britannica*, "founded upon an Italian story, was received very kindly at the time of its appearance, and was often acted after the Restoration. It is somewhat strange that it should be omitted in Mr Langbaine's catalogue of our author's works, notwithstanding it is mentioned by Winstanley, and, which is more, in Mr Langbaine's own catalogue of plays."

The same authority in reference to this play and the tragi-comedy of "Love and Honour," suggests:—"it is very probable that the two following pieces were written some years earlier than they were printed, for it can hardly be supposed that after Mr D'avenant had fallen so grievously under the displeasure of the Parliament he could have any great intercourse with his stationer at London; so that it is more likely these plays having been formerly acted with applause, were now printed in the absence, though not without the consent, of the author."

"Both these plays," it is further remarked, "are without any testimonies of the author's friends before them, because published at a time when, perhaps, there were not many who were inclined to inform the world that they *were* his friends."

Pepys, in his diary, has this entry, "8th April 1668. With Lord Brouncker to the Duke of York's playhouse, where we saw 'The Unfortunate Lovers,'—an extraordinary play."

There were frequent subsequent repetitions of it, and it would seem to have been a favourite stock play, and much relished by the public. Geneste, in his account of the English stage, in noticing its performance on the 3d December in the same year, remarks, "It is on the whole a good tragedy."

The text of the first and second editions are identical, but the third, included in the folio edition of 1673, has undergone considerable alteration and curtailment. In the present instance, as before, the original text has been adopted.

Among the *dramatis personæ* the folio has " Frisklin " in place of " Friskin," and " Fibbia " is there called " Orna, Cousin to Amaranta." Further, to render the play more acceptable to the growing taste for the introduction of music into dramatic entertainments, a short dialogue to enable Fibbia to sing a song about " Love's Lottery " has been interpolated in the first scene of the third act. This interpolation will now be found at the end of the play.

The dedication which follows prefaces the first and second editions only, and, as it does not emanate from the pen of D'Avenant himself, affords confirmation of the conjectures of the *Biographia Britannica.*

The nobleman to whom this dedication is addressed was the second son of the lady to whom Sir Philip Sidney inscribed his Arcadia, and in memory of whom Ben Jonson composed the following lines :—

> " Underneath this marble hearse
> Lies the subject of all verse—
> Sidney's sister, Pembroke's mother ;
> Death ere thou has slain another,
> Wise, and fair, and good as she,
> Time shall throw a dart at thee.
> Marble piles let no man raise
> To her name, for after dayes,
> Some kind woman born as she,
> Reading this, like Niobe,
> Shall turn statue, and become
> Both her mourner and her tomb." *

Mary Sydney, daughter of Sir Henry Sydney, K.G., and sister of Sir Philip Sydney, was the third wife of Henry, second Earl of Pembroke, who died at Wilton, the family seat, upon the 19th day of January 1600-1, and was buried in the Cathedral of Salisbury. The

* The last six lines are supposed to have been cancelled by Jonson, "on account ", in the opinion of Sir Walter Scott, " of the outrageous false wit with which they disgrace the commencement." —See *Osborne's* " Secret History of the Court of James I.," reprinted, Edinburgh, 1811, vol. i., p. 225, in which these verses are preserved entire.

Countess survived her husband for many years, and, departing this life in her house at Aldersgate Street, London, her remains were removed to Salisbury, where they were placed in the cathedral beside those of her husband.

Of this marriage there were two sons, William and Philip. The latter was created Earl of Montgomery by James, who also honoured him with the Garter. According to Arthur Wilson, his Majesty "either not finding him suitable to his *humours* or *affections*, or seeing another *object* ' more ' delightful,"* adopted in his stead Robert Carr, better known as Earl of Somerset, and the husband of Lady Katherine Howard of infamous memory. Upon the demise of his brother William, third Earl of Pembroke, at his house called Bayards Castle, in the city of London, April 10, 1630, without surviving issue by his wife,—a daughter of Gilbert, Earl of Shrewsbury,— Philip succeeded to his honours and estates. There is a remarkable anecdote, to be found in Clarendon, connected with Lord Pembroke's death, worthy of notice. It was prognosticated that he would not outlive his fiftieth year. The prognosticator was "his tutor Sandford," who seems to have cast his nativity. Some friends of the Earl, persons of quality, meeting at Maidenhead, drank the health of the Earl, upon which another of them said, "that he believed his Lord was very merry, for he had now outlived the day which his tutor Sandford had prognosticated upon his nativity he would not outlive ; but he had done it now, for that was his birthday, which had completed his age of fifty years. The next morning by the time they came to Colebrook, they met with the news of his death." This singular story .resembles the anecdote of the warning said to have been given to the second Lord Lyttleton, who had a party assembled on the day assigned for his death, and who, supposing the hour was past—some friends having put forward the clock—observed "he had jockied the ghost," and, retiring to the adjoining apartment, was found dead on his bed.

The character of Pembroke, by Clarendon, is said by Walpole to have been "one of the best drawn" of his

* "History of Great Britain," London, 1653, folio, p. 54.

portraits. Wood, "Fasti," vol. i., describes him "as the very picture and *viva effigies* of nobility. The person was rather majestic than elegant, and his presence, whether quiet or in motion, was full of stately gravity. The mind was purely heroic, often stout, but never disloyal, and so vehement an opponent of the Spaniard, that when that match fell under consideration in the latter end of the reign of James I., he would sometimes rise to the trepidation of that king, yet kept in favour still; for his Majesty knew plain dealing as a power in all men, so was it in a privy counsellor an ornamental duty, and the same trueheartedness commended him to Charles I."

Osborne, Master of the Horse, and afterwards Chamberlain to Lord Montgomery, after devoting, in his memoirs, some pages to his lordship, says he was "a man carressed by King James for his handsome face, which kept him not long company, leaving little behind it so acceptable as to render him fit society for any body but himselfe, and such bookes as posterity may find ordinarily dedicated to him, which might yet have prompted his understanding to a more candid proceeding than he used at Oxford, where he exercised greater passion against learning, that had by teaching books to speak English endeavoured to make him wiser, than he did towards Ramsay, who, by switching him on the face at Croydon, rendered him ridiculous." *

James, whose aversion from duelling is notorious, was the only person who approved of the pusillaninous conduct of his well-featured favourite. He was raised to the peerage in token of the Monarch's approbation of his adoption of the royal maxim, *Beati Pacifici,* Blessed are the Peaceful. Ramsay, for appearance sake, and to appease the English nobility, was banished the Court for a short time, and, upon his return, was presented as Viscount Haddington of the kingdom of Scotland. Thus Philip got his peerage for submitting to be switched, and Ramsay his for switching him. In 1620, Ramsay was created Earl of Holderness in England.

The Countess of Pembroke, Montgomery's mother, could not be reconciled to this pacific mode of pocketing an affront, respecting which Osborne remarks, " I have

* P. 219.

been told, the mother of Herbert tore her hair at the report of her son's dishonour, who, I am confident upon a like opportunity, would have ransom'd her own repute, if she had not redeemed her countrie's. She was that sister of Sir Philip Sidney to whom he addressed his Arcadia, and of whom he had no other advantage than what he received from that partiall benevolence of fortune, in making him a man; which yet she did, in some judgments, recompense in beauty."

Sir Egerton Brydges reprinted in an elegant form the poems written by the Right Honourable the Earl of Pembroke, Lord Stewart of His Majestie's Household, whereof many of which are answered, by way of repartee, by Sir Benjamin Ruddyer Knight,—being several distinct poems, written by them occasionally and apart, London, 1660, — and, in commenting on their merit, remarks that Pembroke "was an infant when his uncle, Sir Philip Sydney, died; but he must have imbibed from his mother much of that uncle's romantic cast of mind. Thence he must have learned not only the chivalrous spirit by which both the life and the writings of Sir Philip were inspired, but a veneration of that genius and those forms by which Spencer had clothed, in the most powerful verse, all the gorgeous imagery of such a romantic cast of intellect."[*]

These poems had been preserved in manuscript by Christian, Countess Dowager of Devonshire, for whom his lordship had formed a platonic[†] attachment, and, more than thirty years after the death of the writer, were given for publication to Donne, usually called Dunne, a son of Dr. Donne, the famous Dean of St. Paul's. As regards these he used no discrimination, but included other verses found in the lady's common-place book. From Donne's preface, it appears that the sonnets were "set" by the "greatest masters of music."

The new Earl of Pembroke presents a remarkable contrast to his accomplished brother. He had not a particle of the chivalrous feelings either of his paternal or maternal ancestors. Although, as Chancellor of the

[*] Poems of William Herbert, third Earl of Pembroke, K.G. Second edition, London, 1817, 12mo. Preface p. xxi.
[†] See preface to the Platonic Lovers in our second volume.

University of Oxford, he had taken an oath to defend its
privileges, he joined with the Presbyterians in their
attempt to abrogate them.   "In private life," says
Gilpin, "he was vicious, ignorant, and unlettered in a
surprising degree."   In public his character was stained
with ingratitude and tergiversation, as appears in the
noble historian of those unfortunate times.   This worth-
less man and his unhappy lady lived nearly twenty years
together.   During the latter part of his life, he became
so dissolute that she was obliged to leave him."

The Countess was Anne, daughter and heiress of
George, Earl of Cumberland—the representative of the
Shepherd Earl—and widow of Richard, Earl of Dorset.
She survived her second husband, to whom she had
given her hand upon the 3rd June 1630, many years,
and died at the advanced age of eighty-seven upon the
22nd March 1675, having had no issue by either of her
espousals.*

Sir Walter Scott observes, that " this unworthy nobleman had no qualities to recommend him as a royal
favourite, saving two, any one of which would have made
him acceptable to James.   These were comeliness of person and indefatigable zeal in hunting.   His character was
that of Squire Western, choleric, boisterous, illiterate, sel-
fish, absurd, and cowardly.   He was besides a profligate, a
gambler, and, above all, an ungrateful rebel to the son of
the prince who raised him, as he adhered with great
vehemence to the cause of the Parliament and afterwards
to that of Cromwell."   In this ingratitude to his
monarch he was not unlike his namesake, Philip Lord
Wharton, one of the masquers in Britannia Triumphans,†
who persecuted Strafford and Laud, and allied himself to
the Great Protector, taking good care after his death
to suit himself to the times that he foresaw must
follow.   The Earl of Pembroke and Montgomery died
upon the 23rd January 1649, having had by his first
wife Susan, daughter of Edward Vere of Oxford, seven
sons and three daughters.   His Lordship is the direct

* See Brydges' edition of Collins, vol. iii., London 1812. 8vo,
pp. 135 to 139.
* See our vol ii., p. 295.

ancestor of the present Earls of Pembroke and Montgomery, and Carnarvon. *

Inigo Jones who assisted D'Avenant in the mechanical portion of the Masques seems to have incurred the dislike of the Earl. Lord Orford, in his Anecdotes of Painting, informs his readers that "in the Harleian Library was an edition of Stonehenge which previously belonged to the Earl, and the margins of which were full of strange notes written by him, not on the work but on the author or any thing else. I have another commonplace book, if one may call it so of Earl Philip—the life of Sir Thomas More. In the Stonehenge are memorandums, jokes, witticisms, and abuse on several persons, particularly on Cromwell and his daughters, and on Inigo, whom his Lordship calls Iniquity Jones, and says he had £16,000 for keeping the king's houses in repair.

"Earl Philip's resentment to Jones was probably occasioned by some disagreement while the latter was employed at Wilton. There he built the noble front and the grotto at the end of the water."

It seems strange that D'Avenant should have selected such a man as Philip, Earl of Pembroke and Montgomery as the fitting patron of a drama, the beauties of which, from what posterity has learned of him, he was altogether unable to appreciate, and, it is still more wonderful that he should have selected as its patron an opponent of the cause he served. The dedication, which is signed W.H., suggests that it did not emanate from him, but was the device of some satellite of the Herberts, who was desirous of propitiating the wealthy nobleman by ascribing to him excellences he never possessed. It appeared only in the two early impressions of the play in

* Lord Orford must have fallen into error as to the name of the book on which these notes were written, for Pembroke died previous to the publication of Jones' work, which was first published by Mr John Webb, in small folio, in 1655, after the death of Jones in 1652. As Lord Orford had in his own possession a common-place book of Pembroke's, he must have been familiar with the Earl's calligraphy, so that it was not likely he could mistake the hand-writing, although he might the name of the work in which they were written.

See introduction to Britannia Triumphans in our second volume.

4to, but was omitted in the collected folio edition of
our Poet's works.  The first edition of 1643 was wholly
printed from the acting copy without the knowledge of
the author, who was at the time not engaged in providing amusement for the factious citizens of London, but
as a gallant and consistent gentleman endeavouring to
serve the crown, under the noblest cavalier that ever
bore the name of Cavendish.

The part of Arthiopa was originally sustained by the
boy-actress, Edward Kynaston.  See further respecting
Kynaston in the Memoir of D'Avenant, vol. i. page lxv.

### THE UNFORTUNATE LOVERS.

*The Prologue spoken at Black-Friars.*

WERE you but half so humble to confess,
As you are wise to know your happiness ;
Our author would not grieve to see you sit
Ruling, with such unquestion'd power, his wit :
What would I give, that I could still preserve
My loyalty to him, and yet deserve
Your kind opinion, by revealing now
The cause of that great storm which clouds his brow,
And his close murmurs, which since meant to you,
I cannot think, or mannerly or true ?
Well ; I begin to be resolv'd, and let
My melancholy tragic Monsieur fret ;
Let him the several harmless weapons use
Of that all daring trifle called his Muse ;
Yet I'll inform you, what this very day,
Twice before witness, I have heard him say.
Which is, that you are grown excessive proud,
For ten times more of wit, than was allow'd
Your silly ancestors in twenty year,
Y' expect should in two hours be given you here ;
For they, he swears, to th' Theatre would come
Ere they had din'd to take up the best room ;
There sit on benches, not adorn'd with mats,
And graciously did vail their high-crowned hats
To every half dress'd Player,* as he still
Through th' hangings peep'd to see how th' house
    did fill.
Good easy judging souls, with what delight

* "To vail bonnet," which occurs in the Plays of Edward II.,
Edward III., and George-a-Green, signifies to "uncover in
submission."

They would expect a jig, or target fight,
A furious tale of Troy, which they ne'er thought
Was weakly written,,so 'twere strongly sought ;
Laught at a clinch,* the shadow of a jest,
And cry a passing good one, I protest.
Such dull and humble-witted people were
Even your fore-fathers, whom we govern'd here ;
And such had you been too he swears, had not
The poets taught you how t'unweave the plot,
And tract the winding scenes, taught you to admit
What was true sense, not what did sound like wit.
Thus they have arm'd you 'gainst themselves to
  fight,
Made strong and mischievous from what they write ;
You have been lately highly feasted here
With two great wits, that grac'd our Theatre.
But, if to feed you often with delight,
Will more corrupt than mend your appetite ;
He vows to use you, which he much abhors,
As others did your homely Ancestors.

  * A witty saying, or repartee. —*Howell's Lex. Tet.*

## THE PERSONS IN THE TRAGEDY.

HEILDEBRAND, *King of the Lombards.*
ASCOLI, *Prince of Verona.*
ALTOPHIL, *A Duke and General.*
RANGONE, *A Count, Captain of the Guard to Ascoli.*
GALEOTTO, *A politic stout ambitious favourite to Ascoli.*
MORELLO, *A Gentleman, and creature to Galeotto.*
GANDOLPHO, *Brother to Morello, Captain of the Fort in Verona.*
RAMPINO, *A young gallant Soldier, much indebted and vexed by Creditors.*
BRUSCO, *An old Captain, his companion.*
HIRCO, *A Soldier, companion to them both.*
FRISKIN, *An ambitious Tailor, to whom Rampino owes money.*
ARTHIOPA, *Mistress to Altophil.*
AMARANTA, *Her Rival, daughter to Galeotto.*
FIBBIA, *A precise widow, to whom also Rampino is indebted.*

*A Carthusian.    Soldiers of Heildebrand.*
*The Guard to Ascoli.*

*The Scene :* VERONA.

# THE UNFORTUNATE LOVERS.

## ACT I. SCENE I.

### *Enter* RAMPINO, BRUSCO, HIRCO.

RAM. Come, gentlemen, I'll shew you the whole
    Court :
Hirco, I think, was never here before.
    BRU. Never ! He takes these o'er-grown babes,
These tender sucking giants of the guard,
For Colonels of Switzerland ; each usher
Of the presence for a famous leader.
    HIR. Yes, of women in the dark.
    RAM. Why dost thou sneak and tread so bash-
    fully
Behind ? Come boldly on ! they'll think thee else
A City-spy that seeks for leave t' arrest.*
    BRU. He looks as if he had a black jack under
His cloak, and came to beg budge at the buttery.
    RAM. Move on! This is the presence, gentlemen !
Hence is your passage to the privy chamber.
You should erect your fingers to your hair,
Which being order'd thus——or, having us'd
Your little Tortoise-combs to titubate†
Your empty heads, you may salute those of
But half a fortune thus with half a face,
The favourite with your entire frame ; here,
He is your idol, your religion else
Will be believ'd heretical.
    HIR. Rampino, walk no farther into sight !

---

\* *Folio*—A City-dun that sues for leave to arrest 'em.
† Qy. Tittivate ?—To dress neatly. *Var. dial.*

Our General's pleasure was, we should not be
Discover'd yet, for fear it chance to make
His coming known : 'Tis sudden and by stealth.

*Enter* ASCOLI, GALEOTTO, AMARANTA, *who whisper*
*together.*

RAM. Young Ascoli, our Prince ! Brusco, retire !
BRU. Since my last visit to the Camp, he's grown
Tall, man ; and he becomes his growth.   We that
Pursue the sullen business of the war,
Long much to shew him to the foe ;  not in his
Perfume and his silks, but iron vest.
There he must change his gentle looks, and learn
To frown.   Men think his courage great.
RAM. Brusco, he will make good in future acts
Of Chivalry men's best belief, and has
A nature uncorrupted yet with exercise
Of guilt.   His ignorance in sin makes all
His errors seem mistakes ; and well
That false Galeotto knows how to subdue
A heart whose innocence is all
The armour of his breast.
BRU. Is that Galeotto his dear favourite ?
RAM. It is.   He was a soldier in his youth,
And had the luck of early victories,
Which rais'd him to a restless pride, such as
He since maintains by wicked arts of Court ;*
The horror of his thoughts ought make him sad,
'Tis a melancholy doth cause him groan
At night, but they're mandrakes' groans and still
Bode death.   Nor is his mirth less dangerous ;
For, like the wanton play of porpoises,
It prophesies a storm, and when he shakes
His foe by the hand 'tis not in kindness but
To reach his pulse, that he may feel how soon

* The accession of Charles evidently caused this word to be
altered to " power " in the *Folio.*

Nature would kill whom he hath long proscrib'd.

BRU. What lady's that his eyes so overlook ?

HIR. I could lie perdue with her all night i'th'
 snow !

RAM. 'Tis fair Amaranta, Galeotto's daughter !
The beauty of her mind shines in her face :
For she is good as fair, and more to urge
Her excellence, her virtues are so great
They overmatch his vice ; but, luckless maid,
She mourns within, and loves the noble Duke,
Our General, ev'n with a sick and waking heart.

ASCO. This news hath much of joy, and some-
 what too
Of wonder in't. Duke Altophil, our General,
So near the town ! stol'n hither to prevent
The triumphs due unto his victory.

GAL. It is your Highness' custom to give trust
To my intelligence, and this hath truth
Enough to merit your belief; but as
You ever have vouchsaf'd your help to make
Me prosperous so I beseech you now
Assist my daughter's pensive love. This Duke
Is high in worth, as in his blood, and may,
If you procure * him, choose her for his wife :
By his alliance so confirm my family,
That I shall need to fear no change of time,
Nor angry fate, but from your princely self.

ASCO. Fair Amaranta, do you love Duke
 Altophil ?
It is a choice so excellent, you need
Not blush to own the passion of your heart.

AMA. Sir, since it was his virtues taught me how
To love, I hope my modesty may give
Me leave still to confess it to the world.

ASCO. His judgment seldom harbours near his
 eyes,

* Provoke.—*Folio.*

III. B

If he can look on so much beauty, and
Not wish to make it his.    But, gentle maid,
Trust me I shall persuade him to this happiness
With all my pow'r and skill!

     AMA. It is a favour that
My prayer shall endeavour to requite,
Though I am doubtful how to own it from
Mine own doubts.

     GAL. Amaranta, peace!
I am the elder beggar, Sir, and by
Continual practice want no confidence
To ask * your help at all necessities.

     ASCO. This, Galeotto, is a kindness to myself:
I long to see those nuptials consummate,
Where each so much deserves the other's love.
Let's in to make enquiry of the cause,
Why his arrival is so much conceal'd.

         [*Exeunt Ascoli, Galeotto, Amaranta.*

     BRU. But why, Rampino, since this lady is
So rarely qualified, and being heir
To all her father's wealth and hopes, doth not
Our general make her lawful mistress of his bed?

     RAM. The cause is evident: for his
Affections and his faith already are
Engag'd unto the beautiful Arthiopa.

     BRU. Arthiopa! the daughter of our old
Dead General? Alas! his fame was greater
Than his fortune, for he left her poor.

     RAM. Most true!
So poor, she was constrain'd to live conceal'd
Here in Verona, and become, 'tis thought,
Her lover's chaste and thankful pensioner;
And you have heard what strange reports were oft
Disperst into our camp of her disloyalty:
Some saucily would style it lust, and those
Were punish'd for their loose and slippery tongues.

         * Crave. *Folio.*

BRU. It seems then, our Duke Altophil retains
Her still in's breast with's former confidence.

RAM. She grows the faster to his heart, for he
Had strong suspicions to believe these tales
By Galeotto forg'd, who strives, it seems,
By this poor lady's infamy, to make
More easy room for his fair daughter's love!

HIR. O, how full of mischief are these wise men!

BRU. It would be long, Hirco, ere we could squeeze
Such another plot out of thy lean head.

RAM. Never! though it were crushed to a circumference
So small that he might make a helmet of
A hazle nut.

HIR. Well, gentlemen! you'll find
Our General an angry man ere night;
Take that from my intelligence, though I
Receiv'd it since we came to town i'th' streets!

BRU. How, Hirco? Come, the news!

HIR. The lady that
You call Arthiopa, this morning, was
Arrested in her chamber by the officers
Of the purgation-house, and 's thither sent
To suffer for unchastity!

RAM. The devil made thee drunk with spirit of sulphur.

HIR. I'm sure this is the people's language now,
And talk'd on too, by children two foot high.
And more; three witnesses, whom they believe
Brib'd and suborn'd, have all depos'd against
Her maiden-head; that was the phrase.

RAM. Here will we knock * ere long. Let them that have
No money take up plasters upon trust.

* Here will be knocks. — *Folio.*

BRU. Away! let's to Saint Laurence Port: it
  was our
General's will we should be expected there.
                                    [*Exeunt omnes.*

*Enter* GALLEOTTO, MORELLO.

GAL. Morello, I'm subdu'd with thy fine arts;
Thou art as swift to execute as to
Contrive.   How did our witnesses behave
Themselves when they beheld Arthiopa?
    MO. Good faith, my Lord, [like] valiant rogues
      that had
Full oft o'ercome their consciences before;
And, therefore to resist her blushes, thought
It but an easy victory.   The Articles
Were many they had t'accuse her chastity;
Which they both read and swore to in a breath,
And wish'd them longer for your Lordship's sake!
Protesting their good natures checkt them, 'cause
They earn'd their money with so little pains.
    GAL. How did the governors o' th' severe house
Digest th' employment my request did lay
Upon their gravity?
    MO.                    They are a kind
Of more solemn villains; and, like old fishes,
Choose to demur and swim about the bait
Awhile, ere they would catch what afterwards
They swallow'd greedily.
    GAL. I thank their tenderness!
    MO. It seem'd at first as if her innocence
And beauty would pervert their justice to
Rebel against your Lordship's power.
But then, presuming pity was a little too
Effeminate for ancient magistrates,
They thought upon your gold, and had decreed
Her to the whip, but that I interpos'd
To mitigate their purchas'd wrath!

GAL. 'Twas safely done, for such severity
Would too much exasperate her friends.

MOR. Their sentence is, she must from that
Devout chaste college march, vested in white,
And with a purifying taper in her hand,
To the Cathedral Church !

GAL. If Altophil do breed his honour with
Strict discipline, or have but any taste
Of wisdom in her love, this imputation will
Divorce him from her eyes.   My Amaranta then
Hath no impediment to terrify her hopes.
These mischiefs make me more indebted
To my brain, in that they are obscurely laid,
And I their guilty author am unknown.

### *Enter* AMARANTA.

AMA. O, sir, if either tears, or fervent prayers
Can move you to compassion, show it now !
My woman, half depriv'd of breath with her
Astonishment and haste, imperfectly
Hath told me news so sad, would make a fierce
Young Thracian soldier weep before his bride.

GAL. This news were sad indeed !   What is it ?
   Is it, hoh ?
Or if it be too fearful for [thy] speech
Bring here thy lute and breathe it in a song.

AMA. My virtuous rival, poor Arthiopa,
Is in distress ; she suffers shame, such vile
Abuse, as lips well taught will blush to utter of
Afflicted enemies.

GAL. What is this to me ?

AMA. Sir, she's guiltlessly betray'd ;
I'll gage my yet unspotted fame, nay, all
The treasures of my soul, she's most innocent :
Therefore I beg you would employ your power
To take her from the rigour of the law,
And punish those that have perverted it

To exercise their cruelty!

GAL. Away! thou meek religious fool, get thee
    to
Thy closet: go! and with thy needle form
In shadow'd works some ruthful lover's death,
Then weep the silly story out, until
Thy tears stain all thy silk! Hence, from my sight!

AMA. Alas! thou wrong'd Arthiopa! Thou canst
Not hope for truer grief than mine,
When other virgins shall lament thy death. [Exit.

GAL. Morello! haste, and lay out several spies
For Altophil's approach, and bring me word
To whom his earliest visits are addrest. [Exeunt.

Enter ALTOPHIL, RAMPINO, BRUSCO, HIRCO.

ALT. Hah! gone? There's treachery of State in
    this!
From her small solitary mansion ta'en,
Where she liv'd cloister'd up, cag'd like a bird,
To mourn my absence in a pensive song;
Forc'd thence, and by stern officers:
Hirco, what did the people say?

HIR. I know not, sir,
There is no trusting to their whisperings;
Their murmurs are but noise, uncertain, sir,
And not to be believ'd!

ALT. Good soldier, speak!
Deal justly with my griefs: what did they say?

HIR. Why, sir, they talk'd as if—pray do not
    hear't—
All they discourse is out of rage or drink.

ALT. I pray thee vex me not with thy o'erwise
Ill-manner'd love. It is not safe; what did they
    say?

RAM. 'Slight, tell the General!

HIR. Why, if you needs will know, 'tis given out
She was convey'd to the holy college, sir;

The new purgation house, where witnesses
Have severally depos'd she was unchaste.

ALT. Blisters and rottenness consume thy tongue!
Villain! thou hast talk'd away thy life.
[*Draws upon him.*

BRU. Oh! hold sir, hold! can you enforce
A slander from him, and then punish it
Yourself? Your sword upon your vassal too!

HIR. If rogues will bear false witness, can I
    help't?
Cause they lose their souls, must I lose my life?

RAM. Galeotto, sir, the favourite may be,
With argument enough, suspected chief
In this conspiracy.

ALT.                       Thou dost receive
My jealous fears with truth too naked,
And evident to be conceal'd. What is
That holy college he's in madness nam'd?

RAM. A place to whip offenders for their lust.

ALT. O heavens! why is your business so remote
And high, that you can take no notice of
Such wrongs as these? Was this the house thought
    fit
To entertain Arthiopa? Furies
And fiends ascend! take up your dwelling here:
For all this goodly city I'll convert
Into one spreading fume—a fire so large
And hot, shall make the rivers seethe, and seas
To boil without the trouble of a storm.

RAM. Kill all you meet, and burn the rest that are
Imprison'd or asleep.*

BRU. Let's think of rifling first, then fire shops
    after.
Though I must never wear silks, I do not like
Flame-colour'd taffeta.

* These two lines are, in the folio, given to Altophil, the next
three to Rampino, and the following two to Hirco.

HIR. I'ld fain to the mercers too,
And fall a measuring with my iron yard.

ALT. Why, Brusco, dost thou stand so lamely*
    now ?
When I perceive my injuries so great,
Our patience will be held no virtue but a sin.
Draw up the scatter'd troops that winter'd here
Since the last siege.

BRU. O sir! ease your distemper with
Your wiser thoughts ; the prince, you know's, in
    town ;
He's gracious, and will do you right.   Lose not
The fame your noble youth hath justly gain'd
With one rash act, which must be treason call'd
And so interpreted by all the Court:
Then think what danger a commotion here
Would urge, since Heildebrand, the Lombard's
    King,
Our watchful enemy, is now within
Ten leagues strongly encamp'd.

*Enter a* CARTHUSIAN, ARTHIOPA, *who is held by him,
clothed in white, a taper in her hand, people and
boys following her.*

ALT. What means this sad and bashful spectacle,
My friends ?   What penitential lady's that
You wait on with such needless courtesy ?
You sir, speak, can you tell ? are you all dumb ?
          *[They run from him as afraid.*
Here's one whose habit promises so much
Civility as will afford me a reply.
          *[Speaks to the Carthusian.*
Pray, Sir, instruct me in this lady's name !
And what's the cause her penance is expos'd
Thus to the public view ?

RAM. He's a Carthusian, and, by's order, tied

          * Tamely. --*Folio.*

To a concealment of his tongue.   He
Must not speak.

   ALT. Sure I have had some knowledge of her face!
   ART. 'Tis Altophil, the Lord of all my vows !
Sweet Heaven let fall a cloud and hide me in't,
That my shame, since undeserv'd, may be
Conceal'd from all but you.   I ask not for
Revenge from men : their justice I have felt
So cruel on myself, that I not dare
Write it to those who thus have injur'd me !
   ALT. Mine eyes have been too bold.
It is not fit they should discover her
In so much shame : yet it must be she.
O heart ! heart ! if ever thou wert made for love,
Love would  have weaved  thy strings  not of such
    tough
And stubborn wire, but silk, such as would crack
With half that weight which hangs upon his grief.
Arthiopa !
   ART. Fly ! fly ! my Lord, and follow not this
    light,
It is that walking fire which in the night
Misleads the traveller, and, like an
Unwholesome mist about it, needs must blast
Whom it shall tempt to wander from his wits.
   ALT. Stay ! stay ! 'tis instant death to take her
    hence :
Though all your tyrants of the law were here,
They would fall down, down at her feet and hide
Their antic faces that do fright poor prisoners more
Than their false sentence when they're half asleep.
Forgive me, reverend Sir !  I know, in this
Your office, you but serve some high command.
Lend me this lady for a short discourse,
And, on my honour, I'll restore her to
Your charge.   The laws shall be exactly satisfied.
                  [*Takes her aside.*

ART. Sure, Altophil, thou'rt lately come from
    Heaven ;
For this is more than human courtesy
To own a luckless virgin, so much lost
In sorrow and distress !
    ALT.                  Preserve thy tears !
This is a wicked place ; such precious drops
Should not bedew unhallow'd ground.  Thy infamy
Is meant to me, and thou art punish'd for
My envied love.  Ay, 'tmust be so, the proofs
Are pregnant that persuade my faith.
    ART. My sorrows will seem easy to me, though
Accompanied with death. Such is the joy
I take, that you believe me guiltless of
A crime, which, though I blush to name, yet I
Must own before the world in punishment.
The angels if they had but leisure to
Descend would testify I am betray'd.
    ALT. And I, Arthiopa, to vindicate
Thy fame, yet shew obedience to the laws,
In these injurious penitential weeds
Will lead thee straight unto that Church
To which thy penance is prescrib'd ; and there
I'll marry thee, in scorn of all the dull
Abused world.  Go on !          [*She kneels.*
    ART.  O ! sir, though I
Am strictly chaste, most true and loyal to your love,
Respect the honour of your house,
Renown'd in war and foreign courts.  How will
It be defil'd when y' are allied not unto me
Alone, but to my shame ? That is a stain
So deep and public now, not all my tears,
Though they could fall in show'rs, will wash't away.
    ALT. Go on !  My resolution needs no vows.
    BRU. Where is your reason, sir ? you that are
    wise
Enough to govern armies in their rage,

In your own fury now should be so wise
To rule your self.   Though this sweet lady's truth
And virtues sacred are, and firm to our
Belief; yet in the high importance of
A wife, you should take care to match where not
A single doubt, though ne'er so weak, could be
By envy urg'd!

ART. Sir, you have borrow'd much
Of time, much have you seen, and speak from all
Discreet experience : and your love, I know :
You love your Duke.   Therefore in this advice
You have my thanks sincerely from my soul !

ALT. Old man, could'st thou convey thy heart
    into
My breast, and so possess my grief; could'st thou
With my subdued moist eyes behold the great
Gonsalvo's daughter, mistress of my life,
Disgraced thus, like th' people's sinful offspring,
[Here]* in the street: how would it stir thy blood?
And then to know her suff'rance treacherously
Contrived by power, one that did malice all
Our holy vows.   I'll not indure't !—burn—burn
The town ! kill, kill all you meet !

HIR. Rampino, raise the old garrison i'th' citadel.
I'll to the sconce behind the bridge.

RAM. Since they do love to see a soldier's mistress
In a white sheet, we'll see their wives in their
Smocks too, before night.

BRU. Stay! stay! is this your love unto your
    General,
Or thirst to pillage and to blood?

ART. Sir, let me quench your anger with my tears.
Upon my knees let me request you leave
Me to mine own misfortune, and the laws.
This dangerous act at once would violate
All your allegiance to the Prince.

* Interpolated in the folio.

BRU. Think on your self, and us that must de-
      pend
Upon your better hopes !
   ALT. My fair white mourner, rise !
You with your priestly office lead the way,
'Tis to the church, she shall obey the law.
Hold high the taper, and move boldly on !
Know, injur'd Hymen, 'tis thy torch, and this
My wedding day.   Dissuade me not ! my soul
Hath vowed it, and 'tis seal'd in heaven.  You that
Affect your General, follow ! and afford
Me straight your shouts of joy.   Not wealth,
Wisdom nor honour, is to me above
The fame and resolution of my love !
      [*Exeunt omnes, and straight several shouts are
      heard within.*]

---

## ACT II.  SCENE I.

### *Enter* BRUSCO, HIRCO.

BRU. Hirco ! have you appeas'd the mutiny
The General's discontents did raise
Amongst his fry of friends, our tattered camp-
Companions in the street ?
   HIR. All's quiet now ;
They sadly wear their fingers in their pockets,
Which they did hope ere this should have been used
In telling pistolets* and chickeens.†

### *Enter* RAMPINO.

BRU. Rampino ! 'tis expected you bring peace !

* See vol. ii., p. 176.
† Also spelt "Zecchin" and "Sequin."  A coin of gold,
current in Venice, worth about seven shillings and sixpence.
The Turkish Zecchine is valued at nine shillings sterling.—
*Glossographia.*

RAM. Two hours I have been preaching
On a stall to certain car-men, that took't ill
In a good cause they might not hang with our
Cast troops to pull down houses and to rob
An heretical new church or two, but they
Are gone swearing and well edified.   Come !
What news ?   Is our General married ?
   BRU. Not yet.
   RAM. How ! not married ?
   BRU. No, some small spy, that watch'd
Which way the current of his discontents
Would run, convey'd it to the Court, and straight
The Prince himself sent to forbid the banns.
   RAM. The embers are but cover'd yet ; I fear
When they are stirr'd the fire will flame again.
   BRU. Our Duke conveyed the lady to his house ;
Repair'd to Court, where the kind Prince, with
   praise
And joy, receiv'd him in open arms.
   RAM. This qualifies the heat of our affairs !
   BRU. He then laid out for those spies that were
Suborn'd against his lady's fame ; who, with
Severe enquiry, being produced, had strict
Examination from the Prince ; a while
They justified their oaths ; but still
Falsehood betray'd itself : for when
He urg'd for names of persons, time, and place,
With doubtful terms, and words disjointed, they
Began to stammer out their evidence ;
Then Altophil claims leave he may present
Their worships with an odd engine of pleasure.
   RAM. Which courteous politicians call a rock ! *
   BRU. The same, and each with painful leisure was
Slowly, sir, wound up.
   RAM. Like a huge jack-weight by a weak sick
   wench !

* Qy. Rack ?

BRU. Right, sir, and then they both confess'd
That Saint, Galeotto, brib'd them to this perjury.
And know my joy-sweet, wanting men of war,
He is by th' prince imprison'd in the fort.
   RAM. An excellent Prince, by this hand he sha'
     not want.
First, I'll forgive him all my pay ; then, Hirco,
Thou shalt lend him money !
   HIR. Excuse me, sir,
Upon security not else ; I've been
Too often bit that way already.  Retire, gentlemen !

*Enter* ASCOLI, ALTOPHIL, GALEOTTO, *who is held by*
*the Guard.*

   ASCO. Though thou hast so behav'd thyself in war,
With wise directions and a valiant arm,
That fortune cannot boast a share in thy
Fam'd victories ; yet I must chide thee, Altophil,
Since being mine, and so much lov'd, thou could'st
Unto a lady give thyself away,
Not freed by my consent.
   ALT. Sir, I have ask'd your pardon, and believe
My joys you did lessen with your sorrows,
To make them by your kindness now more full.
   ASCO. This separation will be short, for since
Your mistress' innocence is by her false
Accusers clear'd unto the world,
Your nuptials I will celebrate, with all
The glory I can add to th' triumph of
A friend ; and you, Galeotto, shall receive
Such punishment, as shall declare
My justice equal to your crime.
   GAL. Sir, I confess your favour lifted me
To hope alliance with the noble Duke ;
Which, had I lawfully contriv'd, perhaps
Th' ambition had not much been blam'd.

But I am lost ; nor would I beg
Forgiveness of your laws, but of your self,
And next, my Lord, of you.    Be pleas'd to think
The wrongs were not of malice, but of pride.

ALT.  Not the eldest devil with his long practice
    had
The skill to lay on me so great a wrong,
But I could pardon it ; unless when I
Perceive the whiteness of my mistress' virtue stain'd,
Betray'd to penance too !   It were a cruelty
The fiends would sooner weep at than commend !

GAL.  Then I'll provide to suffer, and to scorn
That fate I cannot alter with my prayers !

ASCO.  Thou, once the health, art poison now to
    sight ;
'Tis wholesomer to look upon the basilisk.\*
Perfidious to my friend !   But where's Rangone,
That went to fetch your Mistress, Altophil ?
I never saw her yet.   Trust me you are
A cunning lover, that so long concealed
The beauty you admire.

*Enter* RANGONE, ARTHIOPA, *richly attired.*

RAN.  Madam ! your sweetness doth deserve the
    best
Of joys, and I have brought you where they are.

ASCO.  What light is this, that ere the day is
    spent
Breaks like a second morning in our eyes ?
Whil'st all that's shining else shews like a shade
About her beams, sweet as the precious smoke
Ascending from the funeral fire o' th' long-
Lived bird of Araby.

RAN.  You sent me for this lady, sir : will you
Not speak to her ?  See, where she kneels !

ASCO.  O ! rise !  If I have trespass'd in neglect,

\* See vol. ii. page 179.

Forgive thy beauty, that hath forced my wonder
To adore what I perhaps by th' laws of courtesy
Should first salute.

AR. Sir, though I never fear'd my stock
Of modesty so small, that I could want
It for my necessary use ; yet I
Shall need to borrow blushes, if you lay
More beauty to my charge than I dare own.

ASCO. Where have I liv'd that I could never hear
Sweet music until now? O, Altophil!
I find the treasure of thy love so great,
That, were it mine, I should not blame
The envy of a friend, since from the excess
Of judgment, when it values things at full,
Our envy grows—it is our nicety
To call that envy sin.

ALT. What means the Prince?

ASCO. Was she that was so delicate, and soft as is
The purple fleece of clouds—was she thought fit
T' endure the rigour o' th' perverted law?
Convey the traitor hence! and never more
Presume to set thy treacherous foot upon
The confines of my land!

AR. If so, you'll vouchsafe
To make my mercy an example unto yours.
I shall forgive his cruelties.

ASC. It were an injury to heaven ; away!
If, the next time I, in my dominions, spy
This loathed face, thy life is forfeited.

GAL. Sir, I'll presume you'll think my daughter had
No share in my unlucky guilt, therefore,
It were not like your usual justice she
Should suffer in my loss.

ASCO. She is too good for thy society :
Her virtues shall preserve her here.

GAL. Peace crown you at home, and victory
    abroad !                [*Exit with the Guard.*

Asco. Know, Altophil, my darkest thoughts are
    not
So secret to myself, but I dare trust
Thy knowledge with them, and be safe.
Why then should thy intentions or desires
Be hid from me? I fain would sound thy breast
With a new question ; prithee, give me leave !
    ALT. Sir, I am born to follow your command :
Ask what you please ; if I want knowledge here
To satisfy your doubt, I'll study to know more.
Pray, speak !                      .
    Asco. It is decreed by th' powers above, whom no
Dull earthly meditation can dissuade
Or alter, I must needs marry fair Arthiopa !
    ALT. I look'd for comfort, sir,
From your consent, not trouble from your doubts.
    Asco. Is it inevitable then, as the
Conjunction of th' illustrious planets are
That needs must meet ; else all the spheres will
    straight
Be out of tune ; time break his glass, and throw
The sand in the sun's eyes to make him wink,
And leave us in the dark. Speak, must it be,
Or else you both will suffer an eclipse?
Make answer from thy kind thoughts.   Is it
Decreed ?
    ALT. It is : and nought can alter it but death.
    Asco. How hardly then hath nature dealt with
    us :
For we are prisoners all; all circumscrib'd,
And to our limits tied : the fortunate,
And luckless, are alike ; for thou art with
As strict necessity unto thy happiness
Confin'd, as others to their evil fate.
    ALT. To be her prisoner, sir, is to be free ;
Nor can I wish my bondage off, whilst I
Am fetter'd in her arms.

III.              `            C

Asco. You'll give me leave
To try how far your mistress hath engag'd
Her faith, and not be jealous, Altophil ?
    ALT. I'll trust such virtue with mine enemy.
                   *[Ascoli withdraws with Arthiopa.*
Ah ! me ! where is a lover's wealth ? what joy
Is there of beauty, when once conceal'd, more than
Of jewels in the dark ? but, when reveal'd,
We stand to th' hazard of another's claim.
    RAN. I do not like this alteration in the Prince :
If he doth love, I fear it is too late.
    Asco. Oh, do not promise so much comfort in
Your looks, and in your language breathe despair;
'Tis like fantastic April, that erewhile
With gaudy sun-beams smiles upon the Spring,
And in a minute's space gathers the black
Thick clouds about his brow to make a storm.
Have you no pity left ?
    AR. My pity, sir, you'll hardly entertain ;
Since it must come alone without relief !
    Asco. Why were you trusted with such bounte-
        ous wealth,
And make such hasty bargains for your self ?
Could you have skill to know the value of
Your love, and give it all away at once ?
    AR. Sir, I beseech you do not urge me
To deny, what in your gentler clemency
You should forbear to ask ; heaven made my vows,
And they are Altophil's.
    Asco. No more ! my trespass I'll decline, though I
Augment my griefs.  My Altophil, farewell !
                   *[Takes him by the hand.*
When thou dost hear me sick, think what disease
Arthiopa's neglect might once have bred
In thee ; then mourn me at that rate.
Rangone, come ! lead me to the cypress grove.
                   *[Ex. Ascoli, Rangone.*

ALTO. Thou art as much unfortunate as fair.
But smile upon thy stars, perhaps they may
Be sooth'd into a kinder influence.
The Prince is noble, and in's wisdom will
Digest this fit that shakes him out of frame.
These gentlemen have shar'd with me the sharp
Calamities of war; give them your hand.
                    [*Brusco, Ramp., Hirc., kiss her hand.*
Take care thy valiant friends, here in the town
You give example of a sober discipline.
                    [*Exeunt Altophil, Arthiopa,*
    BRU. A rare creature!
    RAM. No sweet meat in the world
Is like the conserve of a lady's hand.
    HIRC. She'll think o' th' Hircos this twelvemonth
        by way
Of a full buss.  I laid it roundly on.
    RAM. Why, you came last, sir, and kiss'd but her
        wrist,
Her hand was melted before into my mouth; ah!

                    *Enter* FRISKIN.

                    [*Ram. spies him and starts back.*
    BRU. What, planet-struck!
    HIR. 'Tis his tailor! he owes him money.
    RAM. How did the rascal find me out?  I shift
My lodging as often as conveniently
I can remove my trunks; thrice in two days;
Would's needle stuck across his throat!
    FRIS. Signior Rampino!
    RAM. Signior Friskin! I thought it should be
        you.
And how, dear heart, and how, how does thy wife?
My godson too at nurse?  I've a little whistle
For him, 'tis coming in the General's Court.*
    FRIS. All well, signior.  Do the wars thrive, sir?

* Waggon.—*Folio.*

Is there any money stirring?

RAMP. Faith, some of us here,
By our continual practice, know a ducket
From a counter.* We've mauled King Heildebrand.

   FRIS. We hear he is encamp'd some ten leagues
     hence.

RAM. Yes, we have put him to his sallads, like
A saucy frog upon another's meadow.

   FRISK. Signior, there is an old debt!

RAM. Dost thou think I have forgot it? I prithee
What skirt's in fashion now? the jacket-way
Down to the hams?

   FRIS. No, sir, six in a rank.* But, sir, the debt
     is old.

RAM. Ay, Ay, with all my heart! How are their
     cloaks?
A square full cape?

   FRIS. Just as you left them, sir.
Would you would think upon your debt?

RAM. Dost think I do not? I prithee bring me but
A pattern of a Polish coat, I'd wear it loose and short.
Pray, gentlemen, know my friend! believ't
I'd rather see him sit cross-legg'd than any man
In Lombardy; his thimble on, and's needle thus—
He'll run a tilt through cloth two inches thick.

   BRU. Is he so excellent? he shall make my
     clothes.

   HIR. And mine too, if he please.

   FRIS. Have they any sorts, sir? Are they well
     stor'd?

RAM. A brace of rich close curmudgeonly fellows.
Thou see'st they care not what their outside is,

---

   * "Counters" were pieces resembling money, formerly used
in calculations.
   † "Eight, sir, and short. But, sir, the debt is long."—*Folio.*
This difference in the two readings marks the change of
fashion in the thirty years which had elapsed between the first
appearance of the play and its reproduction.

So their pockets be well lined.

    Fris. It seems they are a little careless, sir,
      indeed.

Where is your lodging now ?

    Ram. In troth, 'twill be in the old mansion near
The palace-yard, till six of clock at night,
But then I must remove ; the fiddlers do
So often waken me with their muttoned gridirons
And good morrows, I cannot sleep for them.
I'll send thee word where I shall fix.

    Fris. And you'll remember, sir, my bill ?

    Ram. Dost think I'll fail ?
I prithee bring thy weights along with thee ;
We shall else wrangle about light gold.

    Fris. Y'are welcome, sir, to town !

    Ram. Away, lest we be vex'd again with new
Solicitors for the old cause.        [*Exeunt omnes.*

    *Enter* Galeotto, Gandolpho, Morello.

    Gal. Is Amaranta sent for by the Prince ?

    Mo. She is ! but for what use I could not learn.
My brother, whom your former bounties have
Preferred and late made captain of the fort,
Is come, sir, to bewail your miseries ;
And proffer all his service ; to make known
Your loss cannot dissuade his gratitude.

    Gan. My Lord, from low deservings you have
      rais'd
Me to the best command, this place affords
A soldier's hope, but, if my life can pay
Your bounty, I will keep it for that use.

    Gal. Your natures are so thankful, gentlemen,
For little benefits, that I am taught,
If ever I can reach my former power,
T' oblige more friends though with a greater charge.

    Mo. My Lord, your wisdom hath the skill to cure
Distempers, stronger than your fortune feels.

GAL. Greatness hath still a little taint i'the
  blood;
And often 'tis corrupted near the heart.
But these are not diseases held till by
The monarch spied, who our ambition feeds
Till't surfeits with his love; nor do we strive
To cure or take it from ourselves, but from
His eyes, and then our medicine we apply
Like the weapon-salve,* not to ourselves, but him
Who was the sword that made the wound; and this
State medicine is compos'd of flattering industry,
And such false cures as like to false alarms
Fright men to fear danger, when none is near,
Still vex'd and busy to no real use,
As drones that keep most noise about the hive,
And then devour the politic Court flies
What foolish bees bring on their weary thighs.

MO. These lectures, my Gandolpho, show a brain
That will preserve him, spite of power.
My Lord, my brother is your own, and we
Will share the hazard of your fortune.

GAL. The captain hath a valiant soul, and I
Perhaps shall use him in a close design,
That i'th' success may richly pay his love.

GAN. When y' are most confident of me, you
  can't
Expect so much as I'll perform.

GAL. Enough! Morello, sir, shall undertake
For my belief, to all you dare
Make promise of; if you will please to bring
Me to the ports where short the allowance of
My time will force me take a sad farewell,
I'll breathe my love and business to you both.
                                          [*Exeunt.*

---

* Weapon-salve was supposed to cure a wounded person by
being applied to the sword by which the wound had been in-
flicted.   It was first discovered by Paracelsus.

*Enter* ALTOPHIL, ARTHIOPA.

ALT. Gladness possess my mistress' thoughts. I'm
    told
The Count Rangone from the Prince is now
Alighted at my gates.   Good news, I hope?
For though we live as in a convent here,
You as my nun to-morrow may proclaim
This house a Court, and you my cheerful bride.

AR. The frowns of heav'n are to the virtuous
    like
Those thick dark clouds poor wand'ring seamen
    spy,
Which oft foretell their happiness, and shew
The long expected land is near.

*Enter* RANGONE, AMARANTA, *her face veiled.*

RAN.             Felicity and everlasting fame
Betide the noble general! Thus I
Am bid salute you from our mighty Prince.

ALT. I am the creature of his power and will.

RAN. I, with this gentle greeting, must present
The richest treasure nature in her last
Declining stock of beauty could afford
The world. Behold it, and admire!
               [*Unveils Amar. who weeps.*
Her eyes, dissolving thus in tears, should teach
Thy heart to melt: for know, thou cruel Lord,
She long hath chastely sickened for thy love.

ALT. Alas! unlucky maid! How can thy griefs
Expect comfort from him, that knows not to
Redress his own?

AMA.           Yet, Sir, I hope 'tis in
Your power t'excuse th' unwilling error of
My modesty. I surely am the first
Sad lady that ever was constrain'd to seek
Her lover, and then woo him too. But 'tis

The Prince hath forc'd me here to nourish my
Affection with your real sight, that else
Had been conceal'd, and with your shadow fed.

AR. Poor Amaranta! I must needs lament
The malice of thy fortune, though
My pity shews unkindness to myself.

RAN. Sir, my commission is to ask, if you
Can love and celebrate this lady for
Your wife ?  And our kind Prince, besides the for-
    feited
Possessions of her father's wealth, will to
Her dowry add honours and lands, until
You share his royalty.

ALT. Too soon this am'rous riddle is resolv'd.
He loves Arthiopa, and would
Enforce me wed this lady, to assure
More easy way for 's own desires.

AR. O ! Altophil !  Were I not well
Instructed in thy loyalty, how soon
Her beauty and these soothing hopes would throw
Me cold into the arms of death.

ALT. Sir, you must carry to the Prince, what I
Was never wont to send : a harsh denial of
His suit ; and, give me leave to say, 'tis trouble-
    some,
And too severe.

AMA. How am I lately hardened with the use
Of sorrows, that I can listen to
My angry doom, and live ?

RAN.                        Summon your wise
And kinder thoughts, and make such reply
As I may joy in the delivery,
And soon procure a mutual happiness.

ALT. To court me to a better knowledge of my
    bliss,
Than I already understand, were but
A vain attempt ; I am resolv'd within

The chaste embraces of these arms to live
Or die.

AMA. My ears have forfeited their faculty ;
Why should they still preserve their sense, that
could
Not for a while be deaf, but needs must hearken
To my evil fate ?

RAN. Sir, pardon mine obedience to my Prince,
For I shall execute a sad command.
You of the guard, lay hold upon the Duke !

*Enter the* GUARD *and seize on* ALTOPHIL.

ALT. Fear not, Arthiopa ! some joy remains
I' th' hopes we shall not be divided in
Our sufferings.

RAN.                    She is my pris'ner, sir,
And must to court, whilst you and Amaranta stay
Confin'd together in this house,

ALT. False Prince ! how cunning is thy cruelty.

AR.   Lest we had courage left t' expect an end
Of our calamities, this way was found
To make us yet more certain of despair.

RAN. In this, Sir, you perceive the intricate
Though pow'rful influence of love, that doth
Pervert most righteous natures to attempt
Unjust designs.   His God-head 's not full known
And's miseries have been but dully taught
To men : for I am charg'd to say this new
Constraint is but a sad experiment
To try if you to Amaranta can
Pay equal love for hers, and nice Arthiopa
Return unto the prince what's passions now
May challenge as a debt ?

AR.                    O, my true Lord,
Shall we ne'er meet again, and tell our thoughts,
Which still we found too like, as if we two
Had but one heart, wherein we gave them forms ?

ALT. 'Twere sin to have no hope. We'll change
    our stars,
For there are many more will gladly take
Protection of our loves.

RAN. My time was limited; my witness is
Become my charge, and must to Court.

AR. Sir, give me leave but to salute this lady,
Whose friendship, though of noble worth, I shall
Too soon receive, too soon, I fear, forsake;
You, gentle Amaranta, must enjoy
Your blessed habitation here, here with my Lord,
Whom I would fain commend, not to
Your care, but your neglect: for know,
We, in our virgin bashfulness, esteem
Solicitation and address a more
Undoubted sin than our disdain.

AM. Madam! I'm here a prisoner too, and will
Expect, like others, in harsh times distress'd,
His pity, not relief; I'll hope for that,
If you'll permit without a jealousy.

ART. Preserve me in your kind remembrance,
    Altophil.

ALT. What other use have I of memory
When I have conceal'd the records of thee?

ART. Sir! I am loth to leave this lady here;
Imprisonment is cruel to a maid.
Was it the Prince's will she needs must stay?

RAN. I have receiv'd it in a strict command.*

ART. O Altophil! sir, let me hide mine eyes;
It were some crime 'gainst them, thus to forsake
Their chiefest joy, and let them see it too.

ALT. Since Amaranta, we
Must strive to woo, let's learn no mortal love,
That's dangerous, and quickly ends; but try
To make eternal which is first to die.

                                    [*Ex. omnes.*

      * See Addenda to this Play. No. 1.

## ACT III. SCENE I.

*Enter* BRUSCO, RAMPINO, HIRCO, *their swords drawn.
A noise of drums first heard afar off.*

RAM. All's lost, the town is taken, w' are betray'd!
That cursed traitor, Galeotto, sold
Us like tame feeble sheep to Heildebrand
The Lombards' king; whom false Morello, taught
By 's master's art, gave, in the sleepy* hour
Of night, a secret entrance through the western port.
  HIR. No courage left? Is the citadal surpriz'd?
  BRU. Past all recovery! Gandolpho, he
That was preferred to the command of it
Some two years† since, by th' treacherous favourite,
At his design made a surrender to
The filching king that hath not overcome
But stolen us to captivity.
  RAM. What drowsy ignorance possess'd the
      Prince
To trust, with such important power, one whom
He knew a traitor, to that villain's lust?
  BRU. Ay, there his reason shew'd herself be-
      witch'd;
When he had banished Galeotto, and
Incens'd his very soul to all malignity,
That his envenom'd gall could e'er produce;
Then to put trust in those he had preferred!

### *Enter* RANGONE.

RAN. O gentlemen! To what unseasonable use
Do you advance your weapons, as you meant
To threaten the victorious foe? when we
Are so much past the likelihood of help,
That all resistance you can make is but
To hasten on the forfeit of your lives!

* Darkest.—*Folio.*         † Hours.—*Ib.*

BRU. If channels must o'erflow with blood, they
   shall
Be fed from proudest veins that highest swell ;
Theirs who would empty ours shall open too.
   RAM. Why should we calmly die, as if we had
Drunk cold mandragora, and breathe our souls
Out in our sleep, departing with less noise
Than men who dream they die ?   Let's venture to
Regain the fort.
   HIR. There are enow to make
Scalladoes left, that have not yielded up
Their arms ; if we must fall, it is as good
We do it climbing as thus standing still.
   RAN. Your forces are too weak ! 'Tis fortified
Already with two regiments of Switz.
I know you think I am as much inclin'd
To hazard, as that man, who dares the most
In glory or revenge : but this attempt
Will only serve t'incense stern Heildebrand
Against our prince and Altophil ; who, with
Arthiopa, are prisoners, and given
To Galeotto's power, as a reward :
First promis'd him to purchase his lost faith.
   BRU. The Prince, our general, and his mistress too !
All ta'en ? the destinies are grown too curst !*
                     [*Drums afar off.*
Stand close, and make this passage good.

Enter HEILDEBRAND, GALEOTTO, MORELLO,<br>GANDOLPHO, SOLDIERS.

   HEI. What left mistaken souls are these, who, but
A piece and remnant of discourag'd strength,
Presume defiance still, when all the rest
Have safely yielded to our power ? Bid them,
Galeotto, give their weapons up.
   GAL. Why, gentlemen, do you vainly tempt

* Cruel. -- Folio.

A danger from his wrath, that not delights
To ruin where his mercy is implor'd?
Present him your unprofitable swords,
And I'll procure a full assurance of
Your lives and liberties.

RAN. Kindness sounds ill in a traitor's tongue.
If you had loyal held unto your Prince
Such mediation had been out of use.

GAL. This language is too bold; it doth proclaim
Your anger great, and your discretion small.
But such untimely choler, know, I can
As easily forgive as scorn; and will
Requite it, if you'll yet submit, with a
Protection of your throats, that else are in
Great danger to swallow no more new wine.

MOR. The counsel that he gives you is not fit
To be refus'd.

GAN. You'r brothers of the camp, is it not better
To live and spend your pay, when you can get it,
Than die, and have't laid out in fun'ral plums?*

HEI. If you will hazard death, we can afford it.
If you with taking but a little pains,
Stand still and smile whil'st it is done; if you'll
Deserve to live, you shall enjoy the same
Kind mercy we afford the town; be free,
And still protected by your former laws;
But first yield up your swords.

BRU. Our swords are all our wealth! Take those
away
And we are left to poverty and shame.

HEI. Your grant already hath allow'd our citizens
The preservation of their lands and goods.

RAM. Shall we fare worse than retailers of small
wares?

HEI. The tribute of your arms we'll but possess

* Qy. Plumes; or the comfits then in use for funerals? See
Engine's remark in "The Wits," vol. ii. p. 192.

Till night, and then, on th' honour of a King,
They shall be all restor'd.

RAN. In our resistance, gentlemen, vainly
We give away our lives; let us preserve
Them rather for our Prince's future use.

BRU. Since, it must be, make answer as you
please.

RAN. Upon your Kingly word we yield!

HEI. Disarm, and lead them to the court-du-guard!
Where, when you have enroll'd their names, take care
That our engagement be made good.

              [*The soldiers take away their swords.*

RAM. I pray look to the ribbon on the hilt:
It was a widow's favour.

              [*Exeunt Rang., Brusc., Ramp., Hirc., soldiers.*

HEI. Where's, Galeotto, your prisoners?

GAL. Safely confin'd in my own house, and now,
According to your royal grant, I crave
The full disposing of their lives.

HEI. Take our consent, we ne'er will lessen what
At first our bounty did assure; but then
Your secret promise must be straight perform'd,

GAL. At night! or let me forfeit all your trust.

HEI. Lead to the city-Senate, that we may
Receive their homage, and confirm their laws.
Still wear your secret promise in your thoughts.*

              [*Exeunt omnes.*

        *Enter* ASCOLI, ALTOPHIL, ARTHIOPA, *their
              arms bound.*

ASC. My fall from sov'reign title and command,
My loss of that which nature worst can miss,
My pleasant liberty; thus being bound
Like a cheap slave, that's sold for less than buys
The conqueror the riots of one meal.
Not all these suff'rings make me mourn so much

              * See Addenda to this Play, No. II.

As that short separation of your loves.
Yet when I saw her faith was so obliged,
And knit unto your virtues, Altophil,
I did resign my nuptial hopes, and gave
Her loyalty the praise and rev'rence due
Unto a Saint.
 ART. Your usage, sir, I have
Confess'd was noble, though unfortunate,
And I shall find scarce tears enough left to lament
My own captivity, when I behold
My mourning lord's and yours.
 ALT. Would there were here
Some flow'ry bank, shaded with cypress, yew,
And sycamore, whose melancholy brow
Hung o'er a little discontented brook,
That ever murmurs, as it wisely knew
It travell'd to some river that must soon
Convey it to the sea ; where they are both
In trouble with the bounds, and lost.   Here we
Would sit, comparing mighty Courts to greater seas,
Where lovers like small rivulets are vex'd
A while, and then o'erwhelmed.  A rural residence
Near woods and meads, though it be humble, is
The place where we may love, and be secure.
 ART. Why then did my too valiant father, and
Thyself disquiet all the peaceful world
With hunting after fame ? Loaden and crushed
In heavy armour for the chase ; toiling
To get us this renown and eminence
Which since hath ruin'd our content ? Oh that
We first had met in shepherd's homely weeds !
 ALT. Ay, my Arthiopa, or that we now
Might so enjoy our liberty ; then if
Ambition did inflame my thoughts to aim
At victories, I should not combat for a crown,
But wrestle for some chaplet wreathed by thee
Of daffodills and pinks.

Asco. How kindly we
Should take o' the celestial governors,
If they would make these wishes real truths ;
And me some neighbouring villager, that came
To joy and wonder at your loves, to court
The beauties of your mistress' mind, my Altophil.
Such rivalship is noble though 'tis new.

*Enter* GALEOTTO, GANDOLPHO, MORELLO, *Soldiers.*

ALT. Appear, and let thy rage inflict her worst!
'Las I, poor traitor, how dull thy mischiefs are,
How weak that canst invent no punishment
To quit thy daughter's still neglected love
But what we'll suffer, and embrace with scorn.

Asco. Perform thy malice ; come, that we may
Laugh to think how all posterity will urge
Thy deed in railing proverbs to express
Disloyalty.

ART. And maids, when they but hear thy name,
Shall cross themselves in superstitious fear.

Mo. These are but crabbed compliments
To him that has your lives in his command.

GAL. Right sir ! if I could easily remove
My gull from off my liver to my heart ;
But now I take no joy in bitterness.
Thus I requite their wrath : unbind them straight !
[*Soldiers unbind them.*

ALT. How's this ? what may this courtesy portend ?

GAL. Waste not your wonder, sir. It is no dream.

ALT. His sinful nature is converted, sure !

GAL. Now being all made free, you Altophil,
And fair Arthiopa, have but exchang'd
These fetters to be join'd in everlasting bonds,
Start not ! they are but matrimonial cords ;
And easy to be worn, though ne'er untied :
Such manacles you'll gladly enter in.

ART. My prayers did find the nearest way to
heaven :
How quickly they were heard !
ALT. Those stains are all
Wiped off that so disfigured thee, thy brow
Is quite unwrinkl'd now, and grows so smooth,
Thou wilt not know it in thy former glass.*
ASCO. Galeotto, this restores thee to my kind
Esteem again ; whilst I behold their happiness,
I can forgive thy stealth upon my state.
GAL. Convey those lovers to their bridal-chamber !
And let the ceremonial rites be such
As I directed them.
ALT. Come, my Arthiopa, gladness shall leave
No room for virgin blushes in thy cheeks.
[Ex. Morello, Altophil, Arthiopa.
ASCO. Is my employment void? must I not go
And help to celebrate this blessed hour?
GAL. No sir, you have a greater business of
your own,
And may be thought as happy too,
If you will prove as wise in your consent,
As I am kind to offer it.
ASCO. Instruct me better what you mean.
GAL. You see how your most rig'rous doom
upon
My person and my wealth, enforc'd me to
Such ways in my revenge, as since have made
Me apt for more ambitious hopes than those
I lost. This froward Duke held my alliance in
Unhallow'd worth : Now he is more in my con-
tempt ;
For you, his master, sir, I think
Fitter t'embrace my daughter as a wife.
ASCO. There's mystery in this discourse !

* These, as well as the preceding two lines, are, in the original edition, given to Arthiopa but thus corrected in the *folio.*

GAL. 'Tis easy, sir, when you conceive, that I
By marriage now remove Arthiopa,
From your devices.

ASCO. But I have made a vow,
Since she severely did refuse the first
Most lawful passions that I ever felt,
All other beauty shall appear too late.

GAL. Those are silly vows, which amorists *
In choler make, when they have vainly spent
A frosty night with singing madrigals
To some coy mistress, whilst her window's shut.
Consider, this perform'd, my power with Heilde-
    brand
May keep you yet in your dominions free,
Some slender yearly tribute being paid.

ASCO. It is not in your will to force my love ?

GAL. Sir, if I should, it were but justice and
Divine; since in my absence you conspir'd
T'inforce brave Altophil to make her his,
That your desires might suffer no impediment
When they should court Arthiopa.

ASCO. Thou rudely dost awake
Those thoughts that fain would sleep ; I'll hear no
    more.

GAL. Go ! bind him then ! and lead him where
    he was
Before restrain'd ; you shall have time to meditate
And make your resolution of more worth.

GAN. My lord! I'll watch him like your sentinel.

ASCO. Slave ! dost thou use me as fond children
    do
Their birds, shew me my freedom in a string,
And when th'ast play'd with me enough, straight pull
Me back again, to languish in my cage ?
This insolence will make her † chief in hell.

                       [*Exeunt.*

* See Vol. ii., p. 36.         † "Thee " in *folio*.

*Enter* HIRCO, FRISKIN, FIBBIA.

FIB. Well, this is a good king, the laws shall
   have
Their course ; it matters not who reigns, as long
As every one may come by their own.   If
Signior Rampino pay me not, I can
Arrest him now.
   FRISK. Troth, mistress Fibbia's in the right.
For thus to fail his day is such a thing,
Heaven will ne'er bless him.
   FIB. Never! 'tis impossible he should come to
      good                                 ⋮
That fails his day.   Heaven keep my friends
From failing of their day !
   HIR. Who would have thought, 'thad been so
      great a sin ?
But the truth is, I ne'er studied divinity,*
All that I read is in the muster-book.
   FRISK. But as you, told us, sir, is he so great
Already with the king ?
   HIR. Upon my honour he sent him just now
A sword for a present, and this to me,
Because I am his friend !
   FRISK. Yours, Signior, is not very rich !
   HIR. No. a plain bandall hilt,† it was his great
Great grandfather's, but there are no such blades
      worn now,

*Enter* RAMPINO.

I've told your friends here, how much you are
In favour now at court, and they rejoice heartily.
Bear up, and make it good !
   [FRISK.] Sir, we have reason to be glad.  I pray

* The Casuists, *folio.*
† Vandall hilt, *folio.*—" Bandolet," in architecture, "any
little band, flat moulding, or fillet."

How came't about ?   May we learn a little
Of the state devices ?
 RAM.  Troth partly merit, for you know
I wear my clothes as well as another man ;
Besides I had the luck to be most near
Akin to him who did betray the fort.
 FRISK.  Ah ! signior ! if you could have betrayed it
Your self, then we had been all made.
 RAM.  Well ! no time lost ; we may have occasion
To betray somewhat hereafter : men that
Will rise, must not be tender of
Their labour and good will !
 FIBBIA.  Signior ! y'are in the right :
For, if we labour in our calling, Heaven
Will help us to betray something or other
For our good.
 RAM.  Mistress Fibbia, I owe you
For much profitable counsel.
 FRISK.  Ay, sir, and money for other things !
 RAM.  We'll talk of that anon.
Shew me another of thy standing that bears her
  years like thee,
It shall cost me four ducats but I'll
Get thy picture, and by thy side I'll have
Young Antiphones, thy son, drawn too,
Eating of cherries in a green coat.
 FRISK.  Signior ! this was the day you promis'd me.
 RAM.  Ay, I must talk with you; d'you hear, you
  shall work for the king.
 FRISK.  Who ? I, Sir.   Alas !
 RAM.  Come, it must be so, his tailor died this
  morning.
 FRISK.  I pray, signior.
 .HIR.  'Tis very true,
He fell mad with studying of new fashions.
 FRISK.  I shall be thankful if you'll use your
  pow'r.

RAM. You can i'th' long vacation ev'ry year
Travel to Paris, and instruct your self
In the newest model and best cut ?

FRISK. I have a brother lives there, sir.   He is
A shoe-maker, and lately sent me post
A pattern of the finest spur-leather ;
'Twas so admir'd at court.

RAM. Write for him straight ! he shall be pre-
    ferr'd too ;
If he be known so trim at's pareing knife,
He cannot miss th' reversion of that place.

FRISK. If the house of the Friskins rise, none of
Your worthy issue shall want a second.*

FIB. Signior, my money's due since Lammas last.
Shall I know your mind ?

RAM. Sweet Mistress Fibbia,
You shall receive our whole discourse ;
I'm studying to prefer your neighbour here
At court : now, if she'll chuse any employment
In the Queen's side, her hopes stand fair, she now
Lies in at Mantua : let me see —— what think
You of a rocker's place to the young Prince ?

FIB. Why truly, sir, so I may carry my
Small son along.   I would be loth to leave him
Behind in a lone house.

RAM. You must buy him a new hat, and d'you
    hear
Let him abstain from ginger-bread ; 'twill spoil
His growth.

FIB. A little, sir, on holy days.

RAM. You will be self will'd.

FIB. He always had a care of my son.

RAM. Friskin, you may visit me to-morrow
And know more.

FRISK. I'll bring my measure with me.   It is long

* The *folio* reads,                " Your sons
       Sha'not want. They shall be pages, sir, to mine."

Since I wrought for your worship!

RAM. Do, do, farewell! Hirco make haste, and
    shift the air ;

There's nothing so contagious as the breath
Of creditors.                    [*Exeunt.*

*Enter* MORELLO, ALTOPHIL, ARTHIOPA.

ALT. Rich hangings of the antick Persian loom,
Venetian tapers gilt, and bedding
Of Italian Nuns' embroidery, purl'd* and imboss'd.
Galeotto shows his bounty great to deck
Our bridal chamber with such foreign pomp ;
But where's the priest, that with his holy words
Should make us fit to enter here ?

MOR. Roasting the pig he receiv'd in his last
    tythes.

ALT. Your mirth is somewhat strange : does it
    become you ?

MOR. How little are you prais'd† in the affairs
And souls of men, to think this sumptuous bed
Within, and furniture could entertain an enemy ?

ALT. For whom was it prepar'd ?

MOR. For mighty Heildebrand, the Lombards'
    king,
Who, when he gave the Prince and you secure
Undoubted pris'ners to my master's will,
He had a promise made, th' ensuing night
He should enjoy that lady in his arms.

AR. Ah, me ! what prodigies are here ?

ALT. Villain ! take that for thy intelligence.
                    [*Strikes him.*

---

* This term comprehends an inversion of the stitches, which
gives to the work, in those parts in which it is used, a different
appearance from the general surface. The seams of stockings,
the alternate ribs, and what are called the clocks, are *purled*.
—*Halliwell's Archaic Dictionary.* See also our Vol. ii., p. 27.
   † Practis'd. —*Folio.* Qy., appraised—skilled ?

MOR. So fierce in your rewards! What ho! !
   seize on the duke,
Tie his offensive arms ! the lady too.

   *Enter* SOLDIERS *and lay hold on him.*

ALT. My sense is so much dull'd with often use
Of my calamities, that they are now
Become my sport. What follows, sir ? I do
Beseech you would proceed.
   MOR. Soldiers, avoid the room ! [*Exeunt soldiers.*
Know sir, the wise Galeotto to make full
Witty and new his bounty to the king,
Ordain'd that you, this lady's lover, should
Upon your knees present her to his lust.
Your proud neglect of Amarantha then
Is subtilly repaid.
   ALT. O ! damn'd infernal dog !
   MOR. I'll leave you, sir ! take leisure, and resolve
T' accept of this employment, or to die.    [*Exit.*
   ALT. How divers are the changes of his tyranny ;
Erewhile he flattered us with pleasant shows
Of comfortable hope, then suddenly
Presents us with more horrid forms than death.
   AR. Death is our happiest expectation now.
The grave is ever quiet, though 'tis cold ;
But, Altophil, alas ! when we have slept
A thousand years, who is't can tell
If I again shall know thee when I wake ?

   *Enter* AMARANTA.

AM. The chiefest blessings that are bred above
Fall on you both, like summer flowers, that come
To ripen what before was but i'th' infancy
Of growth ; first, Altophil, on you, that are
Most noble to the world, though much behind*
To me ; next on your bride, whose virtues shine
So clear, that I must check my envy, and
     *Unkind, folio.*

Pretend some joy to see her fortunate.

ALT. Can this be Amaranta's voice ? is she
Perverted too, and taught to mock at our distress ?

AR. This ill becomes a maiden's tenderness !

AM. Forbid it goodness ! if you suffer aught,
That I should make your miseries my scorn ;
For just heaven knows, my father, with great shows
Of kindness and of haste, lately disturb'd
My orisons, with news he had design'd
The prince to marry me, which, Altophil,
Was but unwelcome hope, since my best love
Must die with thy disdain ; then told me all
These preparations were to celebrate
Your nuptials with Arthiopa.

ALT. My nuptial rites ! this was a feign'd dis-
guise
To hide his foul lascivious purpose from
Thy bashful sight.

AM. My lord, though he hath wrong'd you much,
Do not misconstrue him, as fit for all impieties.

ALT. Alas ! it is too dire a truth !
Witness these bonds, witness those griefs
Which hang upon Arthiopa, like black
Wet clouds upon the morning's cheek ; know she
Is here designed for th' lust of Heildebrand ;
And I, by your obdurate father's will,
Must be enforc'd to see and suffer it.

AM. Horror ! why should I tarry here,
And listen to such things as are not fit
To be believ'd ?                    [She is going out.

ALT. Stay ! Amaranta ! stay !
If thou art pitiful, and hast that heaven
Within thy heart, that with such lively truth
Is figured in thy face, express it now !
Thou knowest the secret passages and doors
Of this thy father's house, convey, with thy
Best skill, and trust my mistress to some dark

Unusual place, where she may rest secure
And safe from violence !

AR. Upon my knees I beg,          [*Kneels.*
If yet the softness of thy mother's nature
Have any residence within thy breast,
Look like a virgin on a virgin's moan ;
And let thy mercy find some way to hide
My honour from the reach of wicked men.

ALT. This sad necessity hath made my joints,
Stiffen'd with winter marches in the war,
Now supple as a courtier's knee that waits
Upon a tyrant's throne.   Behold how low
I fall to be my mistress' advocate.          [*Kneels.*

AM. Let me henceforth in darkness dwell; for why
Should I again make use of day, that could
Endure to see th' elected monarch of
My vassall'd love thus humbled at my feet ?
Rise, sir ! rise, sweet Arthiopa ! though it
Seems strange, though thou my rival art, I should
Assist your fortune, whose felicity
Must ruin mine, yet I will justly do't
With hazard of my life.

ALT. What strange malicious courtesy, you stars !
Was this ? to make the first election of
My love so excellent, and with Arthiopa
So fill my breast, that there no room was left
To entertain the lady's true affection
Till it came too late.

AR.                    And I could not confirm
My own chief happiness, but whilst I foiled
The chaste proceedings of her hope.

AM. First, I'll untie these mis-becoming bonds.
                              [*Unbinds them.*
Now follow me with slow and wary feet.
Strong guards are severally dispersed beneath,
You cannot void the house ; but there's a vault,
Deep buried under yonder turret's frame,

Where I'll conceal you both, till I persuade
My father cease his irreligious wrath.

ALT. This kindness to thy rival shall become,
In all succeeding times, a story fit
To soften every amorous lady's ear ;
Fame loud shall sing it, and preserve it long ;
The music of her trumpet, not her tongue.*

[*Exeunt.*

---

### ACT IV. SCENE I.

*Enter* HEILDEBRAND, GALEOTTO.

HEI. These ornaments shew much magnificence
And wealth ; the prosperous monarch of the east
Might here vouchsafe to sleep, though when his bold
And superstitious fables made him think
The sun was married, and would send
His glist'ring wife to be his concubine.

GAL.                              These tapers, sir,
And these refulgent stones, will all grow dark
When you behold Arthiopa ; who now,
That you may find my promise just, you shall
Embrace ; where is she? ha ! death on this slave!
Morello told me that he left her here ;
Her lover too! fast bound to my dispose.

*Enter* AMARANTA.

Amaranta ! what devil counsel'd thee
To this untimely visit in the night ?

AM. It was a careful angel, sir, that to
Prevent the dangers on your soul, hath given
Me order to dehort your rage, which so
Pursues Arthiopa.

GAL.                              Where is she ? speak ?

* Whilst lovers make it their eternal song. *Folio.*

Where's Altophil? remov'd and hid by thee?

HEI. Her beauties make his faint description
    more
Like envy, than just praise; the nicest maid
In Lombardy, strictly compar'd, looks like
A wither'd Lapland nurse; my teeming wife
Shews foul and tawny to her, as she'd been
The sooty offspring of a Moor.

GAL. Why dost not speak? I know she can't
    escape
The confines of my house, my guards are made
Too watchful, and too strong; where is she? Speak!
                              [She kneels.

AM. Sir, I confess, I've hid her from your wrath,
And, till this great distemper of your mind is cur'd,
It is not safe she should appear.

HEI. Galeotto, why dost let this lady kneel?
Such humbleness shews ill, the pleasure of
An anxious beauty is her pride.

GAL. The posture's comely, sir. It is my daughter.

HEI. Hah! his daughter! This courtesy is new
And exquisite! I love a parent for my bawd!

GAL. Tell me! thou troublesome delight of holi-
    ness,
Where thy bewitching rival is conceal'd,
Or I'll torment thee till thou wake thy dead
Unlucky mother with thy groans.

HEI. Galeotto, hold! dost thou use force?

GAL. The lady that I promis'd for your solace, sir,
Sh' hath wickedly remov'd from hence!

HEI. What lady's that?

GAL. The fair Arthiopa.

HEI. There's none fair but she! all beauty else
She turns to black companions of the night;
My judgment is too strong, cheat not mine ears
With the false music of a name. Alas!
My gentle excellence, waste not those tears,

Whose sov'reign power would better nature, where
She weakly doth reside ; and, falling in
The spring, convert a canker to a rose.
Come, mourn no more.
    Am.                         Sir ! you are merciful,
And, by the great prerogative of your
Command, may soon procure an easier weight
Than he hath laid upon the innocent.      .
    HEI. Believe 't he shall not practise violence ;
To bed sweet beauty, go ! he is reclaim'd.
Upon thy life pursue her not : Thy looks
Are grown too terrible to court her now.
                                    [Exit Amaranta.
    GAL. But will you then forego my promise, sir !
    HEI. Your first assurance was, her love should
Present her willingly into mine arms,
And that I must expect, there is no ease
Nor pleasure in restraint.
    GAL.                         You mean Arthiopa.
I'll fetch her, sir, if you'll but let me force
This wayward fool to tell where she's conceal'd.
    HEI. This is that fair Arthiopa whom I'll enjoy.
    GAL. Persuade my daughter to your bed.  Alas !
        you
Are married, sir.
    HEI.                         Or thy ambition else
Were happily so bold to think I'll chuse
Her for my wife !
    GAL. In troth, the other way
Is but unwholesome kind of love ;
Yet may be fit enough for lost Arthiopa ;
If you'll take leisure till I find her out.
But to betray a daughter !—
    HEILD. You lately could betray your country, sir,
Why not a daughter now ?
Mock not my rais'd desires, bring her to-night !
Not forc'd by terror, or outrageous strength,

But, by the soothings of thy tongue, wrought to
A willing liberal consent. Go! do't!
Or thou shalt bleed.

GAL. Peace to your majesty!
This fool in a religious pity hath
Destroy'd herself, i' th choicest hour of time,
When I design'd she should be wedded to
The Prince: for dull loose Heildebrand,
If th' other had but satisfied his lust,
In drunken bounty would surrender all
His conquest here, t' endow and make her great.
What is our human cunning, our obscure,
And vicious wisdom, worth? since at this play
Of policy a gamester cannot win
That hath not skill, but power to help his sin.

[*Exeunt.*

*Enter* ASCOLI *unbound,* RANGONE, GANDOLPHO.

RAN. I hear the lady, sir, and Altophil
Are pris'ners still, and by that traitor were
But led to counterfeit delights.

ASCO. My own calamities soon vanish from
My thoughts, when I remember theirs. You see
This captain gives my hands their liberty;
But I expect he's now so far restor'd,
That he'll contrive the freedom of
My person and my mind.

RAN. Gandolpho, know,
The counsel I have breath'd will shortly, when
Your reason and your piety consult,
Advance your profit much, your honour more.

ASCO. Your error past I have forgiven; as well
Assur'd Galeotto's cunning did seduce
Your easy nature in pretence of gratitude,
To do perfidious things to th' State and me.
But your amendment now shall have as full
Reward as if the memory were lost

Of all your former guilt.

RAN. How excellent repentance shows! it may
Perhaps proceed too slow, but when
'Tis real never comes too late.

GAN. Sir, thus dejected on the earth, I beg
Your pardon, and should rise made happy, though
Not innocent, if you believe that I
Was wrought into my crime, by him that found
A subtle use of my unskilful love.*

ASCO. My faith is willingly confirm'd, and you
Call'd back to all the favour you forsook;
The citadel continues still in your command,
Though with bold strangers new-enforc'd;
And by your power a secret entrance may
Be soon devis'd for a surprise.

RAN. The absence of your person, sir, which is
So much lamented now, when you appear,
Will add a courage equal to the joy
Our soldiers shall receive; and, though dispers'd,
The town may yield enough for this design.

GAN. What valour, or long practice in the war,
Made perfect with much doubtful enterprise,
Can do, we shortly will achieve: but for
A while you must rest close in durance here.

ASCO. My patience is so wise, it will persuade
Me to 't. Rangone, come! the dangers which
These lovers fear are such as we would fain
Prevent, or else adventure to revenge. [*Exeunt.*†

*Enter* HEILDEBRAND, GALEOTTO, ARTHIOPA.

GAL. The beams of your bright beauty could not be
So hid, but I must find them out.

AR. My life I now esteem not worthy of my care,

---

* Here the folio interpolates this stage direction. [" *Kisses his hand.*"]
† See Addenda, No. III.

Since you have sever'd me from Altophil.

GAL. Your lover yet is safe ; but if you use
The King with cruelty, expect the like
On him.  I knew, when he beheld          [*Aside.*
Her lustre shine, my Amaranta would
Be free ; already he grows hot : this fire,
Like those that chymists keep, must still
In secret burn, whilst gazers void the room.
                                        [*Exit.*

HEI. Which way shall I redeem the error of
My former wonder, that, in ignorance,
Committed fond idolatry to one
Who in her greatest beauty may become
Thy worshipper, and not decline her own
Prerogative ; though she excel a throng
Of others that are comely too.

AR. Sir! I am hither forc'd
By a perverse and treacherous counsellor ;
His tongue hath much envenom'd your chaste
    ears,
And would persuade you [to] a horrid sin :
But all my comfort is, your nature hath
Been still so rightly taught, you'll easily
Resist temptations of [a] greater strength.

HEI. Know, thou art hither come, to lay thy
    white
Attractive hand upon my sceptre, and
Give laws to me to make decrees of war
And peace : fold up my ensigns, then command
Them straight unfold again, until they spread
Their bloody streamers in a foreign land :
But then, my precious sweetness, you must love.

AR. Your goodness, sir, I will ; but if your
    thoughts
Are prompted to attempt unlawful deeds,
Sure all the righteous world must hate you then ;
Nor would I be the last should frown upon

A wicked lover though a King.

HEI. Such cold discourse befits an hermitage,
Where age and hunger make a rev'rend
Pretence to hate the pleasure, when, alas,
They have out-liv'd the appetite. You must
Come nearer yet.

AR. O! think upon your honour, sir, and what
Protects it,—Heaven.

HEI. It is some pleasure to
Delay those thoughts a while. Draw near! make me
Acquainted with your lips. Why should they want
Impression that so easily swell; that are
So soft, and fit to take the seal of love?

AR. You'll fright my soul from this unfortunate
Weak tenement, where she unwillingly
Hath dwelt of late; and now 'tis shaken so
With that strong tempest in your looks,
She dares not longer stay.

HEI. Let her come forth, and in my bosom rest.

AR. No, sir, her second dwelling is above
The stars, where she will tell such tales of you,
If you persist, that th' earth shall grow too hot
For your abode, and shortly after, hell
Too cold; they'll mend and multiply their fires
Against you come.

HEI. Were you less fair, such coyness would
    dissuade.

AR. If you continue in this exercise
Of impious power, be still a king; but may
You live to know your title given you for
A scorn, no subjects left you to obey;
More enemies to conquer what you have,
'Till be so little and so cheap: this in
Your age, when miseries do most perplex,
And strength is quite decay'd that should support
The weight, which younger patience thinks no load.

HEI. Are you so excellent at curses, lady?

AR. But better far at blessings, sir.  If you
Subvert the furious danger of your will,
Be still a King ; and may your sceptre grow
Within your hand, as heaven had given it
A root; may it bud forth, increase in boughs,
Till't spread to the Platan tree,* and yield
A comfortable shade, where other kings
May sit delighted, and secure from all
The storms of war and tyranny.
  HEI. Leave me ! away !
That closet make your prison until night,
Where you shall harbour safe from him that would
Betray your virgin-wealth ; but look not back !
For then you share the guilt of my next crime.
You carry in your face the fire that feeds
My flame, which, if I see, 'twill kindle soon
What I will strive to quench. [*Exeunt several ways.†*

*Enter* ALTOPHIL, *bound again.*

  ALT. Arthiopa, Arthiopa ! O that
The double concave of this dismal place
Could but reverberate her name ; I would
Be mock'd, though with a sound of happiness,
Rather than quite depriv'd ; the ghosts
Of impious men walk and revisit the
Relinquish'd earth : but she is gone like things
Most excellent : the souls of votaries,
Who, once departed, know this foulsome world
So much unfit to mingle with their pure
Refined air that they will [ne'er] return.
Arthiopa !

*Enter* AMARANTA, *with a sword drawn.*

  AM. What voice is that, which with
Such fatal accent doth bemoan some great

See ante, vol. ii., p. 313.        † See Addenda, No. IV.
III.                                E

Eternal loss ?

ALT. Arthiopa is gone !
The secret vault, where thou did'st leave us safe
Enclos'd, was by Morello found ; who with
Rude help of murderers enforc'd her from
Mine arms, and left me bound.

AM. I fear'd some danger near,
Which made me haste to thy redress ; once more
My lord, let me give freedom to your strength.
                                        [*Unbinds him.*
Here, take this sword, 'tis a most precious jewel,
And like a relic hath hung long within
Our armoury.  If false Morello shall
Return to threaten death, defend your self.

ALT. I would this bounty had been earlier
            brought.

AM. My fears are so increas'd, I dare not stay
To see the end of thy uncertain fate.
Be watchful and conceal'd.                 [*Exit.*

ALT. Th' unwearied courtesies  ·
Of this soft maid afflict my memory :
Since my affections were so far bequeath'd,
And spent ere they became her due, that now
I cannot pay her equal love for love,
But to another's loss.—What noise is that ?
A second door reveal'd ?  It opens too.
                        [*He steps behind the Arras.*


*Enter* GALEOTTO, MORELLO.

MOR. He's truss'd and pinion'd like a pullet,
        sir,
And you may spit him when you please.

GAL. Yes, he must die, for Amaranta loves
Him so, her wishes else will ne'er be quieted,
Nor she admit the Prince, though I could win
His heart : he suffers for disdain of her ;

She shall appear, and see it too ; 'twill breed
Her up to greatness, whose chief nourishment
Is blood.   When you have lockt the door, give her
This key, and send her hither.
   MOR. If she suspect the cause, she will not come.
   GAL. I say she must, and wait you close about
The King, to watch th' event of his hot enterprise.
                               [*Exit Morello.*
Duke Altophil, where is your mighty grace ?
   ALT. Who is't that  makes my title his bold
     mirth ?
   GAL. His fetters off ! his sword too in his hand !
This argues treachery.
   [*Strives to go back to the door, Altophil steps between.*
   ALT. Nay, no retiring yet.
I have been here reserved your prisoner,
But your dull bounty now hath made you mine.
   GAL. The very sword I won in duel from
The fam'd La Roche, i'th' Vale of Chamberie !
If 'twere taught t'observe as wizards do,
This chance is so sinister, 'twould infuse
A superstitious trembling through my veins.
   ALT. What is it makes your admiration still
Employ'd ? this object of your cruelty ?
   GAL. Who furnish'd thee with  such  a  rich
     defence
For rescue of thy life ?
   ALT. Your daughter, Sir !
   GAL. So true to him that hates her ! and so
     false
To me !  Destruction on her soul !
   ALT. Your curse will find such little entertain-
     ment
Where her virtues are, that it must soon return
Unto yourself ; the memory of her
Would fain dissuade my just revenge on thee.
Where hast thou left Arthiopa ?

GAL. With Heildebrand.

ALT. That fatal word calls back my absent and
Relenting spirits to my arm, which grew
With thoughts of mercy weak, but now it hath
A strength too dangerous for thy repulse.

> [*They fight awhile and part.*

GAL. Yo' are active, Sir.  Your nimble joints
 are bath'd
In jessamine oil.

ALT. And you are known a master in
This angry art : your rapier-miracles
Are chronicled by the hot-fencing French.
But I'll adventure some small practice, Sir.

> [*Fight again and sever.*

GAL. Pause! pause! a while, and keep your
 little breath,
Since 'tis your last, to make your friend more sport.

ALT. So merry? 'Cause your Devil is so learn'd,
And taught you faigne* in subtle lines
Proportion'd by a rule.  Still statue-like!
Standing as stiff as if your posture were
In brass.  I'll discompose it straight.

> [*Figh! again, Galleotto is wounded—they sever.*

GAL. I did not think your skill so excellent.
I shall drop down without revenge, hewn† with
A hatchet, like a senseless tree.  This to requite
Your kindness, Sir!

> [*Fight, Gal. is wounded ; again they sever.*

ALT. Laugh and be merry now!
You are not tickled with a straw, you see
This is a kind of sport will make you bleed.

GAL. O my false fame, where art thou now?
 He bores
And drills me where he list, as I were dead

---

* Fence—folio.
† The original editions have "hence."  The folio alters the
word to "hewn."

Already, and my breast a board us'd to
An augur, not a sword ; as if he had
Forecast how many holes would serve to make
My obscure heart transparent to the world.
The Furies greet you, Sir !

[*Fight, Galeotto falls.*

ALT. This for my much wrong'd Prince—this for
 Arthiopa—
And though a glorious villain, yet like to
A villain fall, despis'd upon the earth ;
Not pity'd in thy parting groan.*

GAL. Oh ! oh ! your wrath and I together end !

[*He dies.*

ALT. 'Tis strange I scap'd without a wound ;
 he was
A cunning duellist. Whose tread is that ?

*Enter* AMARANTA.

AM. Fear still makes others swift to fly from
 danger,
And me thus slow t'encounter it. Sure I
Have stay'd too long. Where are you, sir ?

ALT. Sweet Amaranta, hide thine eyes !

AM. Can they be weary grown of seeing you ?

ALT. But here's another object that will make
 them start
Till they untie their strings.

AM. Hah ! my Father ! mercy ! How far is thy
White throne remov'd from earth, that wretched I,
Thy daily orator, could not be heard ?
My blood will turn to tears at his dire obsequy ! †
O Altophil ! thou cruel lord, did I
For this with several hazards of my life,
And filial faith, keep thee from death ? That sword
I gave you for defence, and straight,

---

* The originals have "grove."
† The folio puts this line into Altophil's mouth.

Perverting all my courtesies, you did
Present it to my father's breast.

ALT. He was a wicked man.

AM. Were your uncivil accusation true,
Yet for my sake you might have spar'd his life.
For me, whom though you could not love,
I ne'er deserved your hatred in
Such fierce extremes.

ALT. There was no help, but one
Of us must fall, and I preserv'd myself.

AM. On such wise sure cautions my
Indulgent nature scorn'd to meditate,
When I deliver'd you from murthering hands;
But made the danger hastily mine own.

ALT. Those words like subtle light'ning pierce,
    and soon
Will kill me, though they make no wound.
Here, take this sword! revenge thy father's cause!
Revenge thy cause, whose love I have been forc'd
To pay with some neglect.   Kill me, and be just!

AM. Did you but call't neglect? and said that
    you
Were forc'd to it?

ALT. So forc'd, as I shall ever be, since my
First plight was seal'd; there is no ease, no end
Of that constraint.

AM. Still to lament, and never to be loved!

ALT. I am the source of all thy grief; make
    haste!
'Tis fit I die.—

AM. That sentence is my doom.

                    [*She falls on the sword.*

ALT. Hold, Amaranta, hold!
Where are our better angels at such times
As these?  Sweet virgin, breathe awhile!—

AM. Go, tell Arthiopa she needs not fear
Her rival now, my bridal bed is in

The earth.

ALT. Oh stay ! there may be help !

AM. When you come near my grave, if any flower
Can grow on such unlucky ground, pray water't with
A single tear, that's all I ask : Mercy, heaven !

*[She dies.*

ALT. For ever gone ! make much of her, you
  stars !
She is the brightest e'er shall come into
Your numberless society. Her last
Salute was sent unto Arthiopa :
Till she be safe I must not follow thee,
But I will hasten, gentle maid, to wear
Immortal wings, and thy new lustre then
Will be so known above, that if I stray,
It can direct and light me in the way.  *[Exit.*

---

## ACT V. SCENE I.

*Enter* ASCOLI, ALTOPHIL.

ASC. Whilst we confine ourselves to this dark
Division of the house, we are secure ;
The guards beneath Rangone did corrupt,
And made my entrance hither easily
Achiev'd. But thou hast told a piteous tale ;
The latter part will give posterity
A lasting cause to mourn ; for though
Galeotto suffer'd justly for his crimes,
And I must ever praise that victory,
Yet Amaranta's fate was most severe.

ALT. Alas ! it is not good to name her, sir ;
It shall but spoil our thoughts, and urge them to
A desperate belief.

Asc. Can your intelligence
Aim at no report that may declare
Your mistress' usage with the King?
     Alt. As passages are stopp'd, no soldier's voice
Is louder than a whisper now, and those
Are breath'd in the dark.

*Enter* Arthiopa, *her hair hanging loose about her.*

     Asc. Look, where she comes!
     Alt.                          If that be she
That gives her sorrow so much ornament
With hair dishevel'd, and unwilling looks
Declin'd with sighs that well may penetrate
The spacious vault of heaven, though it were arch'd
With Onyx and hard Chrysolite;
If that be she, persuade yourself to know
Her, sir, for I would fain preserve her still
A stranger to my sight.
     Ar. I came to seek
You Altophil, but thou art found too soon.
Why should I vex a lover's tenderness?
My lamentations are so great, they'd serve
T' infuse a virtue in a furious ear,
If pity may be call'd a virtue, but
I hope it is not so, for then the world
Would much offend, that long hath wanted it.
     Alt. What dismal story hangs upon thy tongue?
Speak it aloud, to wake the destinies,
Who sure are fast asleep; thy sufferance else
Will make us think they take no care of what
They can so easily create.
     Ar. Fierce Heildebrand,
That tyrant King! O! that my memory
Can keep a name should be forgot by all
The world.
     Asc. He finds our military souls are now
Grown tame, and meek as doves; he'll shortly use

No iron sceptre here.   We can be aw'd
And govern'd by a reed.
   AR. To this perfidious King I was convey'd
By Galeotto, falser than himself,
Endur'd his sinful courtship, and subdu'd,
At first with threat'ning vows, the fury of
His will : so that he seem'd restor'd to grace.
   ALT. And did he fall again ?
   AR.                              His piety
Grew soon too high a bliss for him ;   .
With tedious steps he labour'd up the hill,
Whose top being reach'd, his elevation shew'd
So strange, that it amaz'd his ignorance,
And giddily he tumbled down, in far
Less space than he could climb.
   ASC. Ah, swift inconstancy !
   AR. In a short moment he was quite
Declined from good, ev'n to the extacy of vice :
For in the blackest and most guilty hour
Of night, he came and found my curtains drawn ;
But so uncomely rude were his intents,
That though I there had slept as in a shrine,—
A place which death or holiness did privilege
With reverend esteem,—yet he would force
His way.   You sacred powers ! conceive how fit
It is the rest should make me dumb.
   ALT.                              I have begun
In blood, and must go on.   Inhuman guilt
Is so dispers'd and grown so strong, that now
Revenge from every valiant hand will be
Acknowledged lawful and divine !
   ASC. Let's hasten to our furious business ! Come
I have some strength in ambush near the fort,
And bold Rangone waits within, t' expect
What hidden troops I will command t' assault
My palace which this monster hath usurp'd.
   ALT. That charge confer upon my care.

Away! let's give him swift and silent death,
Like cannons, that destroy ere they are heard.
Yet, since we're sever'd in our enterprise,
We'll take a solemn leave, for ever, sir.
Farewell! Our usual fortune can persuade
Us to no better confidence.

ASC. Yes! noble Altophil,
We'll meet again. I'll find thee, though i'th' clouds.

ALT. I have of late been so much us'd
To weep, that I suspect the chrystal of
Mine eyes is but a kind of ice, which still
Each warmer change of weather straight doth thaw.

ASC. The sweetest, though most injur'd of thy sex,
Farewell! and think such comfort yet remains
As must not be despised, though but in hope.

AR. Sir, reason soon would ruin mine, if I
Had any left: the clean nice ermine not
Endures to live when once the hunter doth
Her whiteness soil, though with a little stain.

ALT. Arthiopa! Come! we are lovers still,
Though too, too much unfortunate. Time ne'er
Could find in all his old records, nor will
The like succeed in's future register. [*Exeunt omnes.*

*Enter* BRUSCO, GANDOLPHO, RAMPINO, HIRCO.

BRU. What lazy elephants are these? Huge
  rogues
That cannot dig through mould as soft as dough.

RAM. Is not the mine yet finish'd?

GAN. Have patience, gentlemen! I'm confident
Th'ave reach'd off the parapet,
And straight the powder will be laid.

RAM. But is the ambush well supplied that
  should
Break in upon the garrison when fire is given?

BRU. Those follow my direction, and are all
Prepar'd to execute at their just time.

HIR. Then one success is sure, for the old troops
Have sent a private message they'll assault
The city gates before the sun can rise
To shew them to the enemy.
I know th' are led by brave Piscaro, the
Lieutenant to our General, and I
Have planted those will give them entrance, though
They tread upon their mothers and their wives.[*]

BRU. It recreates my very lungs to think
How this luxurious stupid Heildebrand
In pleasure snorts, and little thinks
He shall be wak'd with an alarm.

GAN. You, sir, must take important care, lest in
The streets your consultation be with throngs
Of friends betray'd : for busy numbers will be soon
Observed. Your quarter is the Western-bridge.

BRU. But first attend about the palace to
Expect your orders : they must be given you there.

RAM. Direct your selves ! I am more watchful
than
A sick constable after his first sleep
On a cold bench. Hirco, along with me !
[*Exeunt Omnes.*

*Enter* HEILDEBRAND, MORELLO, RANGONE.

MOR. This is the Count Rangone, sir, who was
Before your conquest here chief captain of
The guard unto the captive Prince.

HEI. From Galeotto, sir, is your affair ?

RAN. This ring he humbly sends a present to
[*Gives him a ring.*
Your Majesty ; it was the first rich pledge
You gave him to confirm his new integrity,
By which he would persuade your royal thoughts
I am a messenger of trust, with hope
It may procure me privately your ear.

* These four last lines are, in the folio, given to Gandolpho.

HEI. Leave us, Morello, and attend within
[*Exit Morello.*
What is the cause he can so soon neglect
The homage of his duty here ?   He did
Not wait to-day !
    RAN. His daughter, sir, is sick,
O'er whom so fondly he laments, that he
Supplies both her physician's art and diligence.
    HEI. Proceed to his request !
    RAN. Your wisdom, sir, will much admire
To what a calm and easy sufferance
He hath reduced Arthiopa ! reclaim'd
Her frosty nature to such warm, such soft
And feminine desires, as it is fit
Her beauty should possess.
    HEI. Thou dost bewitch me with thy news.
    RAN. Sir, she no more retains the seeming fro-
          wardness
And peevish rigour of a maid,
But wonders why the Roman Lucrece did
Complain, because enforc'd, since boldly she
Concludes it now the only subtle way
To compass pleasure without sin.
    HEI. Wise Aretine's philosophy ; he'd read
It to his neice.
    RAN. No question, Galeotto had
Good modern authors for his doctrine, sir,
Else 'twould not thrive so well.   His instant suit
Unto your greatness is, you would prepare
To humble your occasions to this night,
As you may visit him ; and you shall find
The lady altered to your wish.
    HEI. It lay not in the power of all his skill
And vigilance, to send me a request
I would so willingly receive : this glad
Assurance render him with my best thanks !
And then return to be my guide.       [*Exeunt.*

*Enter* RAMPINO, HIRCO.

RAM. Stay here, and watch for more supplies!
    the word
Is gone about I've drawn to our confederacy,
From an obscure blind lane, a race of such
Indebted wights, as have not seen the sun
Since the last great eclipse, when wonder more
Than business brought them out.
    HIR. Have they any clothes?
    RAM. Why, dost thou think they go to play a
    prize?*
Is't of necessity they must appear
In scarlet breeches, and clean lac'd shirts?
Swords they have all, although their scabbards are
A little torn about the chape,† they'll serve
To poke, 'less men are squeamish, and won't let 'em
Enter their bodies because they are rusty.
    HIR. I would not be a sergeant in their way!
    RAM. Straight when the hurry shall begin to rise,
Beware my gossip goldsmith's shop; there be
Among us that will drink our morning's draughts
In plate, without asking how much an ounce.

*Enter* FRISKIN.

    HIR. Look there! you must wear an invisible
    ring.‡

*Enter* HEILDEBRAND, RANGONE.

    RAN. He said I should receive the lady here.
'Tis strange he fails! If, sir, it will become
Your greatness to expect a while, I'll seek

---

* " If ever he go alone, I'll never wrestle for prize."—
                         *Shakespeare.*
  " The raising such silly competitions among the ignorant,
proposing prizes for such useless accomplishments, and inspir-
ing them with such absurd ideas of superiority, has in it something immoral as well as ridiculous."—*Addison.*
  † The hook. The metal part at the top.
  ‡ See Addenda, No. V.

Galeotto out, and send her hither.

   HEI. The object may deserve my patience; but
     take care
Y'are swift in your return.

   RAN. If wishes can
Procure prosperity to the design,
Thou shalt not want them; Altophil, I'll guard
The gates below to hinder all impediments. [*Exit.*
                  [*Strange music is heard above.*
   HEI. This sure is some preparative, although
The sound's not very amorous.

*The Song, to a horrid Tune.*

You fiends and furies come along,
With iron crow and massy prong,
   Come! drag your shackles and draw near,
To stir a huge old sea-coal cake,
That in our hollow hell did bake,
   Many a thousand, thousand year.
[*Chorus.* Until your harvest day at doom,
      No grief like this will ever come,
      From whom you may that pleasure find,
      Which does your malice feed 'gainst human
      kind.]*

In sulph'rous broth Tereus hath boil'd;
Basted with brimstone, Tarquin hath broil'd
   Long, long enough; then make more room!
Like smokey flitches hang them by
Upon our sooty walls to dry,
   A greater ravisher will come.
[*Chorus.* Until your harvest day, &c.

If you want fire, fetch a supply,
From Ætna and Puteoli!
   Yet stay awhile, you need not stir,

    * The Chorus does not occur in the early editions, only in
the folio.

Since if his glowing eyes shall chance,
To cast on Proserpine a glance,
   He is so hot he'll ravish her.
[*Chorus.* Until your harvest day, &c.

*Enter* ALTOPHIL.

HEI. My senses are grown sick! speak! what
   art thou?
ALT. Men call me Altophil.
HEI. He I encounter'd in a battle on
The banks of Sibaris? I'ld rather meet
Thee in that river, stemming against
The tide, than thus wall'd in where horror dwells.
I am betray'd!
ALT. Stir not! you are confin'd,
And cannot scape me now; for such events
As are prescrib'd i' th' secret book
Above, here we shall both receive.
HEI. I fear not mine, my single valour is
Enough, if thou art all mine enemies.
ALT. You come to visit Galeotto, sir!
              [*Draws the hangings.*
See where he rudely sits! ill manner'd lord,
That will not rise to welcome such a potentate!
HEI. Sleeping in death! such nodding likes me
   not.
ALT. Survey him well; he was your traitor, sir.
Go hug him now! cherish that falsehood that
Could ruin States, and draw a nation to
Captivity. Open his head, where all
His plots and policies are treasur'd up,
And take them out: it is not fit such wealth
Should die conceal'd i' th' grave.
HEI. Is there no more
Remaining of those sweating toils, danger,
And studious wit that helps ambition to
Ascend, than such a pale complexion and

A cold dumb mockery of what we were?

ALT. Now, sir, to entertain your precious time
With new variety, although I know
You are in haste, see Amaranta, here!
                    [*Draws the hangings further.*
HEI. Is she so alter'd, and grown silent too?

ALT. This was a noble beauty once, replete
With all that gentle ornament lovers
In their kind passion, or poets in
Diviner fury, could advance with praise.
And this, so sanctified a thing, you did
Endeavour to corrupt.  Pray, court her now,
And thrid her tears like Oriental pearl,
Take rubies from her lips to darken all
The jewels in your crown, y' ave undertook
So much in counterfeit hyperboles.
Blast her fair hand with your false sighs, and swear
'Tis no idolatry.  You may ; for look
How like a goddess a dead lady shews.

HEI. I'll see no more! if they are fit for monu-
    ments,
Why were they not interr'd before I came?

ALT. Yes! you must needs behold all that is gay
And pleasing here, 'twill make your welcome seem
More absolute.  Come forth, Arthiopa!

*Enter* ARTHIOPA, *her hair dishevelled as before.*

HEI. This living spectacle disturbs and frights
My senses more than all that's dismal 'bout
The dead.  No traitor like to that within.
My courage fails me now, which till this hour
I trusted most.

ALT. Look on the ruins you
Have made of such a building! cherubims
Would strive to dwell in it, but that they knew
They then must dispossess a soul as good
As they.  See, how it droops!

HEIL. The period of
My vex'd injurious life draws on apace.

ALT. Prepare your valour and your sword, for love
Unto the sacred title which you bear,
You shall not die surpris'd, without defence,
But try what useful strength is left you, now
Your virtue 's gone. [*Both draw.*

HEIL. Stay, then ! I'll call to my remembrance all
The noble deeds of my heroic youth,
Whilst growing mighty with the thoughts, I may
Behave myself as if I had no guilt.

ART. O hold, my lord ! why should you hazard thus
The treasure of your life ? impoverishing
The needy remnant of the virtuous world
In my revenge ; leave it to th' holy powers.

HEIL. Wilt thou be courteous to her, and desist ?

ALT. Move but a little back, Arthiopa !
Couldst thou believe me worthy of thy love,
Yet doubt my fortitude t' encounter him,
Whose crimes have left him no assistant, but
What comes from hell ? All that is good
Forsook him when he injur'd thee.

ART. 'Tis wearisome to beg your safety now !

ALT. By all the fervour of our mutual vows,
I charge thee give me liberty to try
What anger can perform when it is just.

ART. I cannot disobey, though when I see
Your dangers I can die——

HEIL. I am resolv'd for thy assault, yet stay.
That lady's suff'rings hang so heavy on
My soul, that it foretells a longer sleep
Than I would willingly begin ; I wish
Thou couldst prepare me with a little wound,
That might let out my lustful blood, and leave
The rest to strengthen me for this dire cause.

III. F

ALT. I'm good at opening of a vein.  There, sir!
          [*They fight, Heildebrand falls.*
HEIL. Had that afflicted terror in her face
Been hid, th'adst found more trouble in this victory.
I feel desires of bliss, and those I hope
May prosper, though presented very late. [*He dies.*
ALT. Depart! forgotten, and forgiven.
ART. Why dost thou shrink? speak, Altophil!
    why dost
Thou bow like tired unweildy age?
ALT. His sword has been too busy here, just here
About the heart.
ART. The region of thy love.
I find thou hast a wound by perfect sympathy,
For mine grows sick, and doth desire to bleed.
ALT. How fares my mistress, sweet Arthiopa?
ART. Your pulse must give account of all my
    health.
ALT. Take't not unkindly I shall leave thee now,
My eyes grow dim, and I would furnish them
With everlasting light.
ART. O, my dear Lord!
Let me not think that voice was yours.
ALT. Alas! that, in a loyal lover, death
Must argue some inconstancy, since 'tis
The first occasion to forsake what we
May ne'er enjoy again.
ART. I shall not be forsaken; for I feel
I can decay apace, and keep you company
In this long journey to our last abode.
ALT. First let us seek our vows upon our lips,
They were so strictly kept, that we shall find
Them warm, as if but newly breath'd,
These are the funeral rites of love.     [*They kiss.*
ART.                              Break heart!
It is the way to show that thou wert true.
                              [*They both die.*
WITHIN. Victory! the fort is taken! Victory!

*Enter* ASCOLI, RANGONE, GANDOLPHO, RAMPINO,
    BRUSCO, HIRCO, *and the Guard.*

ASCO. Your brother died, Gandolpho, in the first
Assault : you and the soldiers still shall share
My best affection and rewards.

OMNES. Long live your Highness!

RAN. O, Sir, the splendour of our triumphs is
Eclips'd ; we came too late. Behold
The tyrant is not only slain, but here
The valiant General lies, his mistress too,
Embracing, though insensible of love.

ASCO. Friendship and love are dead ; I find
My sorrows are too mighty for my tongue.

RAN. The King thus sever'd from them, it appears
He first was kill'd by Altophil, who straight
Fell after on a ling'ring hurt ; Arthiopa,
This seen, could need no other wound than grief.

BRUS. The pride and comfort of the war is gone!

RAM. A General fit to lead the world against
The force of hell.

HIR. But now we may hang up our arms,
And yield to every enemy.

RAN. Sir, though 'tis fit you mourn, yet take
        some care
So to proceed, as that your subjects may
Be perfectly assured of our victory !

ASCO. Bear hence these woeful objects of our first
True elegy ! thy statue, Altophil,
Shall in my palace stand, with sad Arthiopa
Lamenting still ; and Amaranta fixt
On th' other side, hiding her eyes, that found
Too much of beauty in her rival's face ;
In lasting gold, by old Ephesian art
Design'd, this triple figure I'll advance :
Though it will little credit add to fate
That made such lovers so unfortunate.

                              [*Exeunt omnes.*

## EPILOGUE.

Our poet in his fury hath profest,
Yet gravely too, with's hand upon his breast,
That he will never wish to see us thrive,
If by an unhumble epilogue we strive
To court from you that privilege to-day
Which you so long have had to damn a play.
'Las, Gentlemen, he knows, to cry plays down
Is half the business termers have in town;
And still the reputation of their wit grows strong,
As they can first contemn, be't right or wrong,
Your wives and country friends may power exact,
To find a fault or two in every act :
But you by his consent most kindly shall
Enjoy the privilege to rail at all :
A happy freedom, which y'esteem no less
Than money, health, good wine, or mistresses ;
And he, he hopes, when age declines his wit
From this our stage ; to sit and rule i'th' pit ;
Heaven willingly shall assume a charter firm
As yours, to kill a poet every term.
And though he never had the confidence,
To tax your judgment in his own defence,
Yet the next night when we your money share
He'll shrewdly guess what your opinions are.

## ADDENDA.

The following are among the principal corrections and alterations of the earlier edition, as chronicled in the folio of 1673.

### 1.

The second Act concludes thus : after " in a strict command,"

ART. In pity, Altophil, I'll hide mine eyes;
For though they have unhappy been to me,
Yet I to them will not so cruel be
As to permit they heedful view should take
Of all thy love, and must at once forsake.
            [*Exeunt Rang. Arthi.*
ALT. Since, Amaranta, we are here enclos'd,
And I must learn to woo with love impos'd;
Let us contrive a way of wooing so,
That from constraint love may to freedom grow.
Our mortal love (which narrowly extends
No farther than life's lease, and quickly ends)
We will draw out to vast eternity ;
But to begin that progress, we must die.

### 2.

This scene has been introduced apparently to suit the taste, after the Restoration, for greater variety and song.   It comes in in the first scene of the third act, between the exit of Heildebrand and others with the concluding words : " Still wear your secret promise in your thoughts," and the entrance of " Ascoli, Altophil, Arthiopa, their arms bound."

*Enter* AMARANTA, PHŒBE.

PHŒB.    Madam, your little cousin, Orna, is
Without, and comes to visit you.
    AM.    Attend her in!  [*Exit Phœbe.*
This dreadful storm of war has frighted her.
Can childhood, in a cloister bred, fear danger?
Not being grown to the unhappy sense
Of love neglected and disdain'd.          '

*Enter* ORNA.

ORN.  How do you, Madam?
AM.  Alas, sweet cousin, you look pale!
ORN.  We have been praying all night in the nunnery
For fear of the soldiers.
AM.  The soldiers will not hurt ye.
ORN.  I hear they are cruel black men, cousin.
AM.  Fear nothing! you are safe.
ORN.  I dare stay anywhere but in the dark.
AM.  You come in season, hither; prithee sing
That song which Gartha taught thee ere she died.
ORN.  I'm out of breath.
AM.  Pause and recover it.

THE SONG.

ORN.  Run to love's lott'ry! run, maids, and rejoice:
When, drawing your chance, you meet your own choice;
And boast that your luck you help with design,
By praying cross-legg'd to old bishop Valentine.
Hark, hark! a prize is drawn, and trumpets sound!
          Tan, ta, ra, ra, ra!
          Tan, ta, ra, ra, ra!
Hark maids! more lots are drawn! prizes abound.
Dub! dub a, dub a, dub! the drum now beats!
And, dub a, dub a, dub! echo repeats.
As if at night the god of war had made
Love's queen a skirmish for a serenade.
      Haste, haste, fair maids, and come away!
      The priest attends, your bridegrooms stay.
Roses and pinks will be strewn where you go;
Whilst I walk in shades of willow, willow.

When I am dead let him that did slay me,
Be but so good as kindly to lay me
There where neglected lovers mourn,
Where lamps and hallow'd tapers burn,
Where clerks in quires sad dirges sing,
Where sweetly bells at burials ring.
 My rose of youth is gone,
 Wither'd as soon as blown!
 Lovers, go ring my knell!
 Beauty and love farewell!
 And lest virgins forsaken
 Should, perhaps, be mistaken
In seeking my grave, alas! let them know
I lye near a shade of willow, willow.

    *Enter* PAGE.

PAGE. Madam, your father expects you in the garden.
AM. I fear his pity of me will undo him.
ORN. I pray desire him to speak to the king,
That the soldiers may leave drumming.  I'm sure,
We can't sing matins for 'em in the nunnery.
 AM. Come cousin, I will teach you grief betimes,
Lest when your growth admits of love it then
Should meet you unprepar'd.

     3.

This interpolation occurs in the fourth Act, immediately between the exit of Ascoli, Rangone,
and Gandolpho, and the entrance of Heildebrand,
Galeotto, and Arthiopa.

   *Enter* AMARANTA, PHŒBE, ORNA.

AMAR. Send back my little cousin to her cloister!
She has a soul too musical for mine.
 PHŒBE. Shall she go to-night, madam?
 AMAR. Ay, presently.  My discords are
Unfit companions for her harmony.
 ORNA. Call for the coach.  I am grown weary of you.
'Tis merrier being in the nunnery
Than here.  Phœbe, pray call for the coach!
 PHŒBE. First sing the song to her you promis'd me.

It may put her out of this dull humour.

ORNA. Cousin, leave your melancholy and hear me.

THE SONG.

'Tis, in good truth, a most wonderful thing
(I am e'en asham'd to relate it)
That love so many vexations should bring
And yet few have the wit to hate it.

Love's weather in maids should seldom hold fair ·
Like April's mine shall quickly alter.
I'll give him to-night a lock of my hair,
To whom, next day I'll send a halter.

I cannot abide these malapert males.
Pirates of love, who know no duty ;
Yet love with a storm can take down their sails
And they must strike to adm'ral Beauty.

Farewell to that maid who will be undone
Who in markets of men, where plenty
Is cried up and down, will die even for one.
I will live to make fools of twenty.

AMAR. Music to her who does all comforts lack
Is like to whistling winds before a wrack.

ORNA. Cousin, farewell! I'll go sing with the nuns.
[*Exeunt several ways.*

4.

The following scene occurs in the same Act,
between the exit of Heildebrand and Arthiopa and
the entrance of "Altophil bound again." The
mention of "stage doors" shows the alteration in
the stage arrangements which had taken place since
the first production of the play in 1643.

*Enter* RAMPINO, HIRCO, *at one door,* BRUSCO *at another.*

BRUS. What cabin'd up like sea-sick ladies in
A storm? Abroad! abroad! if you can find
No business now, you may ask leave to sleep
For ever.

Ram. Right reverend Brusco, what news?

Brus. The Count Rangone has had conference with
Th' afflicted Prince.   We must meet at his house,
Where we shall find confed'rates, and with hearts
Of as resistless metal as our own.
We only want now a convenient store-house where
We may convey the arms and ammunition.

Ram. You may have Frisklin's house.
You could not find a safer magazine,
If you should travel through the whole town map.

*Enter* Frisklin.

See, where he comes!

Frisk. Signior, my wife remembers her to you ;
And desires you of all loves I may take
Measure of the King immediately ;
And you know, signior, she's, as they say,
A kind of longing woman.

Ram. Well, you shall:
But I've another employment for you
First.   This night you must watch at your back door,
Where you shall see, come gliding down the stream,
A boat fraught with the Prince's arms and ammunition
Which we have stole.   Receive 'em, for you know
Men that will thrive must labour in their calling.

Frisk. Signior, you say right: I have ever found
It the best way.

Ram. To-morrow I will send you customers,
Whom you may sell 'em to, and afterwards
Pay yourself my debt.                    [*Exeunt.*

### 5.

These few lines, to suit the taste of the ground-
lings, are in the 5th act, immediately before
the entrance of Heildebrand and Rangone together.

Frisk. The chapmen are come, sir, but let me tell you
I do not like 'em.   They look rustily,
Each wears a pound of hair on's upper lip.
Pray signior let 'em not deal on the ticket.*

* On credit.   Since corrupted into "tick."

You know ready money makes the pot boil
Though the devil piss out the fire.

RAM. They shall pay ready money.   Farewell.

FRISK. But hark you, signior, I may tell you in private:
One of them took my wife into the coal hole,
And about an hour after she shriekt abominably.

RAM. No more words.

FRISK. But I hope, Sir, you will remember my bill.

RAM. Away! I will.                    [*Exit Frisklin.*

Hirco, if thou meet'st Frisklin in the dark,
Prithee give him a prick in the belly piece ;
For he has prickt me there often.

HIR. I will do him that kindness for thy sake.

                              [*Exeunt several ways.*

LOVE AND HONOUR.

*Love and Honor. Written by W. D'avenant, Knight.
Presented by his Majesties Servants at the Black Fryers.
London, printed for Hum. Robinson, at the Three
Pidgeons, and Hum. Moseley, at the Princes Armes in St.
Paul's Churchyard. 1649.*

*Ib. in the Collected Edition of D'avenant's Works.
Published by Herringham. Folio, 1673.*

Love and Honour was originally called the Courage of Love. It was afterwards named by Sir Henry Herbert, at Davenant's request, The Nonpareilles, or the Matchless Maids.

The scene is laid in Savoy, but the plot has no historical foundation. The Duke of Savoy, and Alvaro, his son, are apparently imaginary persons; no traces of them, as depicted in the play, are to be found in the annals of that country. It is not improbable that the story may be narrated in some of the Italian novels, although it is rather thought that the plot is original. The play is possessed of great merit, and might, with some alterations, be adapted to the modern stage, and stand a fair chance of becoming as popular as it appears to have been two hundred years ago.

After dramatic entertainments were revived, Mr Langbaine assures us that he has seen this play often acted with applause, at the playhouse in Lincoln's Inn Fields, and afterwards at the theatre in Dorset Gardens. Originally produced at Blackfriars, it was more successful than any other of our author's plays.

"In point of style it resembled Shakespeare rather than Fletcher, and is more correctly finished than any of Sir William Davenant's former plays, which shows that he was not hurt by the applause that he had met with, but thought himself obliged to labour hard, and take so much the more pains to deserve it. Both these plays [i.e., this play and the Unfortunate Lovers] are without any testimonies of the author's friends before them, because published at a time when, perhaps, there were not many who were inclined to inform the world that they were his friends."—*Kippis' Biographia.*

At the opening of the new playhouse in Dorset Gardens this play was acted before the Court, upon which occasion Mr Betterton, who played Prince Alvaro, wore the King's coronation suit; Mr Harris, who played Prince

Prospero, obtained that of his Royal Highness the Duke of York ; and Mr Price, who performed Lionell, Duke of Parma, had a very rich suit that was given him by the Earl of Oxford.

Pepys thus records his opinion of the play, 21 October 1661 :—"To the Opera, which is now newly begun to act again, after some alteration of their scene, which do make it very much worse ; but the play, 'Love and Honour,' being the first time of their acting it, is a very good plot, and well done."

23 October. "To the Opera, and there I saw again 'Love and Honour,' and a very good play it is."

The folio edition of 1673 abounds, as usual, in omissions and alterations by no means judicious.

In 1720 there was produced at the Theatre in Lincoln's Inn Fields a three-act comedy in prose, adapted from this play by Charles Molloy, entitled "The Half-pay Officers." In his preface he says, "This thing was brought upon the stage with no other design but that of showing Mrs Fryar, the house being willing to encourage anything by which it might propose to entertain the town, therefore the author, or rather the transcriber, did not think himself any way concerned in its success as to the reputation of a writer. I say transcriber, the greatest part of it being old. The part of Mrs Fryer is in an old play called 'Love and Honour,' which she acted when she was young, and which was so imprinted in her memory she could repeat it every word ; and it was to an accidental conversation with her this farce owed its being. She acted with so much spirit and life, before two or three persons who had some interest with the House, that we judged it would do upon the stage. She was prevailed upon to undertake it, upon which this farce was immediately projected and finished in fourteen days. It was got up with so much hurry that some of the comedians, who are allowed to be excellent in their way, had not time to make themselves masters of their parts ; therefore, not being perfect in the dialogue, they could not act with that freedom and spirit they are observed to do upon other occasions."

Whincop, in noticing this farce, says that "the part of an old grandmother was performed by Mrs Fryer, who

was then eighty-five years of age, and had quitted the
stage ever since the reign of King Charles II. It was
put in the bills : ' The part of Lady Richlove to be performed by Peg Fryar, who has not appeared upon the
stage these fifty years,' which drew together a great
house. The character in the farce was supposed to be a
very old woman, and Peg went through it very well, as
if she had exerted her utmost abilities; but, the farce
being ended, she was brought again upon the stage to
dance a jig, which had been promised in the bills. She
came tottering in, as if ready to fall, and made two or
three pretended offers to go out again, but all on a sudden, the music striking up the *Irish Trot*, she danced
and footed it almost as nimbly as any wench of five-and-
twenty could have done. This woman afterwards set
up a public-house at Tottenham Court, and great numbers frequently went to satisfy their curiosity in seeing
so extraordinary a person."

The farce of the " Half-pay Officers" was produced on
the 11th January 1719-20, to which was added " a new
farce call'd Hob's Wedding, in 2 acts, being the sequel to
the Country Wake, with entertainments of dancing by
Mrs Fryer, particularly the Bashful Maid and the Irish
Trot." The dramatis personæ were not mentioned in the
bill, but the following cast is in the second edition of
the " Half-pay Officers," printed in 1720, 12mo —

MEN.

| | | |
|---|---|---|
| BELLAYR, | ⎫ | Mr RYAN. |
| FLUELLIN, | ⎬ *Officers.* | Mr GRIFFIN. |
| MAC MORRIS, | ⎭ | Mr H. BULLOCK. |
| CULVERIN, *a sharper*, . . | | Mr SPILLER. |
| MEAGRE, *a scrivener*, . . | | Mr C. BULLOCK. |
| LOADHAM, *a Hamburgh merchant*, | | Mr HARPER. |
| SHARP, *Bellayr's servant*, . | | Mr EGLETON. |
| JASPER, *Meagre's servant*, . | | Mr BOHEME. |

WOMEN.

| | | |
|---|---|---|
| WIDOW RICH, . . . | | Mrs VANDERVELT. |
| BENEDICT, | ⎫ *Her two grand-* | Mrs BULLOCK. |
| CHARLOTTE, | ⎬ *daughters*, | Miss STONE. |
| JANE, *the widow's servant*, . | | Mrs ROBERTSON. |

Scene—Covent Garden.

Mrs Vandervelt and Mrs Fryer appear to have been the same person, and, it is surmised, that the latter was her maiden name, by which she had been known as an actress in her earlier years, although no traces of her are discernible in any list of dramatis personæ appended to the printed plays of Charles II.'s time. The Prologue to the "Half-pay Officers" thus introduces the old lady :—

> " In vain old Shakespeare's virtue treads the stage,
> On empty benches doomed to spend his rage ;
> When we would entertain, we're forc'd to ship ye
> Tumblers from France, mock kings from Mississippi !
> To-night, strange means we try your smiles to win,
> And bring a good old matron on the scene :
> Kindly she quits a calm retreat, to show
> What acting pleas'd you fifty years ago.
> Like old Entellus, long disus'd to fight,
> Fresh in her spirit she summons all her might,
> Season'd by time, and harden'd to the stroke,
> She dares the youngest of us all provoke :
> Blooming a century, like a great oak.
> Unconscious in her limbs what havock time
> Can make, or how deform us from our prime,
> When you behold her quiv'ring on the stage,
> Remember, 'tis a personated age ;
> Nor think that no remains of youth she feels,
> She'll shew you, ere she's done,—she has it in her heels."

It will be observed that Whincop, quoting, terms the Widow "Lady Richlove," while in the printed book she is styled "Widow Rich." This immaterial alteration may have been the result of an after-thought either on the part of the author or of the manager, just in the same way as Lord and Lady Randolph, in Home's tragedy of Douglas, originally stood Lord and Lady Barnet. But Whincop is decidedly mistaken in attributing imbecility to Peg Fryer in the matter of the dance, which is incidental to the piece, and occurs in the second act. The stumbling he refers to, was a part of the stage business. Thus it is :

" Cul. I have brought musick—they shall give us a flourish, and, ladies, let us have a dance before the wedding.    [Flourish.

Wid. Ah! this musick makes my blood dance in my veins.

BEL. Come, madam! will you make one in a dance?

WID. I have made one in a morris before now.

CUL. She dance! she'll totter like an old oak in a storm. I'm afraid too much motion will overheat your blood. What say you, widow, will you venture?

WID. Verily, I will; for I don't think it wholesome to stand idle.          [*Dance: at the end she falls.*

CUL. What's the matter?

WID. 'Tis nothing! I am us'd to it. I am taken so every now and then; once in fifty years or so; but 'twill over, lead me in!—

CUL. Come, my little love, the sound of the wedding fiddles will fright it away. Strike up, scrapers!

          [*Musick plays 'em off.*"

The *Irish Trot*, as advertised, formed a portion of the interlude.

" As to the farce itself," Geneste remarks, "it is professedly a compilation. Fluellin is pretty much as in Shakespeare, Culverin is a bully like Pistol—he is made to eat the leek. The characters of Loadham, Meagre, and Jasper, with the greater part of what they say, are taken from those of Lodham, Rawbone, and Camelion in Shirley's Wedding. Two speeches are well altered from Much ado about Nothing. The half-pay officers are Bellayr, Fluellin, and MacMorris;. Bellayr, Loadham, and Meagre pay their addresses to Benedict—she and Charlotte are the Widow's grand-daughters—Charlotte is a young girl, but ready for a husband. Jasper is Meagre's man, and as thin as his master. Culverin wants to marry the Widow—she is very willing. Culverin is discovered to have been a highwayman, and the Widow's friends prevail on her to marry Fluellin. Bellayr and MacMorris marry Benedict and Charlotte. Fluellin was a new character to a considerable part of the audience, as Shakespeare was not very much read, and his Henry the 5th had not been acted since the Restoration. The author of this farce has put his materials very well together. He acknowledges his obligations to Shakespeare and Davenant, but says nothing of those to Shirley. Some little addition is made to the character of the Widow. The song " for am'rous sighs" &c., is so good it should have been retained. The half-pay officers and Hob's Wedding, (attributed to Leigh the actor), were acted

III.          G

together seven times. The author or authors had two benefits, viz., on the third and sixth nights."

The only other occasion on which Peg Fryer seems to have acted was on the 28th March following, when she appeared as Mrs. Amlet in Vanburgh's Confederacy.

Of Mr Betterton, who played Alvaro, some particulars will be found in the Memoir of D'Avenant introductory of our first volume.

Mr Harris—who acted Count Prospero—as Davies observes, was, like Betterton, a general actor, and like him possessed of varied and opposite abilities. Pepys, in his Diary, notices him very frequently. His forte seems to have been light comedy, in which having been said to be superior to Betterton, and having been praised by the King and the public, he became troublesome to D'Avenant, and in July 1663 had seceded from the Duke's company. D'Avenant appealed to the King, and in December, Harris had returned to his duty.

He left the stage prior to the union of the two companies in 1682. Further accounts of him will be found in the introduction to the Siege of Rhodes in the present volume, and to Juliana in vol. i. of Crowne's Dramatic Works, in our series.

Mr Price, who acted Lionell, Prince of Parma, in this play, very shortly afterwards performed with Messrs Betterton and Harris in a revival of Romeo and Juliet when, as Curll has it, " a merry incident happened " in which Mrs Holden bore a prominent part, but for which the reader is referred to p. 91 of Curll's History. Price's name does not otherwise appear among any of the recorded Dramatis Personæ prefixed to other plays of the time, nor is his biography apparently extant. There was a Mrs Price who acted in 1678 and in the Factious Citizen, printed in 1685, but supposed to have been performed at an earlier date.

Mrs Davenport, who acted Evandra, is styled in Curll's History of the Stage, 1741, " an excellent actress." Malone supposes that she, and not Mrs Marshall, was the actress whom the Earl of Oxford carried off, and Geneste concurs in this. Downes certainly says that Mrs Davenport was " erept the stage by love."—See preface to the Siege of Rhodes, and introduction to Juliana in the first volume of Crowne.

# PROLOGUE.

But that the Tyrant custom bears such sway,
We would present no Prologue to our play,
Since we have learn'd in Prologues all the scope
Is with weak words to strengthen weaker hope.
When with sad solemn phrase we court each ear,
Not to observe, but pardon, what you hear;
Or if there were but one so strangely wise
Whose judgement strives to please, and trust his
        eyes,
Him at an easy charge we could provoke
To a kind doom with this grave, long, old cloak.
Now for the over-subtle few, who raise
Themselves a trivial fame by a dispraise,
Our bold opinion is, they may descry
Some easy wit but much more cruelty.

## DRAMATIS PERSONÆ.

THE OLD DUKE OF SAVOY.
HIS BROTHER.        } *Disguised like Embassa-*
THE DUKE OF MILLAIN. }   *dors.*
ALVARO, *Prince of Savoy.*
LEONELL, *Prince of Parma.*
PROSPERO, *a young Count.*
CALLADINE, *an old counsellor.*
VASCO, *a colonel.*
ALTESTO,   }
FRIVOLO,   } *Officers and soldiers.*
TRISTAN,   }
EVANDRA, *Heiress of Millain.*
MELORA, *sister to Leonell.*
OLD WIDOW.
LELIA, *her maid.*
BOY.
MUSICIANS.
SOLDIERS.
SERVANTS.

.

*The Scene :* SAVOY.

# LOVE AND HONOUR.

## ACT I. SCÆNA I.

*A retreat being sounded as from far,*
*Enter* VASCO, ALTESTO, FRIVOLO.

VAS. Hark boys! they sound us a retreat! This
    skirmish, sirs,
Was no rare pastime to continue at ;
'Tis safer wrastling in a bed. Give me
Henceforth your white-fac'd foe, a plump fair
    enemy
That wears her head-piece lac'd ; I'm for a cambric
    helmet, I.
ALT. And yet these mighty men of Millain got
But little by the sport ; some of them shall
Vouchsafe to wear a single arm hereafter,
Two wooden legs too ; and limp their days out
In an hospital.
FRIV. How ? an hospital.
VAS. A road, a road ! Your highway, sir, is now
Your only walk of state for your maim'd soldier ;
Your hospital and pensions are reserv'd
For your maim'd mercers, decay'd sons o' th' shop,
That have been often cracked, not in their crowns
Like us, but in their credit, sir.
FRIV. And placket* squires, that have bin long
    diseas'd
In their lord's service ; a score of ducats
Shall bribe them into place, where they may sleep,

* See vol. ii., p. 157.

And eat, and pray too ; but with breath so much
Unwholesome, th' air can hardly purify't
And make it fit to reach near heaven.

ALT. Well, the surprize o' th' citadel, wherein
The Duke had plac'd his daughter, with the ladies
Of her train and treasure too, was a service
Of most rare work.

VAS. Just when they sallied out
To cut our rear in pieces, then steal in,
By ambush wisely laid, and make them all
Our prize was miracle.

FRIV. They say his daughter 'scap'd, and fled ;
     with her,
As her best guard, one they call Leonell,

*Enter* TRISTAN.

Whom our Count Prospero pursu'd.

VAS. Tristan ! welcome ! Is all our pillage wag-
     gon'd ?
Shall it to-night see Turin ?

TRIS. All's safe, my lusty leader ! Our horse, too,
Have sounded a retreat, and the foe speaks ;
He walks with's hands in's pockets, like a skipper
In a frost.

VAS. Well, let me reckon my estate :
First, a widow prisoner.

ALT. Mine's a maid prisoner,
Young, my Vasco ; she's yet in her first blush ;
And I've despatch'd her unto Turin, to
My mother's house, thy prisoner in her company ;
They are acquainted.

VAS. You have the luck. These bald chins are
     as familiar
With their good stars as with spur-rowels ;
Play with them and turn 'em which way they please.
I fought as well as he ; and yet, forsooth,
His prisoner must be fair, and young, and mine

So old she might have given Hercules suck ;
Now she sucks too, for she hath no teeth left.
In one month she'll cost me as much in caudles
And sweet candy as her ransom comes to.

FRI. But you have other pillage, captain.

VAS. Let me see ; three Barbary horses with rich
Caparisons, two chests o' th' general's clothes.

ALT. And I two chests o' th' general's plate.

FRIV. In those I share, Altesto.

VAS. How? plate! shall we encounter our sous'd
fish
And broil'd pullen* in silver service, rogues,
Like furr'd magnificoes?

FRIV. We shall, captain :
But you may dip your morsel in good China earth.

ALT. All your plate, Vasco, is the silver handle
Of your old prisoner's fan.

*Enter* PROSPERO, *wounded, and* EVANDRA, *her
arms in a scarf pinion'd.*

TRIST. Here comes Prospero, the valiant Count!

VAS. And with him the brave prize.

PROS. Evandra do not mourn ! I, that have made
You captive thus, with hazard of my youth
And blood, shall think you now as worthy of
My care, as of my valour in the fight.
Can I esteem you less by being mine?

EVAN. What have I done unknown unto my
heart,
That I should tempt your valour to so great
A sin as my captivity? Or are my crimes
Observ'd more than my prayers, that heaven shall
leave
Me to become the scorn of victory?

PROS. It is the sad pre-eminence of your
Exemplar birth and beauty, to confer

* Poultry.

Honour on him that is your conqueror.

    EVAN. Honour? Is that the word that hath so
        long
Betray'd the emulous world, and fool'd the noblest
    race
Of men into a vex'd and angry death?
If 'twere a virtue 'twould not strive t' inthrall,
And thus distress the innocent.

    PROS. I am the war's disciple, and, since first
I had the growth to wear a sword, I ne'er
Was taught how to subdue by reason, but
By strength. Altesto!

    ALT. My lord!

    PROS. Take here this lady to your charge; conduct
Her unto Turin, and there guard her in
My house till my approach.

    ALT. I shall, my lord.

    PROS. Let her be safe, Altesto, in thy care,
On forfeiture of life. She is my prisoner,
And th' noblest in the field, the beauteous
Heir of Millain. Had not my niggard stars
Intended me but half a courtesy,
The duke her father had lamented now
Under the self-same fate.

    VAS. I could wish your lordship would be-
        lieve me
A fitter man to take charge of the lady.

    PROS. Why, captain?

    VAS. You could not commit her to an eunuch
With more safety. If the Great Turk knew me,
Honest Achmet, he would trust me in's seraglio,
By this hand, without defalking* one grain beneath
        the waste.

    PROS. Success hath made you wanton, captain.

    VAS. Besides, my lord, I have ta'en an old Abbess
Prisoner. O such a governess for a

          * Abating in reckoning.

Young maid !  She'll read to her such homilies,
And teach her such receipts out of the fathers :
How to cure the toothache, preserve plums,
And boil amber possets,* will make her, sir,
In three days a very Saint.
 Pros. Well, you shall take my bounty, too.
  Close by
The valley, that doth join to th' neighbour grove,
Lies, conquer'd by my sword, a Millain knight,
His wounds med'cined, and stopt by the best art
I had, but by much loss of blood unable yet
To move him ; and his ransom I bestow on you.
 Vas. I thank your lordship.
 Pros. But use him nobly, Vasco, for he hath
A courage that well merited his cause,
And fought with eager and with skillful strength
To free that lady from my bonds ; but the glad day
Was mine.
 Vas. He shall be kindly us'd ;
Only your sweet lordship must give me leave,
When he pays his ransom, to weigh his gold.
Were he my father, sir, he must endure
The trial of my scales.  Follow, Tristan !
 Pros. Make haste, see him well waggon'd, and
  provide
A surgeon to attend his cure.
         *[Exeunt Vas., Tris.*
 Evan. Sir, can you find no pity yet within
Your breast ?  You have already shewn enough
Of your stern father's spirit ; is there not
In all your heart so much of softness as
Declares you had a mother too, must I
Be led a captive, and in a cruel land
Lament your victory ?
 Pros. Altesto, bear her from my sight ! make
  haste !

    * See vol. ii., pp. 121 and 244.

I am not safe when I converse with tears.
                    [*Exeunt Altesto, Evandra.*
I would ambition were not brave in war!
Or that the rage of Princes had not made
It lawful to subdue whom they dislike,
Or 'twere ignoble to inflict a misery
Or to indure't ourselves.   Frivolo, where
Did'st thou leave the Prince ?

    FRIV. In pursuit of the Duke, who since we
      hear
Recovered Millain, which caus'd him sound us.
                    [*Drum march afar off.*
A retreat,—hark, sir ! his march leads hither :
It is his way to Turin.

### *Enter* CALLADINE.

The Prince ! the Prince ! my Lord Prospero
You have been sought for, the valiant Prince
For this day's action hath advanced you to
The public ear, and we, your friends, rejoic'd.

    PROS. I did but as his bold example gave
Me, sir.  I saw him conquer, kill, and lead
In fetters sad faces, which I ne'er saw
Before, and I believed 'twas good.  I wish
That heaven may think so too ; I not converse
With books, but I have heard our enemies,
Although they wrong'd not me, must be so us'd.

### *Enter* ALVARO, *soldiers stripping off his corslet.*

Unbuckle, Calladine ! the day is hot,
And our great business cools like to their heats,
That fled to humbled Millain, and have left
Their fainting honour hovering o'er our crests.
Lead on my horse in triumph ! I will march
On foot.  He hath perform'd his work, as he
Had equall'd me in sense of what he did.

CAL. Sir, Prospero, the Count! whom your kind
   fears

                [*Pros. kneels, kisses his hand.*

So heartily inquir'd for i'th retreat.

ALV. Rise, noble youth! and let me hold thee
   near

My heart; join thy stout breast to mine, that we
May grow a while together in our love,
Yet when divided, be the same in thought
And act. This day thou hast begot an history
And given our Savoy chronicles a theme
To teach them boast, and be believ'd.

PROS. Alvaro! my dread Prince! why should
   you lose

Your praise on me, that did but imitate
The faintest of your vigour and your skill?
You bred me from my childhood to do things
That they call glorious, though, dull and much
   unlearned,
I cannot reach the cause of what I do
More than your example, and command.

ALV. Since thou got'st strength to wear a sword
   thou hast

Been mine, and't hath been drawn to execute
My will, and though, I know not why, thou wast
Averse to arts and written labours of
The wise, yet discipline of war thou lov'dst;
And bring thee to a fiery steed him thou
Would'st sit, and manage with such gentle rule
That our idolatrous philosophers
Believ'd thou had'st created whom thou taught'st.

PROS. Your love will breed me envy, sir; something

I've done, since you are pleas'd to value so
My weaker toils, which may perhaps deserve
Your father's thanks, and yours, and's yet unknown
Unto you both: Evandra, heir of Millain,

I have fought for, ta'en prisoner, and sent
To Turin ; a reward for our just war.
    ALV. Hah ! the fair Evandra made prisoner ?
And Prospero, by thee ?
      PROS. Why should you think him whom you
        prais'd
So much unfit for such a victory.
    ALV. Now all the blessings of my faithful love
Are lost : she, whom I doated on with my
Most chaste and early appetite, is sent
In bonds t'appease my cruel father's wrath.
    CALL. My Lord ! he lov'd her much, though
      temp'rately
Concealed from gen'ral knowledge and his friends.
    PROS. Then mount my courser, Frivolo, and
      try
If, by the happy quickness of his speed,
Thou can'st recover her return, and use
Her with such fair respective homage as
May expiate my violent surprize.    [*Ex. Friv.*
    ALV. Fly, fly! I would thy nimble motion could
O'ertake the arrow from th' Assyrian bow,
Or swifter lightning whom our sight pursues
And is too slow to reach.
    PROS. What have I done that I should thus
      mistake
An act of valiant glory, for a deed
That argues an austere ignoble rage ?
    ALV. Fair Evandra, the pride of Italy !
In whom the Graces met to rectify
Themselves, that had not cause enough to blush,
Unless for pity they were not so good
As she ; think, now the Eastern spices sweat,
And that the blossoms of the spring perfume
The morning air, necessity must rule
Belief, let's strew our altars with them now,
Since she's imprison'd, stifled, and chok'd up,

Like weeping roses in a still, whose inarticulate
   breath,
Heaven thought a purer sacrifice than all our
   orizons.*

PROS. Is she not fitter then
For Turin than for Millain, sir ? I saw
You take prisoners, and in my fury had
Discretion to achieve the best.

   ALV. O thou hast lost my heart! hence doth
   proceed
This recreant act, that to thy savage courage
I could never join the temperature
Of sweet philosophy. Had'st thou been learn'd,
And read the noble deeds of gentle knights,
Reason had check'd thy rage, thy valour would
Have been more pitiful than to have led
A virgin into harsh captivity.

   PROS. I thought I had done well.

   ALV. How ? well! Draw back that falsehood in
   thy breath
Again, or I will pierce thy heart, that thou
May'st die impenitent.
               [*Draws his sword. Call. stays him.*
Unhand me, Calladine! I've already met
My better thoughts : why should I waste my
   breath
On such a forester, wild as the woods ?
Where he should graze with the brute herd, who,
   though they want
Discoursive soul, are less inhuman far than he.

   PROS. She was the daughter of our greatest
   enemy,
And so I us'd her, sir.

   ALV. A choleric bear, or hungry panther would
Have us'd her with more soft remorse ; had I

* " Like weeping roses in a still, and is
  Like them ordain'd to last by dissolution." *Folio.*

Encounter'd her in the mad heat of chace,
In all the fury of the fight, I would
Have taught my angry steed the easy and
The peaceful motion of a lamb.
She should have set his back, soft as the air,
And in her girdle bridle him, more curb'd
Than in his foaming bit, whilst I, her slave,
Walk'd by, marking what hasty flowers sprung up,
Invited by her eyebeams from their cold roots ;
And this would each true soldier do, that had
Refin'd his courage with the sober checks
Of sweet philosophy.

PROS. Would you had taught me some philosophy
Before I learn'd to fight.

*Enter* FRIVOLO.

All hope is past ! she was convey'd in one
Of your swift chariots, sir, which, it doth seem,
Altesto did unhappily o'ertake,
And she's ere this within our Turin walls.

PROS. Such language and such news better
become
The fatal birds of night ; so ravens croak
When they fly o'er the mansions of the sick
And bode their deaths.*

ALV. Prospero, see me no more !
Th'art a disease unto my injur'd sight.
Fly to some lustfull coast, where none but goats
And satyrs live, where the name of virgin is
As strange as this thy cruelty ; there thou
May'st hope to wander not contemn'd.   Should I
Behold thy face again, and let thee live,
My patience would become my vildest† guilt.

---

\* " Thus, like the sad presaging raven, that tolls
The sick man's passport in her hollow beak,
And in the shadow of the silent night
Doth strike contagion from her sable wings."
*Marlowe's Jew of Malta.*
† Vilest.

CAL. See, sir, he weeps! Can you endure him
  mourn
And languish thus, whom heretofore you did
Embrace in the chief rank of love, not mov'd,
Sir, with his tears?

ALV. No more than to behold
The puddled channel overflow. He saw
Her weep and could endur't; the drops fell down,
Methinks, as when the piteous pelican
Wounds her remorseful breast.

PROS. Sir, have I, in one hasty moment, so
Far merited my ruin that no means
Are left to win me to your former grace?

ALV. Never, unless thou couldst restore
Evandra's liberty. She is, ere this,
Within my father's reach, whose nature is
Severe and mortal to her father's blood;
An ancient vow he took will make her destiny
So sad, I fear to think on it. Poor Evandra!

PROS. I sent her in good conduct to my house,
Where is a cave, so artfully conceal'd
Within my garden's verge, that not the sun's
Most prying beams, nor human search
Can e'er discover it. I'll hide her there,
Till time and apt convenience can dispose
Her unto Millain.

ALVA. Fly, then! loose not the sick hope with
  slow
Pursuit. Fate keep her from my father.

PROS. I'll strive to groan away my breath, and
  die.                                    [*Exit Pros.*
                          [*Cornet flourish afar off.*
FRIV. Hark, sir! the Duke, your father, sure
Doth ride in triumph through the town, to meet
And celebrate your victory.

ALV. Give order that our troops march! march
  slowly on.

Our drums should now in sable cases beat,
Our colours folded, and our muskets be
Revers'd, whilst our dejected pikes we trail,
But that, I fear, 'twould breed enquiry in
My father of a cause he must not know.
O Callandine! Evandra is in bonds.     [*Exit.*

*Enter* VASCO, TRISTAN, LEONELL *wounded and led.*

    VAS. Prepare the waggon, Tristan! spread a
      mat in't;
And, dost hear? bid my Ancient tear off's colours
For a coverlet; 'tis thine, sir, all our shift.
    TRIS. All's ready, sir, i' th' bottom of the hill;
He shall be us'd like a queen when she lyes in.
    VAS. Softly, Tristan! he moves as weakly as
His sinews were of spinners' threads, so cut
And carv'd; he hath made your skin, sir, only
Fit to be worn in summer. This Prospero
Is a Turk when's whinyard's drawn and shines
    in's eyes.
    LEO. He us'd me nobly, sir, when I had bled
My self past strength to conquer him, nor could
I hope to find such mercy in an enemy,
'Less I had fallen beneath the force of your
Alvaro, Prince of Piedmont.
    VAS. Ay, there's a man! 'tis true, Lord Prospero's
      valiant,
I think he dares meet the devil in duell,
And give him two flashes of lightning odds; but
He wants that they call learning, sir. Prince Alvaro
Is, as they say, a philosophy man:
He talks of Rabins, and strange Hebrew roots;
Things we dull soldiers rather eat then mention.
    TRIS. He can tell you, sir, how many showers fell
Since Noah's flood.
    VAS. Ay, and how many cloaks those showers
    have wet.

LEO. Have you no knowledge of the lady, sir,
That was surpriz'd from my protection by
Young Prospero?
    VAS. Good! was ever creature of heaven's mak-
        ing
So libidinous as paltry man? Now,
Has he a mind to the lady? She, sir,
Is safe in Turin, whither strait we mean
To lead you too.
    LEO. Some comfort yet; it is decreed I must
Indure my bondage where she suffers her's.
Poore Evandra! was fate so niggardly,
She could allow no more protection for
Thy beauty than my single fortitude?
    TRIS. Come, move on, sir, it will be late ere we
Shall reach the town.
    LEO. What other fortune had the battle?
    VAS. We swadled your Duke home; he and the
        rest
Of your bruis'd countrymen have wondrous need
Of capon's grease.
    LEO. Strange giddiness of war; some men
        must groan
To further others mirth. What fury rules
O'er human sense, that we should struggle to
Destroy in wounds, and rage, our life, that heaven
Decreed so short? It is a mystery
Too sad to be remembred by the wise,
That half mankind consume their noble blood,
In causes not belov'd, or understood.    [Exeunt.

---

## ACT II.  SCÆNA I.

*Enter* VASCO, FRIVOLO, TRISTAN.

FRIV. Have you heard the proclaim'd law, Vasco?
III.                    H

VAS. I would there were no law, or that no man
Were learn'd enough to read 'em, or that we had
Courage enough not to obey them.

TRIS. Frivolo, what law is this?

FRIV. It is proclaim'd, all female prisoners
After a year should have full liberty
To return to Millaine, and ransomless;
Only a year is given to us the conquerors,
That those we took of birth and dowry may,
If we can woo them to consent, marry us,
But we've no power to use constraint, nor to
Inforce a maidenhead, on pain of death.

VAS. My beldam hath tane order with her
      maidenhead
Ten years ere I was born.

FRIV. I' th' mean time, Tristan,
As a requital for our hopes, we must
Maintain them at our own charge.

TRIST. Must not the men we took pay ransom?

VAS. Yes, yes, they pay. I have a knight
      given me
By young Count Prospero, shall sell his spurs
Ere he 'scape free. I will pawn him, till he
Be worn to th' title of a squire.

FRIV. Thou art as cruel as a constable
That's wak'd with a quarrel out of his first sleep.

VAS. Hang him, bold Cataian, he indites finely;
And will live as well by sending short epistles,
Or by sad whisper at your gamester's elbow
When the great by* is drawn, as any bashful
Gallant of 'em all.

TRIST. But what's the cause our Duke is so
      severe

---

* *Bye.*
  " By loss in play men oft forget
      The duty they do owe
    To him that did bestow the same,
      And thousands millions moe.

Unto the heir of Millain ? whom, 'tis said,
Shall suffer instant death, yet is thus kind
To others of her sex.
    FRIV. She dies to satisfy
A vow he made in's youth, when those of Millaine
Took his brother prisoner, and would not be
Appeas'd without the forfeiture of's head.
    TRIS. I am not yet instructed, Frivolo,
Why should not then the rest we took die too ?
    FRIV. Evandra is a sacrifice for all.
His other mercy takes from th' cruelty
He shows on her.

*Enter* ALTESTO.

    VAS. From whence, Altesto, comes your loftiness?
    ALT. Why, from the Duke ! I had laid me
For breakfast a fine comfortable gin.
    VAS. What was't, a wench ?
    ALT. A rack, Vasco, a rack ;
A certain instrument that will extend and draw
Our sinews into treble strings, and stretch
Our great shin bones till they become slender
As knitting needles, or a spider's legs.
    VAS. Didst thou commit treason ? 'tis well thou
      hast
A brain for anything; the age requires parts ;
We cannot eat else. But quick, the cause ?
    ALT. 'Twas to discover where I left Evandra,
Whom Prospero delivered to my charge ;

I loath to hear them swear and stare
  When they the *main* have lost ;
Forgetting all the *byes* that were
  With God and Holy Ghost."
    *Portion of " A Penitential Sonnet, written by*
    *a lord, a great gamester, a little before his*
    *death, which was in the year 1580."-- From*
    *the Compleat Gamester.* 16mo. 1710.

I answer'd a full truth, that I restor'd
Her to his hands, at his return to his house;
And this, as fortune would vouchsafe, the
Duke believ'd without applying, gentlemen,
The recreation of the rack.

    FRIV. But she is not yet found.

    ALT. No! and the Duke believes her still i' th
        town!
Therefore a guard is plac'd at all the gates
To hinder her escape.

    VAS. I do not like
This cutting off young wenches' heads; 'tis thought
They cannot kiss handsomely without them.

    TRIS. But how does Prospero excuse her flight?

    ALT. He says, she's stolen away, but shews no
        manner how;
And th' angry Duke, though he be precious in
His love, threatens him much.

    VAS. Some angel stole her from him: and,
Gentlemen, if I have any skill in magic, you
Shall see her three days hence pirking* in a cloud,
Southward of yonder star. Look up! just there;
With her ivory lute hanging at her back,
And working me a scarf of sky-colour'd satin.

    ALT. A halter, Vasco, to save the poor State
Th' charge of a penny: thou'lt have need on't.

    VAS. What's become of Melora, your fair
        prisoner?
You hear the proclamation!

    ALT. Yes, and am well pleas'd:
I mean to woo and marry her. She hath

---

  * *Qy.* "perk "—To hold up the head with an affected brisk-
ness.

    " If after all you think it a disgrace,
      That Edward's miss thus perks it in your face!" — *Pope.*
" My ragged routs wont in the wind, and wag their wriggle
    tails,
Peark as a peacock: but nought avails." - *Shakespeare.*

Twelve thousand crowns by good intelligence.

VAS. If she consent—but I am of the faith
Such suckets* are but seldom swallowed by
Us wealthy Aldermen o'th' camp—a jointure
Is the word, Altesto, and then you'll shew her
A young back with a sword hanging over't,
Worse than a hand-saw.

ALT. Just now, I left her at my mother's house ;
And sirrah Vasco, she looks——Oh rogue, rogue !
A Flanders peak† i'th' middle of her brow,
Which straight I spy ; and shake, and melt, then
    speak
Fine language to her, and am duteous with
My bonnet at her instep, thus——

VAS. Th'ast found the way.

ALT. Then, Vasco, she moves back, discovering
    but
The very verge of both her picked‡ toes,
But in white§ shoes, and then I'm taken, that
I stand like one of the Turk's chidden mutes,
A girl in a bongrace,‖ thus high, may ravish me.

FRIV. Alas, poor gentleman !

ALT. But Vasco, her fingers——by this good day !
I think they are smaller than thy point-tags ;
And she behaves them on the virginals
So prettily——I'ld wish no more of heaven,
Than once to hear her play, " Fortune my Foe,"
Or " John come kisse me now."¶

---

\* Sweetmeats.—See vol. ii., p. 145.     † Peak—Lace.
‡ Sharp-pointed—hooked.
§ Lac'd.—*Folio*     ‖ See vol. ii., p. 97.
¶ There are three different copies of the tune of FORTUNE ;
the first as given by Dr Burney, the second from Queen Elizabeth's Virginal Book, and the third from a Collection of English Airs, published at Haarlem in 1626. This tune is invested
with particular interest, from the old ballad of Titus Andron-
icus, on which Shakespeare founded his play, having been sung
to it. A black-letter copy of the original is in the collection of
ballads in the British Museum.

VAS. Those are tunes my old widow prisoner
    sings,
With more division than a water-work,
When the main pipe is half stopt.
    FRIV. You have a year allow'd to woo her,
    Vasco.

The ballad is mentioned in " Lingua," 1607 ; in the " Knight
of the Burning Pestle," 1613 ; in the " Two Merry Milk-
maids," 1620 ; in Burton's " Anatomy of Melancholy," 1621 ;
in " Vox Borealis," 1641 ; in Brome's " Antipodes," 1638 ; in
" The Custom of the Country," 1647 ; in " The Rump or
Mirror of the Times," 1660 ; in " Tom Essence," 1677 ; in
" Loyal Songs," 1731 ; and in " The Merry Wives of Windsor,"
Act iii. Scene 3. Chappell's " Ancient English Ballads," vol.
ii., pp. 63 and 191. The air is given in vol. i., p. 33. Among
Mr George Daniel's collection of black-letter ballads and broad-
sides, printed in the reign of Queen Elizabeth, which were
purchased at the sale of his books for a very large sum, by
Henry Huth, Esq., and reprinted by Mr Lillie in 1867, is a
ballad " to the tune of Fortune," titled "a mournfull dittie on
the death of certaine Judges and Justices of the Peace, and
diuers other Gentlemen, who died immediately after the
Assises holden at Lincolne last past."
*John come kiss me now.*—Of this old ballad the tune and only
a fragment, preserved by Herd, have come down to us. These
will be found in the Vocal Miscellany, the version in Johnson's
Scots Musical Museum is an alteration by Burns. The early
reformers, in order to forward their views with the general
body of the people, " spiritualized," in the same manner as was
done in Holland, many of the popular songs of the time.
Among them was this song. The spiritual version appeared in
" Ane compendious buik of Godlie psalmes and spirituall sangis,
collectit furthe of sindrie partis of the Scripture, with diueris
otheris ballatis, changeit out of prophane sangis in Godlie
sangis for auoyding of sin and harlatrie." The authorship of
this " Compendious book " has been ascribed to two brothers,
John and Robert Wedderburn of Dundee, who lived about the
year 1540. Mention is thus made of it in a " Historie of the
Estate of the Kirke of Scotland, written by an old minister of
the Kirke of Scotland, at the desire of some of his young
brethren for their informatione," A.D. 1560, printed for the
Maitland Club, also for the Wodrow Society : "for the more
particular meanis whereby came the knowledge of God's truth
in the time of great darkness, was such as Sir David Lindsey's
poisie, Wedderburne's psalms, and Godlie ballands of Godlie pur-
poses," &c. A limited impression, a reprint, of " the gude and
Godlie ballates," under the very able editorship of Dr Laing,

TRIS. She's rich. I knew her husband; he
thriv'd much
By a monopoly he had of dead women's hair:
All Millaine talkt of it. She kept another shop
Under Saint Maudlin's wall, and quilted ushers'
calves.

was issued by the enterprising publisher, William Paterson of
Edinburgh, in 1868.

It is noticed in Stenhouse's "Illustrations of the Lyric
poetry and music of Scotland," 1853, that "the celebrated
Wm. Byrd, organist of the Chapel Royal in 1575, author of
the musical Canon 'Non Nobis, Domine,' composed fifteen
variations upon the air of 'John come kiss me now ;' which
are in Queen Elizabeth's Virginal Book. MSS., 1576."

"This favourite old tune," Mr Chappell says, " is to be found
in ' Queen Elizabeth's Virginal Book,' in Playford's ' Introduction,' in Apollo's ' Banquet for the treble violin,' and in ' The
first part of the division violin '" He further observes : "In the
Virginal Book only the first part of the tune is taken, and it is
doubtful if it then had any second part. It is one of the songs
parodied in Andro Hart's ' Compendium of Godly Songs,' on
the strength of which the tune has been claimed as Scotch,
although it has no Scotch character, nor has hitherto been
found in any old Scotch copy. Not only are all the tunes to
the songs in the ' Compendium '—of which any traces are left
—English, but what little secular music was printed in Scotland until the eighteenth century, was entirely English or
foreign."

This sweeping assertion of Mr Chappell, in reference to the
secular music of Scotland, is open to question, and it may as
well be advanced that numbers of the ancient airs claimed as
English were imported from Scotland. A glance at dates will
show whether the present song was Scotch or English. We hear
of it as being current in Scotland in 1560, but not in England till
1575. In the latter instance only the first part seems to have
been known—in the former, it is evident from having been
sung as a ballad of eight lines, with a repeat, that there was
a second part, which had not found its way into the sister
country. In England, also, the air does not appear to have
been wedded to words, but used only for dancing, in which
capacity it is mentioned in Heywood's "A woman killed with
kindness," 1600 ; in "'Tis merry when gossips meet," 1609 ;
in "Westminster Drollery," 1671 ; in "The scourge of folly,"
N.D. ; and in Henry Bold's "Songs and Poems," 1685.

In the same capacity it is also noticed in Burton's "Anatomy
of Melancholy," 1621 : "Yea, many times this love will make
old men and women, that have more toes than teeth, dance
'John come kiss me now,' mask and mum."

VAS. Well, gentlemen, let's waste no time. I'll to
My barber's straight ; purge, shave, and wash, for
    know,
If cleanness and good looks will do't, I'll teach
Her grandameship to mump, and marry too,
Or my arts fail.   Frivolo, you and Tristan
Follow me !  I shall employ you both.
    ALT.  I am for Prospero ; he sent to speak with
      me.                              [*Exeunt.*

*Enter* ALVARO, PROSPERO, *with a key and lights.*

    PROS.  Sir, you have made me know my cruelty,
'Twas such uncomely valour,* that I blush
To name't.   And, trust me, could I sink low as
The centre whilst I kneel, still would I thus
Implore your pardon and your love.      [*Kneels.*
    ALV.  I have a memory so apt
T' advance my pity 'bove my anger, when
It mentions thee, that I'll forget the cause
That made thy guilt and me to mourn.   But O !
That dismal place brings it again to thought.
This looks, methinks, like to the dark
And hidden dwelling of the winds, as yet
Unknown to men, where storms engender, and
The whirling blasts that trouble nature, till
She trembles at their force, and ruin all
The sumptuous piles of art.
    PROS.  Necessity hath caus'd this choice, till the
Severe enquiry of your father be appeas'd,
And we can shape her some disguise fit to
Convey her from the town.
    ALV.  With soft and gentle summons call, that she
May climb unto the top and verge o' th' cave.
    PROS.  Evandra ! speak ! ascend to us ! I am
Your penitential enemy, that come
To weep away my trespass at your feet.
        * Wretched courage.—*Folio.*

ALV. Evandra, rise ! break from this thick
And silent darkness, like the eldest light.*
          [*The stage opens, Prospero lifts Evandra up.*
EVAN. Ha ! my lord, the prince.†
ALV. O noble maid, what expiation can
Make fit this young and cruel soldier for
Society of men, that hath defiled
The genius of triumphant glorious war
With such a rape upon thy liberty !
Or what less hard than marble of
The Parian rock cans't thou believe my heart,
That nurst and bred him my disciple in
The camp, and yet could teach his valour no
More tenderness than injur'd Scythians use
When they are vex'd to a revenge ?   But he
Hath mourned for it ; and sure, Evandra, thou
Art strongly pitiful, that dost so long
Conceal an anger that would kill us both.

EVAN. Sir, I am nobly recompens'd, in that
You will vouchsafe me worthy of your grief.
And though I die forgotten here, a poor
And luckless maid, lost like a blossom which
The wand'ring wind blows from the bosom
Of the spring, to mix with summer's dust,
Yet so much courtesy deserves to be rememb'red
Even in heaven.

ALV. Was this a subject fit to bear the pride
And insolent calamity of war ?
As well had it become in the world's youth
The giant race to hunt, with mighty spear
And iron shield, the young and tender ermine.
Evandra, I have lov'd thee much and long.
Why do you start, as if some jealous thought
Did whisper that my love devis'd this snare,

* First fair light.—*Folio.*
† EVAN. Sure 'tis the prince whom Prospero brings
          To give me courage in this solitude.—*Folio.*

To keep thee here within my power and reach ?

EVAN. I cannot think you are so cruel to
Yourself, t'afflict the thing that you esteem.

ALV. No, beauteous maid, had I beheld thy
    flight,
In our stern exercise of wrath, I would
Have made the bloody field a garden, fit
T'adorn the shews of a triumphant peace; .
And every soldier like a reaper cloth'd
Fitter to use his sickle than his sword.
Still thou recoil'st ; like the chaste Indian plant
That shrinks and curls his bashful leaves at the
Approach of man.

EVAN. I've lost my reason, and I want the
    courage
To entertain your kindness as I ought.

ALV. Is it because my years a little have
O'er grown my youth, or that the enmity
Our fathers interchange begets in thee
A factious hate, till't make thy duty sin ?
But 'tis not possible thou canst create
A thought will merit such a name.*

EVAN. The gentle business, sir, of love is fit
For hours more calm and blest than those
A captive can enjoy.

ALV. These are not words
To quiet me in sleep, and peaceful thoughts.

PROS. Nor shall I evermore relish delights
And triumphs of the court, or haughty joys
Of war and victory.

---

* The Folio has this speech thus rendered :—
    ALV. Can you participate in any part of that
    Unhappy enmity which has so long
    Disorder'd both our fathers' breasts ? if you
    Whom heaven did purposely ordain for love,
    Should hatred from your parents learn, you would,
    Obeying their example, straight convert
    Your duty into sin.

ALV. Evandra, live ! Be yet some happiness
Unto thy self, and, with the patience that
Becomes a maid's divinity, relieve
Thy heart with easy hope of liberty :
Inforcing a content within this dark
And solitary cave, till I have power
With apt disguise to further thy escape,
Which shall be hast'ned with my ablest skill.
Believe me, good Evandra, the honour of
My birth and soul shall warrant it.

EVAN. You are a Prince renown'd and precious
    for
Your faith and courtesy.

ALV. Think not I'll use advantage or constraint
Upon thy love.  A virgin's heart, I know,
Is sooner strok'd than check'd into a kind
Surrender of her breast.

EVAN. Sir, all the bounties that the heavens
    provide
For truth and clemency fall on you still !

ALV. If thou suspect'st I've not enough of cold
And holy temper to resist the flames
Of appetite, command that I shall see
Thee here no more, and my obedience straight
Shall be restrained within a sacred vow.
For I would have thy thoughts, Evandra, safe
As are thy beauties.

EVAN. It were a crime,
Greater I hope than I shall e'er commit,
To doubt such princely goodness can pervert itself.

ALV. Then thou wilt give me leave to make free
    use
Of every happy opportunity
That may invite me to attend you here ?

EVAN. Not angels, sure, when they converse, can
    meet
With less intent of sin, and more of joy.

ALV. Well, I must see thee' oft : thy wondrous
 eyes
Have soft'ned all my spirits to a calm
And easy temper for thy sway, that I
Could change my corslet and my iron vests
Of rugged war, to move in gentle pace
Unto the tuneful whispers of thy lute,
Still clothed in tender garments of thy work,
And for a plumed helmet wear chapletts
Of flowers, in a mysterious order rank'd
By thy white virgin hand, then like thy neat
O'er busy maid, bind up thy looser philleting
And pleat in curls thy soft dishevelled hair.
I'll make my frequent visits here till thou
Confess how much I am subdued.

 EVAN. I am opprest with fear, [lest] the watch-
 ful Duke,
Your father, should observe unto this sad
Unusual place your stolen approach ; and then
My sorrows would be doubled in your danger.

 ALV. Danger ! How noble lovers smile at such
A thought. 'Tis love that only fortifies
And gives us mighty vigour to attempt
On other's force, and suffer more than we
Inflict.   Would all the soldiers, that I lead
In active war, were lovers too, though lean,
Feebled, and weakened with their ladies' frowns
How, when their valour's stirred, would they march
 strong,
Through hideous gulphs, through numerous herds
Of angry lions, and consuming fire? [*Knock within.*
 EVAN. What doubtful noise is that ?
 ALV. 'Tis Calladine !   I did appoint him here.
Stay Prospero ; let him not enter yet.
O envious chance, must we depart so soon ?
   [*They put Evandra down into the cave.*
Descend like the bright officer of day ;

Whilst darkened, we thy beauteous absence mourn;
And every flower doth weep till your return.
            [*Opens the door, and lets in Calladine.*
PROS.  His looks declare there's hazard, and some
    haste.
ALV.  What wouldst thou speak ?
CALL.  The Duke, your father, sir, is much per-
    plext :
He calls for Prospero, and, it is fear'd,
Will torture him to find Evandra's flight.
    ALV.  He shall not yet appear ; I will endure
His anger's edge, with venture of myself.
Stay till I send.                               [*Exit.*
    CALL.  My lord, I grieve to see your sorrows bear
So great a weight, as makes you groan unto
Yourself.  This silence and fixation of
Your eyes, until unchanged objects cause
Them ache is much unlike your wonted mind.
Suspect not but the Prince will qualify
His father to a peace, and a more just
Interpretation of your worth.
    PROS.  Know, Calladine, 'tis not Evandra's bonds,
Nor all the tortures that th' incensed Duke
From cruelty or art can minister,
Have power to freeze and fix me like a statue thus.
I have another cause that swells my heart,
Till't grow too spacious for my breast.
    CALL.  'Las, sir, your favours have oblig'd me so,
That I must share your grief ; and 'twould perhaps
Afford some remedy to share the cause.
    PROS.  I know not, Calladine, in the vast world
One I more love, or would so boldly trust,
But thou wilt think me mad. ·
    CALL.  My lord, I'll forget then my manners and
My reason too.
    PROS.  Come, thou shalt know, I love——
How wilt thou smile to see m' ambitious eyes

Look higher than the eagle, when he soars
To elevate his sight ?   I love——
    CALL.  Who is't you love ?
    PROS.  Evandra! now mix pity in thy scorn.
    CALL.  'Tis sad, the Prince and you should meet
        with so
Much violence in the same choice.
    PROS.  At first, i'th' rage of fight I gazed on her,
With half discernings of her form, a mist
Of fury hung between us then ; but since
That I have view'd her beauty with some care,
And see how sweetly she demeans her in
Calamity, I have o'erthrown my heart
With liking her too much.
    CALL.  It will require great wisdom to persuade
In this : the cause is dangerous.
    PROS.  Would I had ne'er been born, then I had
        miss'd
The sight and memory of her, and my
Fond errors should have been as much unknown
As m' uncreated self.

*Enter* ALTESTO.

    ALT.  My lord, your servant gave me entrance
        with
Command that I should speak with you.
    PROS.  'Tis true, Altesto, y' have a maiden
        prisoner,
Call'd Melora ; 'tis my request that you
Conduct her hither in disguise ; though law,
Newly proclaim'd, allow no ransom for her,
You shall be paid your own demand.
    ALT.  I'll obey your lordship.  She shall attend
You straight.  What use can he employ her to ?
    PROS.  Come, Calladine, ease me with thy counsel.
                                    [*Exeunt.*

*Enter* VASCO, TRISTAN, FRIVOLO, LELIA.

VAS. Is Lelia your own prisoner, Tristan?

TRIS. The powerful purchase of my sword.

VAS. What is she heir to? a brass thimble and
A skene of brown thread? she'll not yield thee in
Algiers above a ducket, being stript;
And for her clothes, they're fitter for a paper mill,
Than a palace.

FRIV. Let her serve your captive widow.

VAS. Why, Tristan, that's a year's wages for you:
'Tis well thought on.   Will you serve, Lelia?

LEL. I hope, sir, I shall be fit to serve.

VAS. Yes, serve for an hospital, when the sins
Of the camp are retir'd into your bones.
She's vilely out of linen.

TRIS. How can I help't?

VAS. Let her make love to a sexton, and steal
    shrouds.

FRIV. Trust my knowledge, Vasco, she's for thy
    turn;
Present her to thy widow, she may woo
In thy behalf, toast plum cakes for her muskadine,
And brush her velvet hood on holy-days.

VAS. Tristan, convey her to her as my gift.
But, Lelia, you must speak notable words
Of me; first, what a goodly man I am;
That I get matrons at a hundred and ten
With double twins: and how in time of war
I fill up the muster with mine own issue.

LEL. Marry, sir! heaven forbid!

VAS. D'you hear? this wench has been villan-
    ously
Ill bred: and I'll lay my life,
She sings at her work too the holy Carol
O'th' lady's daughter converted in Paris;
" She was of Paris properly," &c.

TRIS. Fie, Lelia, you must now take care! you are
Not now i'th' camp, but in a civil common-wealth.

LEL. I shall endeavour, sir, to learn.

VAS. Nor must you persuade your mistress rise
Too early to her beads; she may catch cold,
Having already a pestilent cough,
And so will die before I marry her.

LEL. I hope I shall not be so mischievous.

VAS. Well, gentlemen, the fruitful hour is now
Drawn near that gives success: this morning must
Expose me to great charge.

FRIV. Thou dost not mean
To court her at her window with rare music?

VAS. No! she's very deaf; so that cost is sav'd.

FRIV. What other charge? she hath no teeth fit for
A dry banquet, and dancing she is past,
Unless with crutches in an antimasque.

VAS. I must provide her culleises* and broths
That may stir mettle in her. In this case
She is: Know, my good friends, I find
Her no more fit for the business of encrease
Than I am to be a nun.

TRIS. Thou wilt take care to trim thy person?

VAS. I came just now from consultation with
My barber; who provides me a large main,
A lock for the left side, so rarely hung
With ribbanding of sundry colours, sir,
Thou'lt take it for a rainbow newly crisp'd
And trimm'd. Bucephalus ne'er wore the like.

FRIV. When you have reach'd Sir Leonell's
　　　　ransom,
And the rich widow's wealth, we are forgot
Like creatures of Japan, things hardly to
Be search'd for in the map.

* Jellies. "In the Editor's MS., No. 11, there is a prescrip-
tion for making a colys, I presume a culhs, or invigorating
broth."—*Preface to " The forme of cury, a roll of ancient English
Cookery,"* compiled about A.D. 1390. Lond. 1780. 8vo.

TRIS. In one short month I shall not know his
name.

VAS. 'Tis then because thou canst not read ; for
thou
Shalt find it fairly carv'd on each new church
And hospital, I mean to build apace,
And have my blue boys march through the streets,
Two and two, provided for in gilded primmers,*
And their chops of mutton. Go haste to the widow's,
Present your damsel, I'll be with you straight.
My captive knight would speak with me.

[*Exeunt. Manet Vas.*

*Enter* LEONELL.

LEO. I am bold, sir, to make free use of your
Most spacious rooms for benefit of air.

VAS. Sir, you are welcome : 'tis a liberty
That I expect, and I joy much your wounds
So prosper in their cure.

LEO. You shew your inclination kind and noble.
But is there of Evandra yet no news ?
You promised to enquire whether her flight
Be true, or to what place she made escape.

VAS. No certainty is known, but all the court
Troubled with doubts. Shortly you will hear more.

LEO. If you could bring me, sir, to Prospero,
Or to the Prince, on some affairs that may
Perhaps advantage them and my own good,
You shall oblige me much to serve you in
My better state of fortunes.

VAS. I will endeavour it ; and, as you find
Me ready to assist all your requests,
I hope, sir, you'll see cause to pay your ransom
With what haste you can ; for I would fain be able
To do good deeds, and we have many poor
I'th' town that want their charities, who have

* See vol. ii., p. 104.

III.                                                        I

A will as ready as their wealth.

LEO. Believe me, you express a soul that hath
Been bred, and exercis'd in holy thoughts.

VAS. Faith, sir, not much ; only you know a man
Would joy to do some good whilst he's alive,
For after death our gifts, I ever thought,
Rather proceeded from a devout necessity
Than any free desire.

LEO. 'Tis wisely urged.

VAS. It hath been a maxim I have held long.

LEO. And it becomes you still ; my ransom
Be suddenly prepared.

VAS. I thank you, sir. Follow ! and I'll procure
You an address to th' prince, or Prospero.   [*Exit.*

LEO. If she were fled, her person is of so
Esteem'd and eminent a rate, that straight
Her instant residence must needs be known :
There is much art in these affairs.   How will
She look on me, that in so great a cause
Could strike, or yield to angry fate ? I will
Endure her scorns as a deserved reward.
Nor should a lover's hopes grow cold, because
The influence that last did govern him
Was sick and cold.   That destiny is gone :
The firmament contains more stars than one.

                        [*Exeunt.*

---

## ACT III. SCÆNA I.

*Enter* PROSPERO *and* LEONELL *with a light
and a key.*

PROS. It glads me to behold your strength so well
Restor'd ; and, sir, I wish the fortune of
My sword had met another cause and enemy.

Your ransom I have paid ; and so much prize
Evandra's happiness, that since you make't
Appear your company will render her
Some quietness and joy, in this her sad
And solitary state, you shall both see
And stay with her. *

LEO. From my first infancy I took my speech
And breeding in her father's court, and by
My nearness to her, both in deeds and place
I'th' day of fight, you may believe I am
Of quality enough to be esteem'd
And welcom'd in her misery.

PROS. Your valour then did speak you more
than all
The praise your modesty can urge.

LEO. My lord! it is your gentleness to have
A courteous faith, but I am bold to think
My sight will comfort her so much that she
Will pay you thanks for giving so free trust
Unto my confidence.

PROS. My kindness to you I shall reserve
Till happier hours : this, sir, is for her sake,
That she may have the benefit of your
Approach. Retire awhile within! that key,
When I am gone, will open you a door
That leads unto a cave.        [Exit Leonell.
Melora, where art thou? This way, the light
Conducts thee. Thou art safe.

*Enter* MELORA.

MEL. How dark, and like the dusty hollowness
Of tombs, where death inhabits, this appears.

PROS. Now, you shall know the cause why I have
bought
Your liberty ; Evandra, daughter to
Your Millain Duke, lies here, imprison'd by

* You shall have leave to make your frequent visits. —*Folio.*

The chance of battle, and thus hidden and
Reserv'd, till we can free her by disguise.

MEL. O sad discov'ry of a sorrow, worse
Than I endure; I hop'd she had escap'd.

PROS. I heard that thou wert taken in her train;
But when the stories of thy beauty and
Thy virtues reach'd mine ear, I did believe
Thou hadst familiar knowledge of her face
And thoughts.

MEL. I know too much of her, to think that
heaven
Could thus permit her languish in a cave.

PROS. None can resist their destiny: but good
Melora comfort her, and prithee for
Kind pity when your conversation shall
Beget some pleasant hour, mention my care,
And then my love; for know, she hath so wrought
Upon my heart, that trust me I shall melt
Like tapers overcharged with flame, and die.
Wilt thou implore in my behalf?

MEL. Your bounties have oblig'd me to perform
My best, else I were cruel, sir.

PROS. Fear no surprise: you are secure, for
twice
To-day my house by stern authority
Was search'd, but vainly they suspect and strive
To find this hidden dwelling, that no art
Can imitate for secrecy and depth.

MEL. Will you be gone?

PROS. I'm sent for to the palace where I'm told
I shall endure, for this concealment, more
Than nature's strength can bear, but I've a soul
Dares welcome it with scorn.

*Enter* EVANDRA.

MEL. Lend me the light! Look, there's Evandra,
sir.

PROS. It is ! Remember me, that I may live.
                                        [*Exit.*
MEL. This mingled passion of strange grief and
    joy
I can no longer quietly contain.
Hail ! the most beauteous virtue of the world.
    EVAN. Lov'd Melora ! what dismal chance, more
        than
My sorrow can digest, hath brought thee here ?
    MEL. Why am I thought on, or enquir'd for as
A creature that deserves a life, whilst you
Remain within the house and arms of death?
    EVAN. I fear thou art a captive too.
    MEL. Or else the tyranny of war had been
Too much unjust ; wer't fit you languish thus,
And I, like to a wanton bird should play
And wing the air at liberty ? and yet
My ransom's freely paid.
    EVAN. Then thou art now no prisoner ?
    MEL. A prisoner to you, or else my heart
Were dull, and rudely mannered to permit
Evandra suffer here alone. This war
Hath quickly nursed strange riddles too of love.
    EVAN. Thou dost complain with cause, 'tis in
        the prince.
    MEL. Another of your enemies. Too much
Of leisure I shall have t' acquaint you with
The accident that brought me to your sight.

### *Enter* LEONELL.

    EVAN. Melora, who is that ?
    MEL. Bless me ! how miracles increase, to fright
Astonishment. Sure there is magic in
This place. Madam, my brother Leonell.
    LEO. Ha ! Melora ! art thou here too ? Such
        mysteries
In change so soon arriv'd I have not read.

EVAN. But what unheard of star directed thee
To see and taste our miserable state ?
　　LEO. Ere I begin the little history
Of the short time that thus hath varied us,
Low as the earth I fall, to make you pitiful. [*Kneels.*
Forgive the crime of destiny, not me,
That left me feeble as an aguish girl,
With the faint loss of blood, when I had took
Upon my youth and strength the noblest cause
That e'er employed the anger of a man,
Your liberty ; but leverets and doves
Are valianter than I, for else what make
You in captivity ?
　　EVAN. Believe me, sir, your passion is so great
I understand it not : pray, rise ! I know
You fought with all the forward will and might
That human rage could shew ; but the success
Of valour they above dispose, that are
More wise and stronger than ourselves.
　　LEO. Sure I could weep, but that my eyes
Have not enough of funeral dew to melt
Away. Sister, pray pardon my neglect !
You'll find I am not courteous to myself.
　　MEL. The time compels distracted thoughts in all.
　　EVAN. There is a bank within, though cold and
　　　　bare,
Where never flower, in despair of sun,
Durst fix his root, there we will sit, talk, and
Compare our miseries ; then sing like Philomel,
That wisely knows the darkness only fit
For mourning and complaint., Lead there ! the
　　　　light ! 　　　　　　　　　　　　[*Exeunt.*

　　*Enter* DUKE, *with letters,* ALVARO, PROSPERO,
　　　　CALLADINE, ATTENDANTS.

　　DUKE. Evade me not with such fond circum-
　　　　stance,

Fit only to persuade the easiness
Of untaught babes ; have I not here receiv'd
Her father's letters, that petition her
Release ?  Why should he soothe me thus with low
Demeanour in his phrase, if she were free ?
Or if not in the town enclos'd, and hid,
Where would she sooner fly than to his arms ?

    ALV. Sir, give my duty boldness to believe
If she were here, and some good man, that now
Conceals her in his piteous fear, shall to
Assuage your wrath deliver her, you would
Not mark her out for death ?

    DUKE. No, sir, how cheap then, and how frail
      will you
Suppose my vows ? what need we trick
And dress our altars with such reverend care ?
Let's rather straight pervert their use, grease them
With gluttony and feasts, defile and wash
Them with the riots of excessful wine.
Is perjury the least of guilt you can
Persuade me to commit ?

    ALV. I wish you would allow m' obedience leave
To utter truth ; the vow you made was rash,
And not confirmed with oath, or church solemnity.

    PROS. And I am taught the cruelties, or the
Revenge we threaten : heaven is pleased when they
Are never acted but forgot.

    DUKE. Her stern and deaf'ned father when we
      sought,
And woo'd his mercy with humility,
More than dejected hermits on their knees
Render to saints, us'd not my brother with
Remorse, but snatcht him from the world in all
His pride of youth, his wise and ripened thoughts,
When he was fit to rule a nation's fate,
And exercise mankind in what was bold
And good, shall I not revenge the best

Of all my blood, whilst I have here
The chief of his?

ALV. Alas! this act, sir, was not hers, nor in
The justice of our reason is it possible
By derivation or descent to share a guilt.

PROS. Would I had lost the benefit of strength
When I surpris'd her, to become the instrument
And pleasure of your rage.

DUKE. How, Count, so bold! Hear me, thou
    saucy child
And minion of the war, whom fortune, not
Success from virtue sprung, hath lifted to
A pride more dangerous than traitors' thoughts.
Though I have search'd thy house, and am de-
    feated by
Some charm of my discovery, I still
Believe thou knowst her residence, and bring
Her to my sight, ere yet the sun decline,
Or thou shalt die.

ALV. I must not live to see it, then, nor can
My business here on earth entice me to
One minute's stay in my mortality,
When I behold your business so decay'd.

DUKE. Alvaro, was that said like one that knows
His duty to a father, and a Prince?

ALV. I would be heir unto your virtue, sir,
As well as to your blood.

DUKE. Have I out-liv'd my courage, office, and
My reason too, tamely to suffer this?
I know thy false ambitious cunning well,
Thou fain wouldst vex my weary soul away
That thou might'st reign, and triumph o'er my tomb.
But hear, and tremble at my vow!

CALL. Sir, for regard of heaven, repent what you
Would speak, ere utter'd it become too great
A sin for mercy to excuse.

DUKE. No more, fond Calladine, I am resolv'd,

Since thou art covetous to own his guilt,
He shall be safe, and thou endure his punishment.
Bring me Evandra here ere yet the day
Conceal his light, or the next darkness shall
Eternally be thine.

ALV. If on my knees I can persuade you to
An easier doom, thus I endeavour it.        [*Kneels.*

PROS. I beg not to entreat your rigour less,
But as 't was first design'd you would convert
It all on me.

ALV. That kindness was ill-manner'd, Prospero.
Dost think thou art more worthy of the cause
When 'tis to be Evandra's sacrifice?

DUKE. Ne'er strive, thou shalt have sufferance
    enough
And gloriously alone.   Hence from my sight!
Thou birth ill-gotten, and my marriage-stain.

ALV. I'll keep my duty still, though not your
    love.                        [*Ex. Alv. Pros.*

CALL. Dread, sir, call back your vow, and then
    the Prince,
Yet comfort him.   What will the world esteem
Of such an act as time ne'er parallel'd,
And no posterity be so unkind as to believe.

DUKE. Thou may'st as well persuade th' assem-
    bled winds
From all their violence at sea.   Lend me
Thine ear——do this!   But, Calladine, take heed
Thy prosecutions are not faint : I have
A younger son in Sicily, renown'd
And dear to fame ; him I will strive to plant
I'th' people's hearts.   As thou art loyal, follow me !
                            [*Exeunt.*

*Enter* ALTESTO, FRIVOLO, VASCO, *fantastically
                accouter'd.*

VAS. Just in the posture as you see me, gentlemen;

Not a hair less i'th' lock; and I believed
The heart of woman was not able to
Resist such amorous forms.

ALT. But she would none?

VAS. Name her the pleasures of the marriage bed,
She cries she is more taken with the grave,
'Cause there we are not wak'd with cough nor
    aches.

ALT. Why, sure she knows, for she looks as she had
Been long buried.

VAS. And then I us'd fine phrases;
And talk't, what call you it? of Hymen's tapers,
Which she interprets, sir, according to
Some modern doctress of her sect,—hell fire!
A warmth, you know, we soldiers do abhor.

FRIV. 'Tis base to need it after death : we have
Been hardly bred, and can endure the cold.

*Enter* WIDOW *and* LELIA.

VAS. She comes! This is her breathing room,
    use your
Endeavours, gentlemen. Tell her, her frowns,
Already have so wrought, that my life now
Will ne'er be fit to come into a lease.

WID. Lelia, a chair! I cannot last; 'tis more
Than fifty-eight years since I had hams to trudge.

VAS. I am your guardian that's come to visit you.

WID. What need it, sir? I practice no escape!
I cannot fly!

VAS. No! were the window open
You would behave your self as nimbly on
Your wings as any witch in Europe.

WID. What, says he, Lelia? a witch!

LEL. He says we must one day all fly upward,
Heaven is the place we——
    [VAS. Ay, widow! that is the place.] *

* Interpolated in the folio.

WID. 'Tis well said, sir ; for thither we must go,
Both old and young ; no remedy.

VAS. As soon as you please, if you'd but marry me.

WID. Does he talk of marriage ?

LEL. He says, if you please, forsooth.

WID. Alas, my vow of widow-hood is not yet
Expir'd.   If he comes some ten years hence——

ALT. About that time she 'll make a good wife
For an antiquary to get records on.

FRIV. Although her skin be parchment, 'tis not
     large
Enough to write her annals in ; sh'ath liv'd
So long already.

VAS. How did you like the culleise, widow,
That I sent you last ?

WID. Why, sir, it went down.

VAS. Though the sea were turn'd
To plum-broth, 'twould all down !
I have measur'd her throat, 'tis wider, gentlemen,
And deeper than a well.   Alas ! the Duke
Considers not my charge.   I'ld rather board
Two young giants, and allow each of them
A wolf, instead of a dog, t' eat their fragments.

ALT. Thou should'st get her mouth search'd !
I'll lay my life, sh' hath new furnish'd her gums,
With artificial teeth ; she could not grind so else.

FRIV. Though you must feed her at your own cost,
The proclamation, believe me, allows none
But natural teeth.

VAS. When she is once i'th' fit of swallowing,
If a capon float in her broth, why she
Considers it no more than a small bee,
Or a May-fly.

LEL. You should bear up ! you are too backward,
     sir.

VAS. Sayst thou so, wench ?   Widow ! prepare
     yourself,

For I must marry you to-night, or else
You fast to-morrow.  If the Duke will not
Afford us fasting days, I shall make bold
To borrow 'em o'th' the kalender.  This night !
No longer time to delay a good deed.

WID. Uh, uh, uh !—

ALT. This cough, Vasco, is of some great anti-
    quity.
How wilt thou sleep by her ?

ALT. A little opium after supper,
And let her cough like a cannon from a fort.
I'll free thee from waking.

VAS. Come, come, provide !
Trim up your hood, widow, and air
Your petticoats i'th' sun : it is a case
Of conscience, gentlemen.  We must all marry,
And live chaste.

WID. Why, sir, if we must needs——

ALT. I thought she would consent ; good heart,
    it is
As towardly an old thing.   Dear Vasco,
Provide us in music ; we 'll dance her to death :
Thou shalt be her husband ere night, and her
Executor before morning.

VAS. Sooth, gentlemen, that's all I desire !
Anything, that is reason contents me.

FRIV. Go, kiss her !  By this hand a Brownist * is
More amorous ; a notch'd prentice a very
Aretine in comparison of thee.

VAS. By your leave, widow.     [*Vas. kisses her.*

WID. Much good may't do you, sir ; these com-
    forts come
But seldom after fourscore ; the world, indeed,
Is grown so wicked, that we never think
Of comforting one another.

* See vol. ii., p. 131.  The poet Burns expresses a similar
sentiment as to the sect called Cameronians.

LEL. I told you she would soften, sir ; alas !
A little raw and modest at the first.

ALT. A very green pippin of the last year's
growth.

VAS. You shall find me a kind of sparrow, widow:
A barley corn does as much as a potato.

WID. Blessing on your heart, sir ; we should do
good

Freely, as they say, without egging on.*

VAS. Rise, and stir your feet ! 'tis healthful for
you.

There——softly——so——     [*They lift her up.*

ALT. If one of the hairs of my eye-brow lie
But in her way, she's gone, and then falls like an
Elephant, whose legs are cut with a chain shot.

FRIV. Her os sacrum needs a little prop.

VAS. Why, gentlemen, there's ne'er a wench in
Italy

Moves farther in a day, provide her litter
Be easy, and her two mules well fed.

Courage, widow ! How is it now ?

WID. A certain stitch, sir, in my side, but
'Twill away in time.

VAS. Ay, you are young enough,
But given too much to hoyting, † and to barley-
break, ‡

* Being urged forward by backers.
† Noisy mirth.
‡ There is a description of this ancient rural game in a little
tract, called "Barley-breake ; or, a Warning for Wantons," 4to
Lond., 1607, some extracts from which will be found in the
Brit. Bibl., i., 66. The game was played by three males and
three females, coupled by lot. A chosen piece of ground was
divided into three compartments, the middle plot being called
*hell*. If the couple placed therein caught one of the other
couples who advanced from the two extremities, they changed
places. The middle couple could not separate till they succeeded in a capture, while the others might break hands when
jeopardized. When all had been taken in turn, the last couple
were said to be in *hell*, and so ended the game.

    *See Brand's Pop. Antiq. also Florio,*

Then dance naked till you take cold. Good faith !
You must look to't, Lelia ! take heed you air
Her wedding-smock.

 ALT. Let it be made of cats'-skin fur.

 FRIV. Or a watchman's rug-gown ; * but that
her skin
Will wear it out too soon.

 VAS. Frivolo, yo' are too loud !

 FRIV. I warrant thee I have measur'd her ears ;
She hears in distance but an inch length.

 VAS. You'll in, and set the house in order,
  widow ?
I'll fetch a priest.

 WID. Truly, sir, I'ld fain ask my friends' advice ;
One that hath seen but little of the world
Would be glad, you know, of counsel.

 VAS. No counsel, widow ; nay, if you want metal
Let them call't rashness, our youth will excuse all.

 WID. Well, sir, you know where marriages are
  made ;
'Tis not my fault. Lelia, provide a broom
And sweep away the rheum near the green couch :
And, d'you hear, look for one of my cheek teeth
Which dropt under the wainscot-bed.

 LEL. And shall I stop't forsooth with salt ?

 WID. Ay, and fling't i'th' fire. †  You are weary,
  sir ?

 VAS. Not quite so lusty, widow, as yourself ;
But shall keep pace, the journey being so short.‡

 ALT. Quick, in with her, Vasco ! whilst the fit
  holds.     [*Exeunt Wid., Vas., Lel.*

 * See vol. i., p. 232.

 † It is a popular fret, that when a cast tooth having salt
thrown over it is cast in the fire, a fresh tooth will spring up in
the place it occupied.

 ‡ In the early 4to, the stage direction "Enter Altesto"
here occurs, which seems unnecessary, Altesto being already
on the stage.

With cable and thong, he drew her along
  So heavily to the priest,
And vow'd to undo her, ere he did woo her,
  Make her up after who list.

FRIV. Ah, rogue! thou art a very lark in the
morning.

ALT. And what at night, Frivolo?

FRIV. A very owl.

ALT. Thou art a coxcomb, beyond all redemption
Of wit, 'less thou straight resolve to marry Lelia;
Thy friends will think the match so fit, none shall
Forbid the banns. I know her mother too.
She's wondrous rich in pewter, small wine casks,
And spits.

FRIV. Yes, I have heard o' th' wealthy dowager,
She kept a thatch'd nunnery in my quarter.

*Enter* TRISTAN.

TRIS. Where's Vasco, Gentlemen? I am in haste.

ALT. Why then for more dispatch answer yourself.

TRIS. The Duke hath sent for him, by Calladine,
Who told me 'twas for business of import;
The Court is all disturbed, but for what use
He is design'd I cannot learn. Where is he?

ALT. Follow! we'll convey thee to him. Strange
  luck!
Sir Leonell's ransom, this widow's wealth,
And now employ'd at Court! Vasco, th' art a gone
  man!
Usury, furred gowns, long dinners, and short sleeps,
Thou art condemn'd to without help or hope.*

*Enter* EVANDRA, MELORA, LEONELL, (*at one door*)
*at the other* PROSPERO, (*muffled and hid*) *a table
and lights set out.* EVANDRA *sits to read.*

LEO. Sister, where is your tenderness? shall I

    * See addenda for an alteration of the text.

Be ever lost through your defect of will
And courage to present me to her ear
In winning characters ? tell her how long
With fervency I have pursued my love.
   MEL. Unhappy Leonell, why dost thou tempt
Me with impossible desires ? how oft
Have I solicited thy suit with a repulse ?
And she hath charm'd me by a vow
Never to mention 't more till her release.
   PROS. False Leonell ! did I for this assist
Thee to enjoy her lov'd society
That thou shouldst rival me, and have more fit
Convenience for thy wishes than my self ?
Melora is his sister too ! what strange
New chances have these later hours produc'd ?
I have no advocate, nor am I bold
Enough to be mine own.
   LEO. I see you love me not ;
And since I am a trouble to your sight,
Ere long thou shalt behold my face no more.
   PROS. Thou art a prophet to thy self, and I
Thy priest, to cut thee out in sacrifice,
Although unworthy of Evandra's deity.
   LEO. Melora, can you shew no kind remorse ?
   MEL. Alas, you do mistake my power and will ;
Think on some other beauty, for the world
Hath many that may make you fortunate.
   LEO. None but Evandra governs in my breast.
   PROS. Her thou shalt ne'er enjoy ; lend me thine
     ear—                                   [*Leads him aside.*
   LEO. Ha ! Prospero ?
   PROS. False knight ! was this the cause
That made thee beg conceal'd admittance here,
To practice love where I had planted mine ?
   LEO. My lord, I understood not of your love.
   PROS. If thou art bold, and since thy vanquish-
     ment,

Darest tempt a second hazard of my sword,
Go, wait me on the garden mount ; there I
Will order, though my heart is doubtful to
Enjoy Evandra's love, thine never shall.

LEO. I will expect thee there, and fiercely long
To ravish from thy crest the honour that
I lent thee in our former fight.                    [*Exit.*

*Enter* ALVARO.

ALV. Evandra reach me thy fair hand, that I
Seal on it my last farewell.

EVAN. Ha ! whither do you go ?

ALV. Where shadows vanish, when the world's
    eye winks,
Behind a cloud, and they are seen no more.
The place of absence where we meet, by all
The guess of learned thought, we know not whom,
Only a prompt delight we have in faith
Gives us the easy comfort of a hope
That our necessity most rather praise
Than fear as false.

EVAN. O horrid mystery !
My tender senses are amaz'd.    I fain
Would learn what it is dangerous to know.

MEL. Why do the stars neglect us thus ? why
    should
We lose the noblest and the best of men ?

PROS. Methinks my spirits climb and lift me to
A valiant envy of his sufferings.

ALV. That you mayst live here safe, till Prospero
Restore thee unto liberty and light,
I must to darkness go, hover in clouds,
Or in remote untroubled air, silent
As thoughts, or what is uncreated yet.
Or I must rest in some cold shade, where is
No flow'ry spring nor everlasting growth

K

To ravish us with scent, and shew, as our
Philosophy hath dreamt, and rather seems
To wish than understand.

EVAN. All this for me! you shall not die ; why
   will
You lay so cheap a value on your self,
To think the world should lose you for my sake ;
Alas! a needless trivial virgin that
Can never shew in hopeful promise half
That excellence which you reveal in art.*

ALV. It is decreed! Evandra, thou mayst live
T' encrease the small example we have left
Of virtue, which hath made thy breast her throne.
Time hath begun to wear away my youth,
And all the good I can perform is to
Preserve the future hope of it in thee.

EVAN. Melora, help! sorrow hath fill'd my heart
With such a heaviness, that I must sink
Beneath its weight.  Here let me lye, and mourn,
And chide that haughty destiny that thinks
Us so unworthy of their care

MEL. My lord the Prince, is it no less than death
Of her, or you, can ease your father's wrath ?

ALV. The doom is past, and the sad hour will
   want
No wings to hasten its approach.  Come hither,
   Prospero.

PROS. It must not be ; though I want phrase to
   shew
My nature smooth, it shall appear in deeds.

ALV. I charge thee by our love, by all my care
That bred thee from thy childhood to a sense
Of honour, and the worthiest feats of war,
Thou keep Evandra safe, till happier days
Conspire to give her liberty.  Use her
With such respective holiness as thou

* Act --*Folio.*

Would'st do the reliques of a saint enshrin'd,
And teach thy rougher manners tenderness
Enough to merit her society.

PROS. What need this conjuration, sir ? I mean
To die for her, that I may save your life.
A brave design ! disswade me not.   Though I
Fail oft in choice of fitting enterprise,
I know this is becoming, sir, and good.

ALV. Thou die for her ? Alas, poor Prospero !
That will not satisfy, the shaft aims here ;
Or if it would, I do not like thou should'st
Thus press into a cause that I reserve
To dignify my self.   Urge it no more.

PROS. What am I fit for then, if not to die ?

EVAN. How am I worthy of this noble strife ?

ALV. Evandra, rise ! that I may see some hope,
And comfort in thy strength, before I take
My everlasting leave.

EVAN. You have the voice of death already, sir.

MEL. Dismal it sounds, like the last groan which
     men
In torture breathe out with their soul.

ALV. I could have wish'd I might enjoy thee and
Be mortal still, mix in a love that should
Produce such noble virtues as would soon
Entice the angels to live here, yet not
B' our conversation grow impair'd : but these
Are wishes made too high and late to thrive.
For evermore, farewell !

EVAN. Oh sir ! where will you leave me then ?

ALV. How pity moistens me ! there, in the cave.

EVAN. It is the mansion, sir, of death ; some-
     thing,
Horrid as midnight thoughts can form, so frights
Me still I tremble when I enter it.

ALV. Ha ! what that is but human dares
Disturb thy quietness ?

Pros. Sir, let me see! It dies if it be vulnerable.
Alv. Still you usurp my business, Prospero.
Bide there! I will go down my self.
  Evan. Sir, 'twill not presently appear.
  Alv. I will attend its saucy leisure, then.
                             [*Descends the cave.*
  Evan. Lock safe the door, Melora, with this key.
  Pros. What's your design? mean you t' imprison
    him?
  Evan. Discover, Prospero, the inside of
Thy breast.  Dost thou affect the prince?
  Pros. Next to the absent blessings that our
    faith
Persuades us to, eternity of joys.
  Evan. Why then wilt you permit that he should
    taste
A long forgetfulness in a dark grave?
Let us invent some way to ease him of
This penance undeserv'd, and suffer it ourselves.
  Mel. O glorious maid! this goodness will confer
A dignity for ever on our sex.
  Pros. I'm strangely taken with this virgin's
    thoughts,
Let me embrace your hand, upon my knee.
I thank you much, you have some mercy on
My dull unknowing youth, and can believe
Me fit for noble enterprise, though he
Unkindly did deny my suit.  I'll to
The Duke, and tempt his fury, till he cause
My death; perhaps when his revenge hath
    quench'd
Her thirst with my warm blood, it may grow cold,
And kindly temper'd to you both, and then
I've fully satisfied the crime
Of your captivity, and his free sufferance.
  Mel. This soldier hath a great and daring heart.
  Pros. But how shall I enjoy her then? I scarce

Can understand the happiness it bears.
'Tis odd ambition this, but yet 'tis brave ;
I'll do't ; besides, though I'm not learn'd enough
With certainty, yet I have hope I shall
Be sensible of all her visits to
My tomb,* and ev'ry flower she strews will there
Take growth, as on my garden banks, whilst I,
Delighted spirit, walk and hover 'bout
Their leaves, comparing still their scent with hers.
O, 'twill be wondrous brave !   Lady, dispatch,
That I may go and die.

    EVAN. Since you express your will, so kind and
      violent,
That small provision there allotted to
Sustain my life, reach up, and straight convey
Into the cave, that he may find it out,
And not exchange the pain his father would
Inflict, for famishment.

              *[Pros. takes from behind the arras a*
                *bottle and bag.   They open the cave.*

    PROS. I had almost forgot false Leonell,
He waits me on the Mount.   I will be with
Him straight, and end his hopes by a long sleep,
Ere I begin mine own.         *[Descends the cave.*

    EVAN. Once more, Melora, lock the door !   Now
      they
Are both secure, 'tis thou and I then must
Take solemn leave, and never meet in this
Our beauty, colour, or our warmth again.

    MEL. I am astonish'd at her excellence,
And scarce have humble grace enough to keep
Ambitious envy from my thoughts.

    EVAN. Why should these mighty spirits lay so
      vast
An obligation on our sex, and leave
Eternal blushes on our souls, 'cause we

        * Urn.—*Folio.*

In acts of kindly pity and remorse,—
The virtues sure wherein we most excel,—
Durst not adventure life to them ? *

MEL. The Prince deserves a lib'ral choice of lives
To ransom his ; would mine would satisfy.

EVAN. How, Melora !  I cannot think thou dost
So faintly love my happiness and my
Renown, to wish to hinder me of both.

MEL. Alas ! th' example is so good, I fain would
follow it.

EVAN. But there is reason that I suffer first.
I have a mourning weed within, which thou
Shalt dress, and teach me wear ; then so
Apparel'd like my cause, I'll walk to th' Duke.

MEL. O leave me not behind, let me accompany
Your mourning too, perhaps my death may be
Accepted best, and you be thought more fit to live.

EVAN. Thy inclinations have a noble sense.
Thou shalt along.  Go, call thy brother in !
And call aloud.   This hollowness is such
He will not hear thee else.

MEL. Hoa ! Leonell ! my brother Leonell !

*Enter* LEONELL.

LEON. 'Tis strange, this Prospero appears not yet ;
Sure he is faint, and 's aguish courage comes
To him by fits.  What is your will ?

EVAN. If thou dost love me, Leonell, as thou
Hast sworn—and with assertions most devout—
I know there is no strict command I can
Present, but thy obedience will perform.

LEON. Bring me to trial straight !   If I prove
weak
Or false, I am unworthy to appear
In the sun's light, or evermore enjoy
The better influence of your eyes.

*       Life for them.—Folio

EVAN. Give me confirm'd assurance on your knee,
That you will execute with real* faith,
And punctual circumstance, what I enjoin.

LEON. Let me salute your hand, I breathe on it
My vow.

EVAN. Now I'll inform thee, Leonell; the Prince
And Prospero are both within the cave,
Shut and enclosed by me, where hourly thou
Through a small and slender wicket shalt convey
Such food, as a disguised servant of the house,
Who heretofore provided our relief,
Shall help thee to. Take here this key,
And not permit their passage forth till I
Am gone t' ordain by death their liberty
Secure, which I will suffer to appease
The angry Duke.

LEON. Furies and fiends seize on my senses
straight !
What have I promis'd in the rashness of
My dull and inconsiderate love ?

EVAN. If thou dost break thy vow, the curses of
The saints, and mine, which dying will not least
Affect thy perjury, fall on thy heart.

MEL. Never be called my brother, nor assume
The honour of my valiant father's name.

EVAN. Melora, come ! we are too slow in such
An act as will outlive all history.

[*Exeunt Evan., Mel.*

LEO. O what a dull inhuman lover am
I grown ! that simply by a forward and
Unskilful duty can consent the Queen
And lady of my life should be a sacrifice
To hinder others' deaths ! This sure is such
A great example of a female fortitude
As must undo all men, and blushing make
Us steal from our unjust advancement o'er

* Steady. -- *Folio*

The world ; tear off our saucy beards before
The scatt'ing winds that give us the pre-eminence
Of sex ; when this is known, let woman sway
Councils and war, whilst feeble men obey. [*Exit.*

## ACT IV. SCÆNA I.

*Enter* CALLADINE *in a night-gown, and a Servant.*

CALL. A lady, say'st thou, in a mourning vest !
What should this early visit mean, ere yet
By full appearance of the sun we can
Distinguish day from night ?

 SERV. Sir, she importunes much to speak with
  you,
Says her affair asks secresy and haste.

 CALL. Retire a while without, and let her in !
         [*Exit Servant.*

*Enter* MELORA, *in mourning.* *She unveils.*

Since first my eyes had judgment to discern
A mean from excellence, they ne'er beheld
A beauty so o'ercoming and exact.
What are the lov'd commands you'ld lay on me ?
I not remember that I ever saw
A face I would more willingly obey.
If it were civil, too, I'ld ask your name.

 MEL. Believe me, gentle sir, when that is known,
You'll think me too unfortunate to live.
I am called Evandra.

 CALL. Ha ! the Princess ? Wisely did Prospero
Preserve thee from my sight ; thy beauty is
Too great and dangerous for youth to know
And be secure. Though I ne'er saw her till
This blessed hour, yet Fame assisted me

T' imagine an idea like herself.
But why have you forsaken your conceal'd
Abode, and thus adventure into th' view
Of men ?  I fear it is not safe.

MEL. 'Tis to employ your virtue, sir.  I know
You love the Prince, though not with so devout
A heart as mine : for that I may restore
Him unto liberty, and 's father's love,
I here present myself to cruel death.

CALL. This is a valiant piety! a gratitude
That shows her mind more noble than her shape.
She is not known unto the Duke more than
By guessing characters ta'en from report ;
She must not die, though lately his commands
Have singled my allegiance out ; it is
Religious, sure, to fail in this.

MEL. Sir, expectation of the ills we must
Endure do more perplex us than the pain
Itself.  I crave you'ld not protract my sufferance.

CALL.  My thoughts have fashion'd it unto my
    wish :
Is there not a captive called Melora,
Most beautiful and young, that hath of late
Familiar been to your society ?

MEL. I fear he hath discover'd me.        [Aside.
D'you know the lady, sir ?

CALL. Only by Prospero's report, and I
In charity desire her person safe.
Your death alone will satisfy the Duke.

MEL. My pray'rs have much endeavour'd that
    it may ;
And, sir, t' assist your kind humanity,
Receive this key, 'twill give you entrance where
She now remains a prisoner by my art :
It is a narrow closet that o'erlooks
The orchard  grove :  you  know  the  house—'tis
    Prospero's.

CALL. I am familiar there with all the vaults
And hidden passages.

MEL. Sir, for regard of honour, suffer not
Her freedom from that place till I am dead.
For she's so much delighted with this cause,
That, with unwilling falsehood, I was fain
To take advantage of her orisons ;
For whilst she kneeling lengthen'd her discourse
With heaven, steal on this funeral habit, and
In haste close up the door to hinder her
Pursuit : where now she stays, lamenting her
Enforc'd secure estate, and envying of
This danger, which I cheerfully embrace.

CALL. My life shall warrant hers : be pleas'd to
     enter there,
And stay till I inform the Duke of your
Appearance and approach.

MEL. Most willingly ; but still, sir, I implore
Your mercy would secure that Lady and the Prince,
Howe'er the angry stars dispose of me.

CALL. 'Tis no less unkind t' importune than
To doubt my care.   There, lady, through that
     door—              [Shews her the way.
Expect my sad return will be too soon.

MEL. Forgive me, best Evandra, that I thus
Assume thy name, and have beguil'd thee of
So brave a death ; the motive that persuades me to't
Did not become thy knowledge nor my tongue.
                                      [Exit.

CALL. This Princess hath a soul I could adore,
Whilst it remains eclips'd on earth, nor shall
It yet reach heaven ; both being utterly
Unknown, will make the plot with easy help
Succeed.  Melora straight I will present
T' appease the fury of the Duke ; and then
This lady, and the Prince, are free.   Through
     blood

Is the best issue if our hopes ; if fate
Ordain it thus I shall prove fortunate.

*Enter* FRIVOLO, TRISTAN, *musicians and boy.*

ALT. Come, boys, lift up your voice to yon bay
  window.
Sing the song I gave you last night and firk *
Your fiddles bravely too.   Bear up the burthen !

### SONG.

#### 1.

BOY. No morning red and blushing fair
  Be through your glass or curtains spy'd ;
But cloudy gray, as the short hair
  Of your old everlasting bride.
CHO. So old, so wondrous old, i' th' nonage of
  time,
  Ere Adam wore a beard, she was in her prime.

#### 2.

BOY. Whose swarthy, dry'd Westphalia hips
  Are shrunk to mummy in her skin,
Whose gums are empty, and her lips,
  Like eyelids hairy and as thin.
CHO. So old, so wondrous old, &c.

#### 3.

BOY. For am'rous sighs which virgins use,
  She coughs aloud from lungs decay'd,
And with her palsey cannot chuse
  But shake like th' trembling of a maid.
CHO. So old, so wondrous old, &c.

* Oh ! how they did jerk it,
    Caper and ferk it
      Under the greenwood tree.
*The Countryman's delight*, in Durfey's Pills, vol. 4.

4.

BOY. And when her nightly labour swells
    To vast extent her pregnant womb ;
Midwives believe, that it foretells
    A hopeful tympany to come.
CHO. So old, so wondrous old, &c.

5.

BOY. What need her husband then vex heaven,
    And for a plenteous offspring beg ;
Since all the issue can be given,
    Is that which runneth in her leg.
CHO. So old, so wondrous old, &c.

ALT. Good morrow to the right worshipful Leader,
Captain Vasco, and to 's right reverend bride.
Now, gentlemen scrapers, you may be gone.
                    [*Ex. music.*

*Enter* VASCO, *dressing himself.*

VAS. My good friends, a certain salt shower
    should have
Season'd your feathers, had not my luck been
To marry with one that consumes all her moisture
In rheum : a mere Egyptian cloud for drouth.
ALT. But why so soon abroad ?   Vasco, are
    these,
A bridegroom's hours ? thou art as early up
As creditors i' th' term.
FRIV. Or serjeants, when
The needy gallant means to steal a journey.
TRIST. And they prevent it by arresting his
Innocent horse.
VAS. Business at Court.  But, gentlemen, this is
A resurrection to me, believe 't
I'm risen from the dead, from bones more dusty

Than theirs, that did begin their sleep beneath
A marble coverlet, some thousand years ago.

*Enter* WIDOW *and* LELIA.

ALT. 'Las, poor Vasco! Widows can strangely
    mortify
WID. Put dates and amber* in the gruel, Lelia;
And let it boil long.
LEL. And shall I make the poultice straight, and
    send
Your other hood, forsooth, to be new lin'd?
WID. First stay till you have ript my velvet muff,
I'll have that lining serve.
VAL. She's risen too; pure soul,
Devotion and aches keep her still waking.
WID. How do you, sir? We must comfort one
    another.
VAS. There is need of't. No mariner ere had
A worse night in a storm.
ALT. This usage, Vasco, will hardly mollify
Her iron chest, and make her bags open.
VAS. Nay, I've ta'en order for her wealth if she
Would be so courteous now to die.
ALT. Believe me you'll find her very obstinate
Touching that point; 'tis true a woman that
Had the least drachm of kindness or of reason
Would for her husband's benefit depart
This transitory at a minute's warning,
Make a low curtsey, take her leave and die,
                        [*She listens.*
With less noise, than flies forsake us in a frost.
VAS. Ay, you speak of kind reasonable women,
Alas! she's of another mould. She 'ld think 't
A strange request if I should urge it to her,
Though it be evidently for my good.

           * See *ante*. vol. ii. p. 244.

FRIV. What is't for her to die once ? Alas !
She knows well she hath eight lives more to come.
    ALT. Frivolo says right.   I think, captain,
    'twere fit
You make a motion to her : see how 'twill work.
    VAS. Never, gentlemen ! if her own good nature
Will not persuade her to't, let her e'en live
Till she be thought so much a ghost, that the state
Command her take a house in a church-yard,
And never walk but at midnight.
    WID. What do they say, Lelia ?
    LEL. Forsooth devising for your worship's good.
    WID. Kind heart ! methinks you are not merry,
    sir.
    VAS. Who, I ? As jovial as a condemn'd man, I
    WID. Will you sit down and eat a little broth ?
    VAS. I shall be caudled like a haberdasher's wife,
That lies in of her first child : but methinks
Upon a stricter view you look not well.
Your blood absents itself.   Are you not faint ?
    ALT. Ay, and her eyes shrink, and retire into
Their melancholy cells ; your breath smells somewhat
Of earth too ; but 'tis not much.
    FRIV. By'r lady but take heed, my grandam thus
Was taken spinning at her wheel, and died
So quickly, as they say, as one would wish.
    TRIS. I've seen a corse look better in a shroud.
If you have any business now with heaven
'Twere fit your prayers were short, for I much fear
You'll not have breath to utter it.
    WID. 'Tis more than I feel.  Look I so ill, Lelia ?
    LEL. As you were wont, forsooth : most strange
    and ugly.
    WID. Come, lead me in ! pray husband do not
    grieve ;
'Tis but a fit that ever takes me once
In fifty years : but weep not ! 'twill away.

VAS. Every tear shall be as big as a turnip
When I weep. The good pox comfort you ! Wench
Follow the game close ; still breathe death to her.

LEL. Warrant you, sir, I can do a better
Deed than put her in mind still of her end.

[*Exeunt Wid. and Lel.*

VAS. Marry a widow and be coffin'd up
With clouts and a skeleton ! By this day,
I lay last night lock'd in a surgeon's box ;
Compar'd unto her bed, a pothecary's bing
Is a Venetian couch and canopy.

ALT. Those that seek gold must dig for it in
mines.

VAS. Well, my camp companions, what think
you now
O' the court ? I'm sent for thither to take charge
Of what is yet the moiety of a miracle.
But you are all content to thrive, to jet
And strut like lustful turkeys with your plumes
spread.

ALT. 'Tis not amiss. My good lord, Frivolo,
I kiss your soft hands : noble sir, keep on
Your cordovan ; I swear your glove is a
Preferment 'bove the merit of my lips.

FRIV. You cherish my ambition, sir. Signieur
Tristan ! your profess'd slave ! I pray keep on
Your way. I'd rather build another wall,
Than to dishonour you by taking this.

TRIST. Believe it, sir, both hands must be cut off
Ere I mistake to place you near the left

VAS. This practice will do well. Follow apace !
I must with speed to Calladine.

### Enter EVANDRA, CALLADINE.

EVAN. 'Tis strange ! it seems he knows me not ;
and that
The falsely kind Melora wears my name.

He speaks as if her life he tender'd more
Than mine. 'Tis a mistake I fain would cherish
    CALL. I did not think the stock of nature could,
In this her colder age, be rich enough
To store the world with two such beauties that
Together take their growth, and flourishing.
And this, unto my instant judgment seems—
If such amazing forms admit of difference—
The more exact, but that the blood and style
Of Princess makes the other claim our reverence
As well as love ; and, for Alvaro's sake, I wish
I could procure that she might live.
    EVAN. I have consider'd what you told me, sir,
And though the princess, through a fond excess
Of love, would hasten a calamity,
That all the world must grieve and wonder at,
Yet I can give her reason an excuse :
For I my self to ease her sufferance
Could willingly endure the same.
    CALL. It ripens more, and swifter than my hopes
Design ; you reach at an ambition, lady,
So great and good, my wonder interupts
My language still, I cannot praise 't enough.
Can such a virtuous courage dwell in your sex ?
    EVAN. If you uprightly love her and the Prince,
Whose care she is, straight lead me to the Duke !
And try how real my professions are.
    CALL. Forgive the office you invite me to ;
Which, by the hopes of my religion, could
My life excuse, I should esteem't too cheap
An offering. This, lady, is the fatal way.
    EVAN. Melora, now my fortune is above
Thy art, and I shall equal thee in love.    [Exeunt.

*Enter* DUKE, *with letters,* VASCO, ALTESTO, FRIVOLO,
        TRISTAN, *attendants.*

    DUKE. Again, in low petitionary stile

He begs me by these letters to release
His daughter ; and doth proffer sums so vast
To ransom her, as would o'ercome the covetous.
But I have sent him such denial, with
Disdain, as must distract and break his heart.
Vasco, yo've heard how ill I am obey'd
By these perfum'd sweet traitors of the court ?
And I have chosen you to shew a duty,
Fitting the stricter discipline of war,
To actuate all my will with instant diligence.

VAS. You must enjoin me, sir, commands that
    are
Most horrid and unnatural, when I
Prove slow, or faint to execute.

DUKE. If these, your officers and friends, become
Disloyal to your will, you may provide
The rack and tortures to enforce 'em to 't.

VAS. If their own appetites will not persuade,
There is small hope from punishment.
Mark, sir, that whey-fac'd fellow in the red,
The rack is his delight, and gives him as
Much ease, as when he's stretch'd with laziness
And a cool morning's sleep.

DUKE. Is 't possible !

VAS. I've seen him suffer the strapado thrice ;
Hang in this politic posture in the air,
As he were studying to circumvent nature,
And no sooner done but calls for a wench.

DUKE. I know you have the skill to govern them.
Be sure that Prospero's house be digg'd, until
The pinacles and the foundation meet.
Unless they deal by sorcery and charms,
I'll find these buried lovers out, and my
False son the prince, that covets darkness more
Than blessed light, or my respect.

VAS. I do not like this bus'ness should concern
The prince. Although the rack be somewhat out

III.                    L

Of season with my old bones, for his sake,
I shall become a parcel traitor too.

*Enter* MELORA *and Servant.*

MEL. I fear'd that Calladine, delaying his
Return so long, might frustrate all my glory ;
And how Evandra's skill might work with him
Was dangerous.   I do not see her here.
    SERV. Pray heaven, my master do not check my
        forwardness
T' obey your will: he meant you should keep home.
    MEL. My presence here will make his benefit ;
I told thee so before : trust my excuse in thy
        behalf.
    DUKE. What lady's that ?
    MEL. One that, to pleasure you with a revenge,
Present my self to execution with
As liberal joy as to the marriage priest.
And when I name my self Evandra, you
Will know enough to satisfy your wrath.
    DUKE. Is the belov'd bird flown from the dark
        cage ?
Their magic was not strong enough to hinder
        destiny,
And you will find small am'rous pity in
My frozen age.   My guard ! seize on her straight.

*Enter a* GUARD, *and bind her.*

    ALT. Vasco ! this is Melora, my prisoner.
    VAS. Peace, devil, peace ! thou wilt destroy
        brave mysteries.
A noble girl ; I conceive all !   Now would
My gracious widow be burnt to a charcoal,
Ere she had brain or nature for a plot
Like this.   I could eat her and her clothes too ;
By this hand, her very shoes were a rare mess.
    MEL. If you expect to find me here a lowly suitor,

'Tis but to hasten, sir, your glad content
With a dispatch upon my life, and that
The Prince may be [restor'd]* unto your love.

DUKE. Her spirit seems to stir my manhood
    more
Than it astonisheth my sense. I am
Resolv'd to farther your desires, brave dame,
With all the help of cruelty and haste.

*Enter* CALLADINE *and* EVANDRA.

CALL. Death, slave, what make you here? The
    Princess too!    ·
Why did you give her liberty?

SERV. She told me, sir, it was with your consent.

CALL. She hath o'erreached my skill. I am
    undone.

DUKE. Stay, Calladine! another prize? Come
    **back**
And render me that lady's name.

EVAN. He knows it not. My name's Evandra,
    sir.

MEL. I fear I am depriv'd of my intent.

DUKE. We must to Delphos sure t' untie these
    doubts
And wonders with an Oracle.

EVAN. Do not believe that lady, sir. She hath
Beguil'd me of my name, and is so sick
And fond with an improper love, she would
Betray herself unto a pain; she knows
Not how to merit or endure like me.

MEL. O, sir, I find her language is most apt
And powerful to persuade; but let your faith
Consider my assertions too.

EVAN. Why dost thou let thy kindness wrong
    me thus;
Undoing thy religion with thy love?

    * "Atton'd."—*Folio.*

MEL. 'Tis you confer the injury, that will
Not suffer me to die in peace.

VAS. Rare wenches both! all this is for the
Prince.

DUKE. Though small inquiry would discover
soon
Who justifies the truth : yet I will end
The difference so as shall afford you equal joy,
And not endanger a mistake in me.
Convey them to the fort! they shall both die.
*[The Guard lays hold on them.*

VAS. Hath this Duke buried all his goodness in's
Revenge! Sure he is lib'd; he hath certainly
No masculine business about him.

DUKE. Lead them away!

CALL. I'll follow too, and mourn the obsequy,
Ere ceremonious death make it complete.

MEL. Forgive this emulation. Madam, you
Shall know a cause that will persuade you to't.

EVAN. Poor Melora! I pity not myself but thee.
*[Exeunt Call., Evan., Mel., and Guard.*

DUKE. Now, let my son and's minion, Prospero,
Rebellious as himself, resign to th' fiends
Their dark and hidden tenements again.
Come forth free and secure, for since they valu'd
death
As a delight, they shall not suffer it.
Go, straight! proclaim their next appearance safe,
For it will pleasure me they should stand by
To see, and not be able to resist the justice
Of revenge.

VAS. Sure revenge is a strange kind of lechery;
How it hath alter'd him!

DUKE. Vascô, now the enchanted house may
stand ;
But be you here to-morrow with some strength,
To guard their execution from impediments

Of rage or pity; they shall suffer early.   [*Exit.*

VAS. I thank your Grace for any employment.
Altesto, art thou a rogue!

ALT. A little, sir, infected with your company.

VAS. Art thou so very a rogue, if I command
Thee, from the Duke, to cut off these ladies' heads,
Thou'lt whet the axe thyself, and do't with the
Dexterity of a Fleming!

ALT. I will see thy head in a leathern case first,
Kickt in a foot-ball match from goal to goal.

VAS. Why, I thank thee. What say you, Frivolo?
Wenches and surgeons have cost you dear;
Have you remorse enough to do't?

FRIV. I've a mind rather to rebel, break shops
Open, and make choice of my silks, without
Taking notice, sir, of the Mercer's book.

TRIS. Such wholesome bus'ness would more take
   me too,
Than cutting off poor ladies' heads; unless
Your fair widow, Vasco, come in my reach.
I could behead her for her left ear-ring,
Though it be but an agate set in copper.

VAS. Come, let's to bed! the sun to-morrow will
Rise black, or I shall think him a dull insensible
Planet, and deserves no more adoration
Than a farthing candle.   [*Exeunt.*

*Enter* LEONELL, ALVARO, PROSPERO.

LEON. Sir, you have heard how she betray'd
   me to
A vow, and with what cruel menacings
My sister and herself petition'd heaven
T' assist their curses in a punishment
Upon my after life, if I were perjur'd by
A breach of what my promise did assure.

ALV. It was a vow no less unkind than strange,
T' imprison us that had no cause nor will

To do a noble stranger injury ;
But I have learnt a tame philosophy,
Persuades me still forgive all but myself.
    PROS. How comes the date of your strict vow
      expir'd,
And that you now afford us liberty ?
Which, if my memory be just, you said
She did enjoin you should not be, ere she
Was gone to suffer death.
    LEON. Sir, she is gone ! my sister too.  One that
Attends, by your command, these hidden walks,
In breathless haste just now distill'd
The poisonous news through my sick ear.
    ALV. Gone ! and to die ? adorn'd,
Methinks, like to an ancient sacrifice,
With flowers, which are not sure the issue of
The spring, but of her beauty, and her breath.
    PROS. Would I had patience to endure calamities
Like this !  But I'm forbid by my gall'd heart ;
Why did you keep us limited and lockt
I' th' cave, when we had power to hinder her
Departure and her death ?  'Twas a bold crime !
    LEON. Sir, I have hope I gain'd your pardon,
      when
I mention'd the misfortune of my vow.
    PROS. I understand not such injurious vows.
Thou lov'dst her, Leonell, and through the pride
Of envy could'st not yield, since thy own hopes
Grew faint, that mine should e'er be prosperous ;
Therefore with a cunning willingness endur'd
Her desp'rate sally to the Duke.
    LEON. That I did love her, sir, is a most true
And fitting glory to proclaim ; but that
I'm guilty of so base a slander as
Your rashness hath devis'd provokes me to
A rage that may prove dangerous ; reclaim
Your thoughts, and teach them more civility !

Pros. The Prince grows solemn with his grief.
  Lest we
Disturb him, let's retire aside, and I'll
Whisper such reasons to thee as shall want
No courage to be truths, though they inflame.
                    [*They walk aside.*
  Alv. Fountains, that ever weep, have in their
    tears
Some benefit ; they cool the parched earth,
And cherish a perpetual growth ; the sad
Arabian tree, that still in balmy drops
Dissolves her life, doth yield for other's help
A medicine in those tears ; but trivial man,
Though he hath sense to mourn, may weep and
    melt
His injur'd eyes to viewless air ; yet all
Th' expense affords is mainly to discern
His mourning gives his sorrows life and length,
But not the guiltless cause a remedy.   [*Lies down.*
  Leon. My lord, I stay'd upon the garden mount,
And in the heat of my impatience was
So kind, much to lament your tardiness.
But now I must have leave to think one that
Delights to heap up wrongs hath fury more
To dare than do.
  Pros. Were this a temple, and the prince
Employ'd i' the rev'rend business of a priest,
I could not suffer such a boast from one
That I have us'd with so much clemency
In fight.   Defend thy life, or it is mine !
                    [*They draw and fight.*
  Leon. Are you so masterly ?—again—I find
No lightning in your eyes, nor in your sword.
  Pros. You have the skill, but I'll distemper it.
  Alv. Hold, hold ! eager and silly ministers
Of wrath, is this a time to bleed, when, ere
The morning sun uncloud his pensive face,

There will be streams of blood let out enough
To make him drink till he be sick with sacrifice !
Give me thy sword !   How, Prospero, are my
Commands grown wearisome and cold ?

Pros. There, sir! I'm still rebuk'd like to a boy.*

Alv. How long shall I direct thy temper to
A gentle and a soft demeanour ere thou
Grow wise and mild enough to govern it ?
Let me entreat you, sir, to sheath your weapon too.

Leon. Sir, you are worthy to command ; and
know
I wear it for my guard, not insolence.

Pros. I am appointed all my actions still,
As my stupidity made me not fit
To know but suffer injuries.

Alv. Why dost thou frown ? the sullen wrinkles
on
A lion's brow carry a grace, 'cause they
Become a beast ; but he that can discern
The nobleness of valour should be smooth
As virgins in their bridal ornaments.

Pros. Sir, I am taught!   Howe'er my senses are
Not so mistaken and so weak but that
They know him false ; he lov'd Evandra.

Alv. Is that a crime ? thou told'st me in the cave
Thou lov'd'st her too.

Pros. I ne'er durst tell you so,
Till you discern'd my passions, and enforc'd
A true discovery of their hidden cause.

Alv. But I esteem'd it for a virtue known ;
And it endear'd thee more to my respect.
Pray tell me, sir, did you love Evandra,
And with a heart sincere as she deserv'd ?

Leo. Sir, the confession may be honour, but
No shame.   I did, and with a fervency

* This stage direction is here interpolated in the folio [" *Gives
him his sword.*"]

Upright as my religion could produce.

ALV. O what a prompt and warm delight I feel
When others' reason are inclin'd unto
My choice! 'Tis strange the senseless world should so
Mistake the privilege of love, the best
Of objects ; heaven affects plurality
Of worshippers t' adore and serve, whilst we
In that chief hope are glad of rivalship.
And why should ladies, then, that imitate
The upper beauty most to mortal view,
Be barr'd a numerous address ? or we
Envy each other's lawful though ambitious aim ?
Come, join your hands ! and seal a friendship here,
Good as inviolate, lasting as truth.

LEON. You give my wishes, sir, a full content.

PROS. I want the skill to promise, sir ; but I'll
Perform all your desires with noble faith.

ALV. And now let me embrace you both, for we
Are lovers all ; though when the morn must rise
To see and blush at th' actions of the world,
Like sad distressed turtles we shall want
Our mate : then we may sit and mourn beneath
The willow that o'ershadows every brook ;
There weep, till we are vanisht quite in tears
T' increase the stream, whose senseless murmurings
Will be excus'd hereafter in our cause.

PROS. O that my heart would be the officer
Of death unto itself, and break without
My irreligious help.   My life is tir'd.

LEO. And I have thoughts so wild, so much
        unsafe,
They would be sin in utterance as in act.

ALV. Give me your hands ! with a slow fun'ral pace
We 'll move to see this dismal tragedy.*
Let's bear it bravely, like such lovers as
Have reason can persuade their courage to

* See Addenda, No. 6.

Attempt things bold and fit ; whilst there was hope,
We cherish'd it with proffer of our lives,
But now the strength of armies cannot free
Her from my father's wrath ; nay, hand in hand,  ·
To shew this truth in love's philosophy,
That as one object equally allures
Th' ambition of our hope, so we not interchange
Malignant thoughts ; but sev'ral lovers, like
Strange rivers that to the same ocean trace,
Do, when their torrents meet, curl and embrace.

                    [*Exeunt.*

-----------

## ACT V. SCÆNA I.

*Enter two* EMBASSADORS *with letters,* CALLADINE,
VASCO, ALTESTO, FRIVOLO.

  CALL. Your letters merit to have power on my
Respect and diligence ; I shall afford
You both.  But when I bring you to the Duke,
'Tis to be fear'd you'll find the privilege
Of all my favour there is lost.

  1. EMB. Access and audience, sir, is all our hopes
Presume to get.  The times befriend us not.

  2. EMB. We had swift notice of these ladies'
     danger ;
And, sir, howe'er it prove, your very wishes must
Oblige us to a lasting gratitude.

  ALT. What are these strangers, Vasco, that envy
Our sleep, and wake us before day ?

  VAS. Embassadors from Millain, whose hopes
    want
Some cordial water, for they're very sick.

  CALL. Vasco, it is the Duke's command that you
Assemble straight some strength from the cast
    regiments,
To guard the palace-yard.

VAS. What need it, sir ? To my knowledge the
    ladies have
No other weapons than bodkins, and their nails
Close pared, besides a thread of Eglantine,
Or a small woodbine stalk, will fetter them
As fast as cables of a galley grosse.*
    CALL. I but deliver what I had in charge.
My Lords Embassadors ! this is your way.
    1. EMB. These preparations are severe ; I doubt
His mind will not be easily reclaim'd.
    2. EMB. You see the gen'rous people like it not.
                    [*Exit Amb. and Call.*
    VAS. Altesto, go and muster up from all
The lanes and allies in the town a troop
Of fine fleet rogues ; such as will turn their backs
To a bullet and out-run it ; yet love
Communion too.   I would have such, Altesto.
    FRIV. Let me furnish you.   Hell shall not yield
        a regiment
Of fiends that will be more invisible
At the approach of justice or religion.
    ALT. O for a tiny short trussed baker that
I knew ; a carman too, that died some three
Months since with eating meazled pork ; they would
Have march'd to such a war with a cowlstaff, and
Batoon like Hercules.

*Enter* TRISTAN, *leading the* WIDOW, *and* LELIA.

    VAS. How now ! whither move you so fast,
        like a
Fleet snail over a cabbage leaf ?   So early too !
She sleeps less than carriers, traitors, or madmen.
    TRI. She requests me to be the staff of her age.
    VAS. But whither, I pray ?               ·
    WID. Why, sir, to see the show.

    * Qy. Galleass ? a heavy, low-built vessel, with both sails and
oars.

VAS. The show ! The motion of Queen Guiniver's
    death,
Acted by puppets would please you as well.
The jade too is as full of remorse as
A bear that wants his supper.
    WID. I would have a safe place where I may
    stand
And weep without having my handkerchief
Stolen away.
    LEL. It is of pure cambric, forsooth,
And made of her grandmother's wedding apron.
    WID. Yes, truly, and wrought when I was a
    maid.
    ALT. That's an antiquity beyond all record.
    VAS. Sirrah, Tristan ! Be you sure you avoid
No throng. A crowd well shuffled and close pack'd,
May do me now a special courtesy ;
Let her be squeez'd, for she's as rooten as
A hollow tree that stands without a root.
    TRI. My shoulder shall help too, at a dead lift.
    FRIV. A scaffold that were weakly built would
    serve.
    WID. We must make haste ! Farewell, lamb !
                [*Exeunt Trist., Wid., Lel.*
    VAS. Lamb ! which my own translation renders
    calf.
    ALT. 'Twill be long ere thou grow up to a bull ;
For few will venture to help thee to horns.
    VAS. Well, gentlemen, pity my case : I have
Endur'd another night would tire a Perdu
More than a wet furrow, and a great frost.
    FRIV. Will she not die ?
    VAS. I have persuaded her, but still in vain ;
And all the help the laws afford us poor
Mistaken men, that marry gold instead
Of flesh, is a divorce ; it must be thought
On suddenly. Altesto, haste to your charge !

ALT. Good morrow, cavaliers.

FRIV. 'Twill be an hour yet before that greeting
Be in season. Pray heaven Tristan remember
the crowd.*         [*Exeunt.*

*Enter* ALVARO, PROSPERO, LEONELL *and* BOY,
*to sing.*

ALV. This glorious hazard in thy sister, Leonell,
Doth equally perplex my sufferance
With what the fair Evandra must endure.

LEO. You now have heard the cheerful art she
us'd
To be the first that should confirm her love
With prostitution of her virgin life.

ALV. But why for me ? How poor they make me
now,
That have betray'd me to a debt the wealth
Of saints, that are in kindness ever rich,
Is not of able value to discharge.
I love them both with equal flame, and I
Distinguish neither's beauty when compar'd ;
'Tis virtue and remorse gives ladies eminence
In the severe discretion of my heart.

PRO. I want the wisdom how to love ; but I
Am sure I find I love, and 'tis too much.

ALV. Come, sing ! would music had the power
to give
A life, as it hath had to move things dead.

SONG.

O, draw your curtains and appear
   Ere long, like sparks that upward fly,
We can but vainly say you were,
   So soon you'll vanish from the eye.

And in what star we both shall find—
   For sure we can't divided be—-

* See Addenda, No. 7.

Is not to lovers' art assign'd,
'Twill puzzle wise astrology.

*Enter* EVANDRA *and* MELORA, *above.*

EVAN. Who is it that assumes the office of
The dying swan? All music now, methinks,
Is obsequy, and he that sings should sing his death.
    MEL. The gentle and most valiant prince, bold
    Prospero.
    EVAN. And there, behold the faithful Leonell!
    LEO. O pardon me that I have kept my vow.
    EVAN. Brave youth! I prize thy truth great as
    thy love;
We now are mark'd here, and inclosed for death,
So you have all a blessed liberty.
    ALV. A liberty! we are more bound than slaves
    unto
Th' unwieldy oar; like harness'd cattle in
A team, we draw a load of sorrow after us
That tires our strength.
    EVAN. There was no way but this
To keep you still among the living, who
Before endeavour'd nobly to procure
Our freedom with your deaths; do not repine
At destiny—all remedy is past.
    ALV. A fatal truth!
For we, but now dejected on our knees,
Did woo my father's mercy, and in vain.
    MEL. Then strive not by untimely rage to help
And further our impossible release
With certain hazard of yourselves. Our last
Suit is, we may begin our willing death
As quietly as undisturbed sleep.
    EVAN. The silly crime of envy which unlearn'd
And haughty lovers use, I shall prevent;
You'll want the object now, that makes you inter-
    change

The vext remembrance of each other's claim.

    ALV. Were you to live we could not share that
        guilt ;
Though number make us three, wise love hath given
Us all one peaceful heart.

    EVAN. O, Melora! were it but timely now
To wish continuance of mortality,
Like them, we should not differ though the same
One virtue were our mutual hope and choice ;
But you should chide her, sir, for she hath lov'd
Your happiness too much, vainly to lose
Her life when mine would satisfy.

    ALV. Why, Melora, didst thou undo my soul
With so strange courtesy ? But why did you
Evandra ? Stay, O stay ! Leave us not yet.

    EVAN. The guard are ent'red here, and now the
        last
And shortest of our hours is come.   Farewell,
Brave prince! Brave Leonell, farewell! Farewell,
        brave Prospero !

    MEL. The gentle valiant prince
Farewell ! And valiant Leonell, farewell !
Farewell, the hardy Prospero.        [*Ex. from above.*
          [*Leonell and Prospero draw their swords.*

    ALV. Nay, stir not, gentlemen !   It is in vain !
They are beyond all human help.   Would you
Scale heaven and cool the saucy sun with your
Frail breath when he doth scorch you with his
        beams ?
For such is now the enterprise that strives
To rescue them from this high fort.

    LEO. Would I were in a cannon charg'd, then
        staight
Shot out to batter it, and be no more.

    PRO. Would all the stones might be ordain'd my
        food
Till I could eat their passage out.

ALV. These angry exaltations shew but poor.

PRO. Sir, whither shall we go ?

ALV. To see them die ; but not,
Like vain and choleric boys, to shew
A fury that can hazard none but our
Disdained swords.   Yet still, my worthy friends.
There is an undertaking left, and such
As valiant lovers may perform.   Why should
The base and dirty guard be honour'd with
Our opposition or our blood ?  Have we
Not grief enough to die without their help ?
Let us with fix'd and wat'ry eyes behold
These ladies suffer, but with silence still,
Calmly like pinion'd doves ; and, when we see
The fatal stroke is given, swell up our sad
And injur'd hearts until they break.

LEO.  I do not find myself unapt for this.

PRO.  My breast contains an angry lump that is
Too stubborn for a quiet bravery.
He that shall strike Evandra's life shall feel
Me till he sink low as the hollowness,
Where devils dwell.

ALT.  This way !  Let us avoid the gazing multitude.                                          [Exeunt.

*Enter* DUKE, CALLADINE, VASCO, *two*
EMBASSADORS, *and* ATTENDANTS.

DUKE. Have  you  unto  your  officers  given
charge
To guard the passage from the fort unto
The palace-yard with bold well-govern'd men ?

VAS.  All is directed, sir, as you command.
But for their government, if it be to be had
In prisons, gallies, or [the] stews, you may
Trust them with a mutiny.

CALL.  His resolution's fixt, and there remains
No comfortable sign to flatter hope.

DUKE. My Lords Embassadors, sit down! And
  though
You now behold a Prince that rather loves
To be thought cruel than to break his vow,
Do not believe to be severely just,
Is tyranny.  You shall have fair admittance,
Yet your request unkindly ought to be
Denied; and though your master, when the chance
Of war rendered my brother his power,
Stole in the dark his noble life, and durst
Not give the wrathful act a gen'ral view;
I'm not asham'd to publish my revenge,
It shall be openly perform'd, to shew
I, not suspect men's censure or dislike.
  1. EMB. Sir, he that ministers revenge may hurt
And damage others, but can bring no good
Or real profit to himself.
  2. EMB. And, with your highness' leave, we think
  it were
More wise to mulct our master's treasure, which
Shall be exhausted freely to your own
Proportion and content, so you will take
His daughter and her lov'd companion from
The danger of this day.

*Enter* EVANDRA, MELORA, GUARD, *at one door*,
  ALVARO, PROSPERO, LEONELL, *at the other.*

DUKE. I will not sell my brother's blood.
The prisoners approach.  Make room! Ere long
They shall enjoy the liberty of souls.
Vasco, lend me thine ear.            [*Whispers.*
  ALV. How beautiful is sorrow when it dwells
Within these ladies' eyes! So comely, that it makes
Felicity in others seem deform'd.
I wish my patience may be strong enough.
  LEO. I now begin to doubt I am not fit
To see their hazard and endure't.

III.                     M

PROS. Nor I. My loyalty already's stir'd
Beyond the temp'rate suff'rance of a man.

DUKE. Thou seest the Prince wears trouble
    in his looks;
Though any opposition he can make
Be but impertinent and weak, yet charge
Thy officers, if he endeavour to
Disturb my will, imprison him i'th' fort.

VAS. I shall observe him, sir.  I do not like
This employment; the prince will find no
Enemies in all my tribe.

DUKE. If you have any words from Millain,
    that
Imports their knowledge, ere they die, be brief.
My Lords Embassadors, I give you leave
To whisper your affair; or, if you please,
To make it public to the world.

1. EMB. Your cruel resolutions, sir, have so
Confined our liberality, that all
We shall deliver to Evandra now
Is but her father's, and her country's tears;
And those we can by deputation pay,
To the endang'ring of our eyes.

2. EMB. And to Melora, that in kindness thus
Hath shar'd her destiny, we do confer
The world's eternal wonder and applause.

EVAN. It will deprive me of some joy in death,
To think my father needs must suffer by
A vain unprofitable grief: and 'tis the last
Request I make, that he would wisely now
Forget my obsequies and name.

MEL. And my desires make sure, that those who
    shall
Hereafter write the business of this day,
May not believe I suffer for the hope
Of glorious fame, but for a secret in
My hidden love.

1. EMB. Question your justice, sir. Must they
both die?

DUKE. Both! and I think my payment is but
short,
When I consider well the measure of
My brother's worth, with their unvalued sex,
And wish some man that boasts your master's blood
Were singly here to undergo their fate;
It would more pleasure my revenge. But, since
There is no hope in that desire, away!
Lead them to death!

LEO. Stay, sir! reprieve them but one minute's
space,
Until you hear a stranger speak.

ALV. What means this noble youth?

DUKE. Be sudden in thy speech for my revenge
Brooks no delay.

LEO. If I produce a man
Allied unto this family you so abhor,
Great as yourself in title and descent,
Will you with solemn vow confirm their liberty
And take his life to satisfy your wrath?

DUKE. By th' honour of a Prince's faith, I will!
And such a miracle would ravish me.

LEO. I dare believe your vow, you were so just
Though cruel in your last, and know my joys
Must take the privilege to boast you now
Have lost the pow'r to make them die.

DUKE. It shall be wonderful if that prove true!

LEO. I am not Leonell the Millain knight
But Leonell the duke of Parma's son,
Heir to his fortune and his fame.

EVAN. O Melora! thy brother will reveal
Himself and quite undo our glorious strife.

LEO. By this you find I am to Millain near
Allied; but more to tempt your fury on
My life, know 'twas my valiant father took

Your brother prisoner, and presented him
Where he receiv'd his death : my father that
So oft hath humbled you in war, and made
His victories triumph almost upon
The ruins of your State.

    ALV. So young, and fill'd with thoughts so
      excellent,
That they surprize my wonder more than love !
Well mayst thou worship, Prospero,
But dar'st not envy him.

    PROS. B'ing your disciple, sir,
I'm better taught ; but 'tis no crime to wish
Fortune had made me heir of Parma and
Not him, then I had died for them.

    VAS. This is some comfort yet ; I'm for the
      ladies.

    CALL. But 'thath not given our sorrows a full
      cure.

    DUKE. Sir, you are boldest with your self : but
      you
Shall see I need no provocation to
Observe my vow.   Unbind the ladies there !
And bear him straight to death.

    1 EMB. Stay, sir ! He must not die.

    DUKE. How ! Age and grief makes thee a fool,
      and mad.

    1 EMB. He must not, sir, if your revenge be wise,
And fix your anger where 'tis most deserv'd.
Behold Millain himself, your enemy !
               [*Takes off a false beard.*
Live princely youth ! and let my years, which time
Would soon determine, be the ransom of
My chiefest blood.   Evandra, do not weep.

    EVAN. O sir, there was less use of me ; why
      would
You, with this danger on your self, destroy
That noble fame I virtuously pursu'd ?

MEL. Our hope of endless glory now is lost.

ALV. Sure heaven intends more blessings to this
day.

DUKE. I have achiev'd my wishes in full height ;
This was a justice, sir, more than I could
Expect from my own stars ; free Leonell
And let him suffer the prepared stroke.

2 EMB. First hear me speak, and, sir, however
you'll
Interpret the discretion of my words,
I am resolv'd he shall not die, nor none
Of these, though all in your command and power.

VAS. Say'st thou so, old shaver?* Make but that
good
And the maids of Savoy shall everlastingly
Pay thee tribute in dainty gloves and nosegays
To stick in thy girdle.

DUKE. This were a mystery would please indeed.

2 EMB. Look on me well! I am your brother,
sir !                    [*Pulls off a false beard.*
And though ten years I have been hidden from
Your sight, this noble duke hath used me so,
I cannot call it banishment, but the
Retir'd and quiet happiness of life.

ALV. How wisely have the heavens contriv'd
this joy !

1 EMB. And though his fortune in the war,
which made
Your armies ever flourish with success,
Taught me prevent my country's ruin by
Detaining him from your employment there ;
Yet he enjoy'd all the delights that solitude

* "This cunning shaver," which means "one closely attentive
to his own interests," is used by Swift ; also by Theophilus
Cibber, in his address "to David Garrick, Esq., with disserta-
tions on theatrical subjects," Lond., 8vo, 1759 ; and this cant
phrase obtains even now. "Young Shaver' is meant to express "a boy."

Affords : and when he chose his happiness
In books and deep discourses of the learn'd,
I search'd the most remote and knowing world
For men to furnish his desires.

2 EMB. It is acknowledg'd, sir,
And with a bounteous thanks.

DUKE. How welcome are these miracles ! let me
Embrace thee as the greatest joy, that since
My birth I have receiv'd.  O my lov'd brother !
Thou seest, though absent, I've been faithful to
Thy virtues and thy memory.

2 EMB. But, sir, too strict a master of your vow.
Yet 'tis a fault my gratitude should more
Admire with thankfulness, than chide.

DUKE. This happy day deserves a place supreme
And eminent i'th kallender.

2 EMB. First, I will give into your courteous arms
The Duke of Millain, sir, good and renown'd,
And now the bold and princely Leonell ;
Then Alvaro my honour'd nephew that
Deserves the best of human praise and love.
　　　　　　　　　　[The Duke embraces them.

ALV. Dread sir, that every one may share the joy
And blessings of this precious hour, let me
Restore poor Prospero into your breast.

DUKE. He shall be cherish'd, and his faults
　forgiven.

PROS. I shall deserve it, sir, in future deeds
Of honour, and of loyal faith.  How I
Am rapt to see those wonders strangely thrive !

VAS. What think you of the stars now, Calladine ?
Do these small twinkling gentlewomen
Look to their business well ?  Have they a care
　of us ?

CALL. It is beyond our merit or our hope

VAS. I'll buy me an optick, study astrology,
And visit 'em every fair night o'er my house leads.

DUKE. The chiefest happiness of virtue is
Th' encrease, which to procure, with Hymen's help
We'll knit, and intermingle lovers' hearts.
Come my Alvaro ! I'll bestow thee straight.
  MEL. A little patience, sir, and hear me speak,
Before you give what lawfully is mine.
  DUKE. Indeed thou dost deserve him by thy love.
  MEL. In love Evandra's interest
Doth justly equal mine ; but I appeal unto
His vow, which sure her goodness will assist.
  ALV. And my religion shall persuade me keep ;
But where, Melora, was it made ?
  MEL. Within my father's Court, when five years
    since,
Disguis'd you stole to see a triumph there,
You promis'd, if our houses' enmity
Were ever reconcil'd, the church should join
Our hands.
  LEO. Sir, what my sister speaks I'm witness to,
And hope this day shall end our parents' strife
In a kind peace.
  DUKE. Which thus I do confirm.
Take him, Melora ! with him all the joys
Thy virtues or our prayers can procure.
  ALV. Didst thou for this with kind Evandra
    strive
Who should encounter danger first ? Although
Thy beauty's changed, it is not lost ; I now
Remember thee, and my vow's prophecy.
                            [Embrace.
  1 EMB. Now, my best Evandra, give me thy hand ;
And here receive it, valiant Leonell ;
That I, may ratify the faith I gave,
If e'er this war expir'd she should be thine.
  DUKE. Then he may challenge present interest
For we may meet to hear voices and lutes,
But never more the angry drum.

EVAN. Alvaro's virtues, sir, and yours, have both
An equal claim.  Persons I ne'er admir'd
So much to make a difference in my choice ;
Therefore my father's promise, and my love,
Have made me yours.
LEO. I am o'ercharg'd with my felicity.
ALV. To Evandra, gladness be still renew'd,
Who since I see so worthily bestow'd,
My love is quieted in everlasting rest.
EVAN. And mine by your exact and perfect
choice.
PROS. These glad achievements are so well
deserv'd,
I not malign your joys.  I'll to the war !
And fight to win you a perpetual peace.
*[Vasco takes Millain aside.*
VAS. I'm bold to crave acquaintance with your
grace,
And to begin it with a suit.
1 EMB. It shall be granted, sir.
VAS. I have married your Grace's countrywoman,
And was a little, sir, mistaken in her age.
Would you'ld procure us a divorce.
1 EMB. If you can make't appear she is too old.
VAS. She writes a hundred and ten, sir, next
grass,
1 EMB. 'Tis a fair age! well sir, you shall have a
divorce,
And what the profits of her dowry would
Have been, I will myself bestow on you.
VAS. Such another good day makes us all mad.
DUKE. Come, to the temple ! and let's join those
hearts,
That with such pious courage have endur'd
The trial of a noble constant faith,
Whom tortures nor the frowns of death could move.
This happy day we'll consecrate to love.

### EPILOGUE.

Troth, gentlemen, you must vouchsafe a while
T" excuse my mirth, I cannot chuse but smile,
And 'tis to think, how like a subtle spy
Our poet waits to hear his destiny ;
Just in the entry as you pass, the place
Where first you mention your dislike or grace :
Pray whisper softly that he may not hear,
Or else such words as shall not blast his ear.

FINIS.

# ADDENDA.

## No. 1.

This alteration is introduced in the folio, in the third act, between Frivolo, after saying " a very owl ! " and the entrance of Evandra, Melora and others, in place of the short dialogue in the early text commencing thus :—

ALT. " Thou art a coxcomb," &c., and ending " without help or hope."

*Enter* MUSICIANS.

ALT. Oh ! are you come ?
Friends of the fiddle pray strike up ! we'll have
A dance before the wedding.
    FRIV. I cannot dance, Altesto, without cork
At my heels ; I must have a woman behind me.
    ALT. Thou shalt lead the widow.  The very tuning
Of a cittern will make her bestir her stumps
Like an old oak.

*Enter* TRISTAN.

THRIST. Where's Vasco, gentlemen ? I am in haste.
    ALT. If you are in haste, you had best for dispatch
Make answer to your self.
    TRIST. The duke has sent for him by Calladine,
And it concerns him as matter of business.
    ALT. Send business to fat heavy fellows, who
Have got formality and grey beards.  Tristan, you must
Dance !  Gentleman scrapers, pray strike up.

*Enter* VASCO, WIDOW, LEILA.

FRIV. Look, she's come already ! some fifty years
Ago she was stung with a tarantula,
And ever since a fiddle makes her frisk.
    WID. Blessing on your hearts, gentlemen

ALT. You must into the dance, Widow.

WID. I have been mistress Marrian in a maurice ere
   now.

VAS. Sweet heart! what think you? I'm only afraid
Lest too much mettle should overheat your blood.
Will you to't, Widow?

WID. Truly sir, it is not wholesome to stand idle,
Come Lilia.

ALT. Well said, Widow.                    [*They dance.*

TRIST. Vasco, now you have done your capring here,
You must dance towards court. The Duke
Commanded Calladine to send me for you.

VAS. Bear up, Widow! performent is striding
Towards me upon high stilts.

ALT. Leonel's ransom, her wealth, and now employ'd
At court. Th'art a gone man, condemn'd to usury,
Furr'd gowns, long dinners, and short sleeps. [*Exeunt.*

## No. 2.

This in the folio in same act, in place of Leonell's
three lines prior to his exit and the entrance of
Alvaro.

LEO. My lord! your valour I have try'd in fight;
But had so little knowledge of your love,
That you misplace your anger now.

PROS. You'll meet me on the garden mount?

LEO. I was your captive when you gave me liberty;
And it has never been my custom, to
Contest with those to whom I am oblig'd.

PROS. If you have love, sure you have honour too.
Disclaim the one, and for the other I
Shall never trouble you.

LEO. Disclaim my love! I'll wait you on the mount.
                                        [*Exit.*

## No. 3.

These passages occur also in act three in the
scene between Alvaro and Prospero, Evandra, and
Melora, after " I will go down myself," and before,
" lock safe the door," &c.

EVAN. I fear some inlet has been counter-digg'd
Into the cave, and gives a passage to
Some man, who is employ'd to fright me with
A dismal shape.
    ALV. Who e'er thou art who dar'st death's vizard
      wear,
Assuming the foul shape which nature most
Abhors, grow bolder yet, and stay till thou
Shalt straight be that, which thou dost counterfeit.
Give me the light!          [*He descends the cave.*

### No. 4.

These lines are spoken by Evandra after she has
said, "Go, call thy brother in!" prior to Leonell's
entrance.

Let us contrive how to secure him too.
He hath not yet heard of the Duke's severe
Decree against the Prince, which quickly will
Involve both him and Prospero.

### No. 5.

These passages occur prior to Leonell's concluding soliloquy, which ends the third act.    They
come in after "To appease the angry Duke," in
place of the few lines which appear in the original.

    LEON. This is a mystery!
    EVAN. It must not be examined, Leonell.
    LEON. Why have you here inclos'd them?
    EVAN. If you already question'd me, to give
A cause for that which I enjoin'd, where is
The strict obedience promis'd by your vow?
    LEON. What have I promis'd in the rashness of
My inconsiderate love?    Can you
A mediator for their safety be,
Without apparent danger to yourself?
    EVAN. Do not inquire what means I have of safe
Access to move the Duke, nor what new chance
Has made me confident t' appease that rage
Which does endanger them and you.

LEON. Dear sister, leave me not in ignorance.
MEL. Dare you believe I will consent to that
Which honour has not heedfully proposed?
LEON. You have design'd I shall remain perplext.
EVAN. If thou dost break thy vow, the curses of
The virtuous at their death fall on thy head.
MEL. Never be call'd my brother, nor assume
The honour of my valiant father's name.
EVAN. Melora, come! we are too slow.

                        *[Exeunt Evan., Mel.*

## No. 6.

These lines in the folio are given to Alvaro as
a portion of the speech with which the fourth act
terminates. They follow " We'll move to see this
dismal tragedy."

We may, befriended by the secret aid
Of Calladine, get safe into the fort,
Where in resistance we at least can die,
If none in favour of our cause revolt:
Evandra's prison window does o'erlook
The western walk : there a sentry,
Dispos'd by Calladine, waits to let me take my last sad
    sight,
And at the morning watch. Nay, hand in hand——
To shew this truth in love's philosophy ;
That as one object equally allures
The virtue of our loves, so it shall still
In rivalship, despite of jealousy,
Unite our hearts. For several lovers, like
Strange rivers which to the same ocean trace,
Do, when their torrents meet, curl and embrace. *[Exeunt.*

## No. 7.

The following scene is in the folio, in place of
that in the original edition. It comes in, in the
fifth act, immediately after " Altesto, Frivolo, and
Vasco," exeunt, Frivolo's last line being " Pray
heaven Tristan remember the crowd."

*Enter* ALVARO, PROSPERO, LEONELL, CALLADINE.

CALL. Their window, sir, is there.  But let me beg
You would not let your sorrows make you known :
For my officiousness to your command,
When by your father found, will cause such jealousy,
As may deprive me of all future means
To serve you.
    ALV. Trust my discretion, Calladine !
    CALL. If rashly you resent the form of his
Proceeding, you may lose the hope I find
In the Embassadors ; who seem to bring
(Though they are secret in the main import)
Such offers, as perhaps, may be receiv'd.
They wait me in the palace, sir, and you
Must please to make this visit short.
    ALV. You may securely leave us !  [*Exit Calladine.*
The cruel doom which fair Evandra must
Endure, cannot perplex me, Leonell,
More than this glorious hazard of your sister.
    LEO. You now have heard, how cheerfully she strove
To be the first who should her love confirm
With offer of her virgin life.
    ALV. How must I stoop and groan beneath the weight
Of so much poverty, as such a debt
Lays not on me alone, but on our sex?
How shall I pay this double debt of love?
Owing to two a heart so constantly
Entire, that it could ne'er divided be.
I must love both, with equal flame, since none
Their beauty can distinguish, when compar'd ;
And both in brighter virtue equal are.
    PROS. I want skill great beauty to distinguish ; but I
Can feel my heart grown sore with love of it.
        [*Evandra and Melora are seen in mourning at
         the window.*
    MEL. Three I discern, and they must surely be
The gentle and most valiant Prince
The noble Prospero, and faithful Leonell.
    ALV. The casement now is open, and ere dawn
Appears, a double day does seem to break
Through clouds of mourning.

EVAN. That is the Prince's voice.

ALV. Your voice cannot but sweet music be
Though you can only now a Requiem sing.
Why should not music, if it e'er gave life
To things inanimate, and made them move,
Now lengthen yours who have the soul of love?

LEO. Pardon me, saint, that I have kept my vow.

EVAN. Your truth I value equal to your love.
But what is praise to men above it grown?
Whose worth we rate so much beyond our own,
That we, to make the world enjoy it, have
Design'd your freedom, and ourselves a grave.

ALV. What can the world enjoy when you are gone?
Time will his hour-glass stop when yours is run.

MEL. Repent not that example which you gave:
You would have lost your lives our lives to save.
Could we do less than you our pattern make?
Refuse not that which you would have us take.

EVAN. Accept of your relief, now ours is past.

ALV. Can we accept relief which cannot last?
Your gift, when by your fatal deaths 'tis sign'd,
Shews us unworthy, and yourselves unkind;
For you reproach us with the life you give,
By thinking we, when you are dead, can live.

EVAN. Let not your love's impatient anger wake
Death's sleep, since 'tis the last we e'er shall take.

MEL. You to your father quiet duty owe:
Let not your love above your duty grow.

EVAN. The trouble of your rivals now will cease;
And all love's civil war expire in peace.
For that which did enlighten beauty, life,
Ending in me, will quickly end your strife.
Love fades with beauty, which your diff'rence bred;
For ev'ry lover does forsake the dead.

ALV. Some comfort let it bring your parting mind,
That you had pow'r to make even rivals kind.

LEO. In love's records it shall your glory be,
That, whil'st you govern'd, rivals did agree.

PROS. You are the first that e'er love's knot so ti'd,
As to unite, whom nature did divide.

EVAN. If 'twere not fit, Melora, now to die,
I could awhile endure mortality.

So soft a peace, here, in love's shade appears,
As cannot be more calm above the spheres.
But you should chide her, sir, who in vain strife
Would, with the needless signet of her life,
Seal her undoubted love, and press to die,
When with my death I all might satisfy.
    ALV. Why, did Melora thus my soul undo?
That is but half the question, why did you,
Evandra, to my father's wrath submit?
                    [*The ladies look back suddenly.*
Love's great examples stay! leave us not yet!
    EVAN. The guards are entering, and have brought our
    doom,
The shortest of our fatal hours is come.
Renowned Prince, and faithful Leonell,
And valiant Prospero, to all farewell.
    MEL. Farewell for evermore, the gentle and
Most valiant Prince, the noble Prospero,
The brave and faithful Leonell, farewell!
        [*Exeunt Ladies from above, Pros. and Leon.*
            *drawing their swords.*
    ALV. Nay, stir not gentlemen! it is in vain:
We have not strength enough to storm the fort.
Make not your purpose known before your deeds.
We must attend the pity of the crowd.
    LEO. Affliction now is urg'd to such extremes,
That patience seems to change her constant face:
She first looks pale with doubt, and then does blush,
As if asham'd of remedy when it is slow.
    ALV. Cover your courage, and pray sheath your swords.
    PROS. Sir, whither shall we go?
    ALV. Where we may best observe,
What looks the officers and soldiers wear.
If they begin to grieve, their grief will soon
To anger grow; from whom the people, prone
To passion, quickly will take fire. Too long
My father has my constant duty known;
And now may find the people's change, when they
My lowness measure with his high success:
For as they still all prosperous greatness hate,
So my affliction may their pity move;
They Princes only in affliction love.     [*Exeunt.*

# ENTERTAINMENT

AT

# RUTLAND HOUSE.

III.

*The first dayes entertainment at Rutland House, by declamations and musick, after the manner of the ancients. By Sir W. D., London: Printed by J. M. for H. Herringham, and sold at his shop at the Anchor, in the New Exchange, in the Lower Walk. 1657, 8vo.*

*Idem, in the Folio edition, 1673.*

*In the copy in the King's Library, British Museum, the date has been altered in writing from 1657 to 1656, with the addition in the same contemporary hand of "November 22d," which was in all likelihood the actual day of publication.*

As noticed in the Prefatory Memoir, with which our first volume opens, this Entertainment at Rutland House foreshadowed the revival of the regular Drama in England, which had been rigidly suppressed all throughout the ascendancy of the Commonwealth in previous years. By the influence of several powerful friends, Sir William D'Avenant obtained authority to present an amusement for the people. In his application for this permission he termed what he intended to represent an Opera; but when he brought it upon the stage, it bore scarcely the most remote resemblance to opera, and when printed, had the following title :—

"First Day's Entertainment at Rutland House, by Declamation and Musick, after the manner of the ancients. Lond. 1656. 8vo."

The *Biographia Britannica* remarks that—"This being an introductory piece it required all the author's wit to make it answer different intentions; for, first, it was to be so pleasing as to gain applause; and next it was to be so remote from the very appearance of a play, as not to give any offence to that pretended sanctity which was then in fashion. It began with music, then followed a prologue, in which the author banters the oddity of his own performance . . . The musick, which was very good, was composed by Dr Coleman, Capt Cook, Mr Henry Lawes, Mr George Hudson."

The object of the entertainment was simply to argue the case for and against public amusement, in a dramatic form. Diogenes, the cynic, utters the views the Roundheads maintained upon that subject, while Aristophanes is brought forward to confute them. Then the Londoner and Parisian are paraded to contrast, in argument, the advantages and disadvantages of London and Paris, all tending towards the introduction of dramatic performances with music and scenery after the style of the latter, a style to which both Charles the Second and D'Avenant, during their residence there, had become attached.

Rutland House was situated at the upper end of Aldersgate Street, near what is now called Charter House Square. The "Entertainment" was given "at the back part of Rutland House."

Although having no pretensions to be called an opera, Anthony Wood makes the mistake that it was the first

*Italian* opera performed in England, and goes on to remark that, "though Oliver Cromwell had now prohibited all other theatrical representations, he allowed of this, because being in an unknown tongue, it could not corrupt the manners of the people."

Of Captain Henry Cook, one of the composers of the music, this much is known. He was brought up in the King's Chapel, but quitted it at the beginning of the rebellion; and, in 1642, having obtained a captain's commission in the Royal army, he ever after retained the title of captain. When Charles the Second's Chapel was established, at the time of the coronation of that monarch, Captain Henry Cook was appointed master of the children. He was, according to Anthony Wood's manuscript memoirs in the Ashmolean library, "esteemed the best musician of his time to sing to the lute, till Pelham Humphrey, his scholar, came up, *after which he died of grief.*" In the continuation of *Baker's Chronicle* it is affirmed that Matthew Lock set the music for Charles' public entry, and Captain Henry Cook for his coronation. Be this as it may, it is generally understood that the coronation anthem was composed by Henry Lawes. A hymn of Cook's composition, in four parts, is said to have been performed in place of the Litany, in the chapel of St George, at Windsor, by order of the sovereign and knights companions of the garter, on 17th April 1660. Burgh, in his Anecdotes of Music: Lond. 1814, 12mo., makes this observation on Captain Cook: " None of his church music was printed; and, indeed, if we may judge of that by his few secular compositions, dispersed in the collections of the times, he was by no means qualified for the office to which he was appointed at the Restoration." This opinion being merely deduced from a hypothesis is not entitled to much weight; the more so, as the immortal Pepys has this entry in his diary. "12 Aug. 1660. After sermon a brave anthem of Captain Cook's, which he himself sung, and the king was well pleased with it."

Cook was one of the original performers in D'Avenant's Siege of Rhodes, subsequently produced at Rutland House. It was the first English opera performed in England. Cook died in 1672.

*After a flourish of music, the curtains are drawn and*
*the Prologue enters.*

### PROLOGUE.

Me-thinks, as if assur'd of some disgrace,
I should step back ere scarce I shew my face ;
'Tis not through terror that I know not how
To fashion my approaches, vail, and bow ;
But that displeasure in your looks I spy,
Which seem to turn aside and stand awry.
Ere yet we can offend, are we disgrac'd ?
Or are our benches, not your looks misplac'd ?
We wish we could have found this roof so high,
That each might be allow'd a canopy ;
And could the walls to such a wideness draw,
That all might sit at ease in chaise a bras.
But though you cannot front our cup-board scene,
Nor sit so eas'ly as to stretch and lean,
Yet you are so divided and so plac'd,
That half are freely by the other fac'd ;
And we are shrewdly jealous that you come
Not merely to hear us, or see the room,
But rather meet here to be met, I mean
Each would see all, and would of all be seen,
Which we but guess, respectfully to shew
You worthy of your selves, not we of you.
Think this your passage, and the narrow way
To our Elyzian field, the opera ;
Tow'rds which some say we have gone far about,
Because it seems so long since we set out.
Think now the way grown short, and that you light
At this small inn, to bait, not stay all night ;

Where you shall find, what you will much despise,
The host grown old, and worse then old, half wise;
Still former time applauds, the present blames,
And talks so long that he, indeed, declaims.
From declamations of a long hour's length,
Made strong to last by some dead author's strength,
Not pow'rful to persuade, but to provoke,
Long, grave, and sullen as a mourning cloak;
I wish, if possible, you could scape free,
But plainly, and in brief, it cannot be.
These you must please to hear, and have no way ·
To give the anguish of your ears allay,
But by our Rostras to remember Rome;
Then hope, such mighty minds in time may come,
As think it equal glory to take care,
To speak wise things, as to do great in war,
Declaiming well on what they well have done;
Being best guides where they the race have run,
Quick'ning by influence of their noble deeds,
Glory in others, till it virtue breeds.
What do I mean? Sure there is something here
Has such infection as I ought to fear!
Here I a short and bashful prologue came;
But strait grow long and bold, that is, declaim.
What patience can endure speech bold and long,
Where sense is weak too, when the lungs are strong?
Yet this will rare abridgement seem in me,
When four shall come and talk a history.
Well, I have now devis'd, for your relief,
How you shall make these long declaimers brief;
When you perceive their voices fall with fear,
As not accustom'd to the public ear,
And that they pause, grow pale, and look about,
Laugh but aloud, and you will put them out.

*The curtains are closed again.*

---

*A concert of instrumental music, adapted to the sullen disposition of* DIOGENES, *being heard a while, the curtains are suddenly opened, and, in two gilded rostras appear, sitting,* DIOGENES, *the cynic, and* ARISTOPHANES, *the poet, in habits agreeable to their country and professions, who declaim against, and for, public entertainment, by moral representations.*

### DIOGENES.

I would you were all old, that, having more experience, I might take less pains to make you wise. Or I would you were all poor, that not being diverted by the gaudy emulations of your wealth, you might mind Diogenes, who, you know, has nothing, unless, most thrifty Athenians, you allow me that which I wish you could spare, understanding. But why should I desire your attention? for, considering, that when you are asleep, you neither hurt your friends, nor provoke your enemies, I think 'tis scarce discretion to keep you awake. Yet presuming I am now in the public Rostra, as securely fortified as in my private tub, I will venture to bid you observe, that you are met to hear what your cynic Diogenes, and the poet Aristophanes can say against and for, public entertainment by moral representations.

Can any entertainment divert you from the mischief to which you are excellently inclined when you meet in public? Are not the winds your orators, and you their many headed waves that meet not but in foam and rage? Have you not yet distinguished the modesty and wariness of solitude from the impudence and rashness of assemblies

Do you not, when alone, design wreaths to the
virtue of those whom, when you are assembled,
you reward with ostracism ? *   As if the mingled
breath of multitude were so contagious, that it
infected reason as well as blood.  Beasts of Athens!
Are you not made gentle when bred single, and
continue wild whilst you are in herds ?   When
you are alone, perhaps some of you have judgment
to consider that the wisdom of governors is
encreas'd by their long continuance in power ;
therefore they ought seldom to be chang'd, but
when you meet in the Agora to make up the body-
politic, 'tis like the meeting of humours in the
natural body, all tending to commotion, change,
and dissolution.  There is your annual feast where
you devour your governors, or shift them nimbly
as your trenchers before they are foul.  Most mischievous Athenians! meet not at all.  Man, when
alone, is perhaps not wholly a beast ; but man
meeting man till he grows to a multitude is certainly more than a monster.

O number, number ; when it consists of men,
how accurst are those who trust to it ?  If for
wisdom, who will rely upon determination, where
the difference of opinions doth often equal the
variety of faces ?  If for strength, call Xerxes, and
bid him, if he dares, come back again with his half
of mankind into Greece.  In numerous councils
you give countenance to each other, to dare to do
injustice ; where you each take anger as you catch
yawning, merely by seeing it in another.  In armies
the number doth often tend more to famine than
to strength.  Fear, which is in armies as infectious
as opinion in councils, is quickly disperst, whilst

---

* Banishment: Expulsion.  See *Life of Aristides in Cornelius
Nepos*, in which, through the medium of ostracism, is depicted
the glorious idiotcy of universal suffrage.

all depending on their multitude are defeated, because each trusted to others and none to themselves.

But Athenians ! I am old, I want memory, and
have displac'd my thoughts ; for I intended not
to declaim against assemblies in civil councils, or
in military attempts, but against such as meet for
recreation. In defence of which the poet Aristophanes is arrogantly resolv'd to plead. What need
you public recreations ? If you are old you are
past the days of mirth, and are come to the even-
ings of contemplation, and contemplation requires
solitude. If you are young, 'tis your time to grow
solemn, which is to become old betimes, that you
may more willingly entertain age when you are
forc'd to feel it. If you had philosophy enough to
make you humble, you would avoid such public
assemblies as tempt you to that cost in vests and
ornaments, which occasions the emulations of pride:
If you have so little philosophy as to desire to be
very rich, you would prevent that vain expense.
If you would live in peace and power, why by such
excesses do you enrich retailers and mechanics
whose sudden acquisition of wealth makes them too
proud to be obedient, and too fantastical to be
quiet ? If you have business, what do you here ?
If you have none, what do you in Athens ? where
wealth is not to be got with idleness, nor the wars
maintain'd without wealth.

But you would meet to receive entertainment
from such as represent the virtuous actions of the
heroes. Is not virtue esteem'd in Athens but as
the particular humour of philosophers ? And,
though it may please some few who study it, yet,
because 'tis singular, it doth offend the generality ;
and 'tis safe in popular governments to content the
people, though to their own prejudice, who perhaps
too can hardly be said to be prejudic'd when they

have no sense of their harm. If Virtue could be
drest in such a fashion as all should be provok'd to
like her, you might open the gates of Athens to her
spiritual tire-women, the Muses, and let them work
freely to her. But since many have very vainly
endeavour'd to make her amiable to all, let the lady
Virtue shrink up her white shoulders, put on her
black hood, and retire to her closet.

But you would meet to behold virtue in the
bright images of the heroes. Gentlemen of Athens!
Be not at charge to pay for glasses which shall
render you the reflection of better faces than your
own, lest you give your selves an uncomfortable
occasion to blush. 'Tis discretion, if you have any
imperfection, to keep at distance from that excellence to which others may compare you. Be you
contented without seeing the heroes, and let them
be satisfied with the reward of their virtues. Are
they not made stars and statues? Let them shine
in the firmament, and rest in our temples. But
what need they be personated, and intrude into
our theatres to disgrace us? If you are exceedingly inclin'd to think that you may draw a benefit
from great examples, and are resolv'd to raise the
heroic ghosts, in hope they will lead you to the
hidden treasures of virtue, pursue the experiment,
and the next day after you have paid your money
in theatres, cast up your account and see what you
have got by your dream. I suspect that your remembrance of the worthies will vanish and be as
short as the vision. The ghost of Hercules rais'd by
a poet can no more make you laborious and patient,
than a rose or lettuce raised in a glass by a chymist,
can make you sweet, or serve you for a salad.

Aristophanes will perhaps make you a small
present of another pretext in behalf of the opera ;
which is, that it will introduce civility. But be-

cause there are some beasts in Athens, does he take us all for bears? We eat not raw flesh, nor live without distinctions of alliance. What means he by civility? Would he make an art of external behaviour, and have it read in the schools? Would he prescribe you a certain comely posture in your sleep, and not to wake without a long compliment to your chamber-grooms? Would he not have you cough but when alone, or, if in public, then with a musical concordance to the rest that have taken cold? Would he have you at table carve with your arm a little extended, as if you were nicely to finish a touch in painting; or more at stretch as if you were to fence for your meat? Would he make a science of salutation, and draw it out to such a length, as if when you met you were always treating to reconcile empires; or when you take leave, you were concern'd as kings that depart from their daughters when they are married by proxy and embarking for another climate? Where will be the end of excesses in civility? Is not extraordinary civility imputed to Courts as dissimulation? Subtle Athenians! If you will 'learn to be very civil, which is, to dissemble with a good grace, yet know that dissimulation is a kind of black art which you must study in private. Let the people be rude still, for if by suffering it to be taught in public we refine their craftiness with civility, you must ere long fling away your night-caps and sleep in your helmets.

Would you meet to enjoy the pleasure of music? 'tis a deceitful art, whose operations lead to the evil of extremes, making the melancholy to become mad, and the merry to grow fantastical. Our city's ancient stamp, the owl, which bears no part in the merry quires of the woods, denotes the wisdom, not the mirth of Athens. I would have

the people of Athens, from the mason to the mer-
chant, look as grave and thoughtful as rich
mourners.   They should all seem priests in the
temples, philosophers in their houses, and states-
men in the streets.   Then we should not need to
be at expense of public magistrates ; but every
man would be freely forward to rule another, and
in time 'grow to such a height and ability in
government, as we should by degrees banish the
whole city, and that ostracism were happy preferment ; for the rest of the world would soon invite
us to rule them.

Does not the extasy of music transport us beyond the regions of reason ?   Changing the sober
designs of discretion into the very wildness of
dreams ; urging softer minds to aim at the impossible successes of love ; and enkindling in the
active the destructive ambitions of war ?   Does
it not turn the heads of the young till they grow
so giddy, as if they walk'd on pinacles ; and often
divert the feet of the aged from a funeral to a
wedding ?   And consider, my malicious friends of
Athens, how you would look, if you should see
me, at the mere provocation of a fiddle, lead out
a matron to dance at the marriage of an old philo-
sopher's widow.

Would you meet to be delighted with scenes ?
which is, to be entertained with the deception of
motion and transposition of lights ; where, whilst
you think you see a great battle, you are sure to
get nothing by the victory.   You gaze on imaginary woods and meadows, where you can neither
fell nor mow ; on seas, where you have no ships,
and on rivers where you catch no fish.   But, you
may find it more profitable to retire to your houses,
and there study how to gain by deceiving others,
then to meet in theatres, where you must pay

for suffering your selves to be deceiv'd. This,
Athenians! concerns your profit; which is a
word you understand better than all the gram-
marians in Greece. And though the ways towards
profit are somewhat dark, yet you need no light
from me, which made me presume to leave my
lanthorn at home.

Virtue, in those images of the heroes, adorn'd
with that music, and these scenes, is to be en-
liven'd with poetry. Poetry is the subtle engine
by which the wonderful body of the opera must
move. I wish, Athenians! you were all poets;
for then, if you should meet, and, with the pleasant vapours of Lesbian wine, fall into profound
sleep, and concur in a long dream, you would ere
morning, enamel your houses, tile them with gold,
and pave them with agates. This is the way by
which the poets would make you all exorbitantly
rich. Yet I doubt you are so malicious as to
think, if Homer, Hesiod, and six more of the
ancients, I dare not suspect the moderns, were har-
nest in a team, they would prove too weak to
draw the weight of a single talent out of Athens.
I allow that in a city where diverse are more than
somewhat guilty, you may suppose satires a profitable commodity for the public; but am confident a
whole ream of odes and epigrams will not be held,
by any man here, a sufficient pawn for a drachma.

I conceive you have now heard me as frowardly
as you used to hear the ambassadors of Sparta,
from whom you seldom like any thing but their
brevity. I shall leave the advantage on your side;
for if my advice be bad, 'tis too late for me to
recal it; if good, you have time enough to follow
it. Go home, and consider! but I fear your
houses are so spacious and so fine, as they will
divert your understanding. Though you are will-

ing to perceive that you have no necessity to consider me, yet I am sure I shall have continual occasion to study you; therefore am resolved to contract myself, and retire to my tub.

*A Concert of Music, befitting the pleasant Disposition of* ARISTOPHANES, *being heard, he thus answers.*

### ARISTOPHANES.

Renown'd Athenians! How vainly were you assembled here, if you met to be made wise by Diogenes? and how much more vainly should I ascend the rostra, if I sought to inform your understanding concerning him, or reform his concerning himself? Diogenes came to persuade you to suspect the good effects of assemblies, and I come to accuse him of the evils of solitude. In which I am prevented by his own behaviour; for you have found him, like a man sure to be condemn'd, reviling even you his judges; as pitifully froward as children suddenly wak'd, and as weakly malicious as witches when they are mock'd. He will quarrel with the wind, merely for playing with his beard, and in his age studies revenge on the posterity of his dead pedant, for chastisements received in his youth. 'Tis well that nature hath inclin'd mischievous men, as well as beasts of prey, to live alone; for if the one should be conversable, and the other walk in herds, mankind might by the first be persuaded from the true use of natural reason; and, by the second, be forced from the original inheritance of natural power.

But as sullen Diogenes is by nature secretly urg'd to live alone, so those who are not misgovern'd by passion have an instinct to communication, that by virtuous emulations each may endeavour to become the best example to the rest; for men meet not to see themselves, but to be seen by others, and probably he who doth expose himself to be a public object, will strive to excel before he appears. Other creatures of the most pacific species incline to society, that they may delight in each other's safety, whilst they are protected by their conjunction of strength. 'Tis not my theme to declaim of the abuse or use of number in civil councils, or military attempts : and since Diogenes was constrained to excuse his digression, by accusing his memory, I shall learn to avoid such presumption as must shamefully require your pardon, and will not treat of busy, but pleasant assemblies; and particularly of such as meet for recreation by moral representations.

But Diogenes is implacably offended at recreation. He would have you all housed like himself, and every man stay at home in his tub. He thinks your dwellings so large as they divert your contemplation; and perhaps imagines that the creation hath provided too much room ; that the air is too spacious for birds, the woods for beasts, and the seas for fish ; especially if their various motion in enjoying their large elements contribute to what he esteems vain idleness, recreation. This discontented Cynic would turn all time into midnight, and all learning into melancholy magic. He is so offended at mirth, as if he would accuse even nature herself to want gravity for bringing in the spring so merrily with the music of birds. When you are young, he would have you all seem old, and formal as simple men in authority. When you are old, he would bring you back to the crying condition of children, as if you were always breeding teeth. Nor hath he forgot to dispose of middle age, when the ripeness of mind and body makes you most sufficient for the difficult toils of affairs : for, in this season of laborious life, he would use you

worse than beasts, who are allow'd bells with their
heavy packs, and entertain'd with whistling, when
they are driven with goads.

Gentlemen of Athens !   If you would admit the
deform'd disposition of Diogenes under the pleasant
shape of humour; or rather, if you would vouchsafe to give him authority, and let him have time
and countenance to breed and enlarge a melancholy
sect; you would find the people so apt to nourish
the seed of small evil, till it multiply to extremes,
that you should not need to be at expense of executioners, nor executioners be at cost to buy the
juice of hemlock to dispatch offenders; for we should
all grow most couragiously sad, and very bounti-
fully hang and drown ourselves at our own charge.

He would have you abstain from such public
assemblies, that you might avoid the costs of vests
and ornaments, which he traduces, as occasioning
the emulations of pride.   Can large dominions be
continu'd without distinction of qualities ?   And,
can the people distinguish more immediately than
by their eyes ; which are always sooner satisfied
with shape than substance ?   And, are they not
safer entertain'd with what they instantly admire,
than with that which busies their judgement ?   If
external glory and gaudery be pride, we learn it
there where there is no sin ; for nature, who cannot err, ordain'd the patterns, even in the various
and gaudy ornaments of birds and flowers ; or if
excelling ornament offend him, why looks he upward to the stars, since of the greatest part of
their infinite number, it is hard to find any other
use than that of beautifying and adorning the
world ?   Whilst he scorns pride, he is ignorant
that 'tis commonly but by a kind of pride more
refined that men disdain the proud.   Most just
Athenians ! I cannot forfeit your esteem, if I con-

vince not Diogenes, who will not be instructed by
the work of nature, nor could be corrected by the
rebuke of Plato.

He conjures you, if you would preserve your
peace and power, to refrain from those assemblies
which occasion such emulation of expense as may
enrich retailers and mechanics : as if the wealth
of the people did not make them cautious of inno-
vation, and slow to insurrection ; who rebel to get
that from others, which makes them obedient when
it becomes their own.   The wealth of the eminent,
contracted and retain'd, offends the people ; but
being disperst and apparently spent prevents their
jealousy, that 'tis more than is suspected ; and
takes away their envy, by giving them evidence that
it will grow less : and none will believe expense
superfluous, who think it necessary to gain by
what is spent.    When the laws enjoin frugality to
the rich, they provide well for particular families,
but ill for the public.

He next takes care you should not assemble,
especially at representations of the actions of the
Heroes.   And in the progress of his discourse, meets
the Lady Virtue, and takes her aside, as if he were
to examine a mere stranger ; as if, because she was
not of his acquaintance, therefore she had never
been in Athens ; or at least was so austere in her
garments and behaviour, that she seemed only fit
for the company of old philosophers.    Noble
Athenians !  You all know that her delightful
maids, the Muses, have given her a pleasant and
familiar dress ; and, I know, you will provide her
such a palace as Diogenes shall not need to straiten
himself by inviting her to his tub.

He again forewarns you from beholding her in
the shining shapes of the Heroes ; as if, because
his own eyes are weak, he may therefore think

III.                   O

yours so sore, as it would hurt them to behold the light. Or, as if the heroic ghosts were insolently rais'd by the poets in such angry shapes, as rather serve to upbraid your defects, than to encourage your endeavours for perfection. Or, as if active examples are reviv'd in vain, and seem not more prevalent then written precepts; yet the first invite imitation by shewing experienc'd possibility in the utmost attempts of virtue; and the latter but presumptuously draw a map of an unsteer'd course to an imagined coast. Heroic virtue, when 'tis busy in the open world, is more deserving, because more laborious and less safe, than when she lazily retires to the cells of contemplative cowards, who securely sit and write against those dangers of temptation, from which out of fear they have hastily and meanly fled. He would likewise infer, that the great examples of elder times are vainly presented, because, being so remote, they are less credible. But he forgets to observe that envy will more patiently behold great actions in the ancients, who cannot hinder our pretences, then in those of our own times, who perhaps are our competitors for the rewards of Virtue, as well as rivals to her person.

He next grows angry, not at the pretence which public entertainments make to introduce civility, but at civility itself; loving so barbarously the uncleanly ease of his own life, that he cares not how much inconvenience it gives to the lives of others. If the Ephori and Kings of Sparta invited him to their mess, he would for indecency's sake eat their broth without a spoon. He often commends the ancient use of fingers, that by tearing his meat he may save the labour of whetting his knife. Never washes any thing but his beard, and that too in the bowl where he drinks to his betters. He lets his nails grow to the length of talons,

seizing and snatching his meat at another's table,
as if it were his prey.   And is against the civility
of making a stranger enter a house before the
owner, because the cooper built not his to contain
more than himself.   He terms it brevity, and saving of time, to salute a magistrate with no more
then a nod ; and only for laziness avoids common
salutation.   Judge you, most civil Athenians !
whether cleanness be inconvenient, because he
imputes it as a troublesome part of civility.   Or
whether salutation should be prohibited, because
sometimes, where the dignities are equal, it draws
respect into length.   Or whether length of respect
is not necessary to shew the distinctions of quality ?
Or rather, whether distinctions of quality tend not
to the conservation of government ?  without which,
governors would soon grow weary for want of
obedience, and age retire to the grave for want of
reverence.

He proceeds next against the ornaments of a
public opera, music and scenes.   But how can
he avoid the traducing of music who hath always
a discord within himself, and which seems so loud
too, as if it would a mile off untune the harmo-
nious soul of Plato.   Music doth not heighten
melancholy into madness, but rather unites and
recollects a broken and scattered mind ; giving it
sudden strength to resist the evils it hath long and
strongly bred.   Neither doth it make the merry
seem fantastical, but only to such as are enviously
sad at the pleasure of others.   If it doth warm
the ambitious when they are young, 'tis but as
cordials warm the blood, to make it evaporate
the evil humour.   If it awake hope in the aged,
where hope is fallen asleep and would take rest,
we may therefore say, since hope is the vital heat
of the mind, that it prolongs life where it would

slothfully expire.  Nor need Diogenes suspect that
it may make his bones ache, by seducing him to a
dance ; for he can only lift up his feet to a dismal
discord, or dance to a concert of groaners and
gnashers of teeth.

He is offended at scenes in the opera, as at the
useless visions of imagination.  Is it not the safest
and shortest way to understanding, when you are
brought to see vast seas and provinces, fleets,
armies, and forts, without the hazards of a voyage,
or pains of a long march ?  Nor is that deception
where we are prepar'd and consent to be deceiv'd.
Nor is there much loss in that deceit, where we
gain some variety of experience by a short journey
of the sight.  When he gives you advice not to lay
out time in prospect of woods and meadows, which
you can never possess, he may as well shut up
his own little window, which is the bung-hole of
his tub, and still remain in the dark, because the
light can only shew him that which he can neither
purchase nor beg.

This worst Athenian, whom you have long contemn'd as your suburb-dog, hath all this while but
bark'd at the Muses.  In the end of his discourse
he offers to bite and worry poetry ; yet, 'tis only
with his gums, for his teeth are lost ; why should a
cynic, who applauds poverty in himself, disdain it
in others ?  He pretends to make it his business
to seek out poverty, and to court her in public ;
but the poets, having more wit than the cynics,
only entertain her when she finds out them, and
then but in private.  Or perhaps poets, the busy
secretaries of nature, are so intentively employ'd
in providing for the general happiness of human
kind, that they have no leisure to make provisions
for themselves.  He upbraids that art which may
be said to be the only art of nature ; which elevates

the harmony of reason, and makes even the severities of wisdom pleasant. But, excellent Athenians ! it were an unpardonable want of judgement in me to tire you with defending that which you already know needs no defence. And my presumption is less to be forgiven in having dared to rescue that from the rage of Diogenes, which you have long taken into your own protection : therefore instead of defending poetry, whose several beauties make up the shape of the opera, I will conclude in excuse and defence of her enemy, who hath much reason to dissuade you from moral representations, because he is himself the worst representation of morality ; and is justly afraid to be represented in the theatre.

*The curtains are suddenly closed, and the Company entertained by instrumental and vocal music, with this song.*

### S O N G.

Did ever war so cease
   That all might olive wear ?
All sleepy grow with peace,
   And none be wak'd with fear ?
Does time want wings to fly,
   Or death ere make a stand ?
Men must grow old and die :
   Storms drive us from sea to tempests at land.
*Chorus.*—This through his tub the cynic saw ;
       Where vainly with time he did strive,
      And in vain from death did withdraw
       By bury'ng himself alive.

The poets they are wise,
   All evils they expect,
And so prevent surprize,
   Whilst troubles they neglect.

Can age e'er do them harm,
Who cheerfully grow old ?
Mirth keeps their hearts still warm,
Fools think themselves safe in sorrow and cold.
*Chorus.*—Then let the sour cynic live coopt ;
Let him quake in his thrid-bare cloak
Till he find his old tub unhoopt,
His staff and his lanthron broke.

*The song being ended, a concert of instrumental music,
after the French composition, being heard a while,
the curtains are suddenly open'd, and in the
ROSTRAS appear sitting a PARISIAN and a
LONDONER, in the livery robes of both cities, who
declaim concerning the pre-eminence of PARIS
and LONDON.*

## THE PARISIAN.

You of this noble city, are yet to become more
noble by your candour to the plea between me a
burgeois of Paris and my opponent of London ;
being concerned in honour to lend your attention
as favourably to a stranger as to your native orator. Since 'tis the greatest sign of narrow educa-
sion to permit the borders of rivers, or strands of
seas, to separate the general consanguinity of mankind ; though the unquiet nature of man, still
hoping to shake off distant power, and the in-
capacity of any one to sway universal empire, hath
made them the bounds to divide government. But
already I think it necessary to cease persuading
you, who will ever deserve to be my judges, and
therefore mean to apply my self in admonishing
him who is pleased to be a while my adversary.

My most opiniater'd antagonist—for a Londoner's
opinion of himself is no less noted then his opinion
of his beef before the veal of Italy—you should

know that the merit of cities consists not in their fair and fruitful scituation, but in the manners of the inhabitants ; for where the scituation excels, it but upbraids their minds if they be not proportionable to it. And, because we should more except against the constancy of minds than their mutability, when they incline to error, I will first take a survey of yours in the long continued deformity of the shape of your city, which is, of your buildings.

Sure your ancestors contrived your narrow streets in the days of wheel-barrows, before those greater engines, carts, were invented. Is your climate so hot, that as you walk you need umbrellas of tiles to intercept the sun ? Or are your shambles so empty that you are afraid to take in fresh air, lest it should sharpen your stomachs ? Oh, the goodly landskip of Old Fish-Street ! which, had it not had the ill luck to be crooked, was narrow enough to have been your founder's perspective ; and where the garrets—perhaps not for want of architecture but through abundance of amity—are so made, that opposite neighbours may shake hands without stirring from home. Is unanimity of inhabitants in wise cities better exprest than by their coherence and uniformity of building ? Where streets begin, continue, and end in a like stature and shape ; but yours—as if they were rais'd in a general insurrection, where every man hath a several design—differ in all things that can make distinction. Here stands one that aims to be a palace, and next it another that professes to be a hovel. Here a giant, there a dwarf, here slender, there broad ; and all most admirably different in their faces as well as in their height and bulk. I was about to defy any Londoner who dares pretend there is so much ingenious correspondence in this city, as that he can

shew me one house like another. Yet your old
houses seem to be reverend and formal, being com-
pared to the fantastical looks of the modern; which
have more ovals, nieches, and angles than are in
your custards, and are enclos'd with pasteboard
walls, like those of malicious Turks, who, because
themselves are not immortal, and cannot ever dwell
where they build, therefore will not be at charge to
provide such lastingness as may entertain their
children out of the rain ; so slight, and so prettily
gaudy, that if they could move they would pass for
pageants.* 'Tis your custom, where men vary often
the mode of their habits, to term the nation
fantastical ; but where streets continually change
fashion, you should make haste to chain up the
city, for 'tis certainly mad.

You would think me a malicious traveller, if I
should still gaze on your mishapen streets, and take
no notice of the beauty of your river ; therefore I
will pass the importunate noise of your water-men
—who snatch at fares as if they were to catch
prisoners, plying the gentry so uncivilly, as if they
never had row'd any other passengers but bear-
wards—and now step into one of your pescod-
boats ; whose tilts† are not so sumptuous as the
roofs of gondolas, nor, when you are within, are
you at the ease of *chaise a bras.* The commodity

---

* The word "pageant," like the Pegma of the Romans, originally signified the vehicle in which Pageants or dramatic
mysteries were performed. These, "being acted with mighty
state and reverence by the Friars of this house, had theatres
for the several scenes [or, pajiont clothes, as they were called]
very large and high, placed upon wheels, and drawn to all the
eminent parts of the city for the better advantage of spec-
tators."—*Dugdale.*

† A covering overhead. "It is a small vessel, like in proportion to a Gravesend tilt-boat."—*Sandys.*

        " The rowing crew,
To tempt a fare, clothe all their tilts in blue." – *Gay.*

and trade of your river belongs to your selves ; but
give a stranger leave to share in the pleasure of it,
which will hardly be in the prospect or freedom of
air, unless prospect, consisting of variety, be made
up with here a palace, there a wood-yard, here a
garden, there a brew-house ; here dwells a lord,
there a dyer, and between both *duomo comune.*
If freedom of air be inferr'd in the liberty of the
subject, where every private man hath authority
for his own profit, to smoke up a magistrate, then
the air of your Thames is open enough, because
'tis equally free. I will forbear to visit your courtly
neighbours at Wapping, not that it will make me
giddy to shoot your bridge, but that I am loth to
disturb the civil silence of Billingsgate, which is so
great as if the mariners were always landing to
storm the harbour ; therefore, for brevity's sake, I
will put to shore again, though I should be constrain'd, even without my galoshoes,* to land at
puddle-dock.

I am now return'd to visit your houses, where
the roofs are so low, that I presume your ancestors
were very mannerly, and stood bare to their wives,
for I cannot discern how they could wear their
high crown'd hats; yet I will enter, and therein
oblige you much, when you know my aversion to
the odour of a certain weed that governs amongst
your coarser acquaintance, as much as lavender
amongst your coarser linen ; to which, in my
apprehension, your sea-coal smoke seems a very
Portugal perfume. I should here hasten to a
period, for fear of suffocation, if I thought you so
ungracious as to use it in public assemblies ; and

---

* Galages, now called galoshes —Upper shoes. "Solea, a
shoe called a *galage* or paten, which hath nothyng on the feete
but onely latchettes."—*Elyot,* 1559. *See also Greene's Ghost-
haunting Coney-catchers.* 1626.

yet I see it grow so much in fashion, that me-thinks
your children begin to play with broken pipes in
stead of corals, to make way for their teeth. You
will find my visit short, I cannot stay to eat with
you, because your bread is too heavy, and you disdain the light sustenance of herbs. Your drink is
too thick, and yet you are seldom over-curious in
washing your glasses. Nor will I lodge with you,
because your beds seem, to our *alcovaes*, no bigger
than coffins, and your curtains so short as they will
hardly serve to enclose your carriers in summer ;
and may be held, if taffeta, to have lined your
grandsire's skirts.

But though your houses are thin, yet your
kitchens are well lined with beef ; and the plentiful
exercise of your chimneys makes up that canopy
of smoke which covers your city ; whilst those in
the continent are well contented with a clear sky,
entertain flesh as a regalio ; and we, your poor
French frogs, are fain to sing to a salad. You
boast that your servants feed better than masters
at Paris ; and we are satisfied when ours are better
taught than fed. You allow yours idleness and
high nourishment, to raise their mettle ; which is,
to make them rude for the honour of old England.
We inure ours to labour and temperance, that we
may allay them ; which is, to make them civil for
the quiet of France. Yours drink wine, and the
strong broth of malt, which makes them bold, hot,
and adventurous to be soon in command. Ours
are cooled with weak water, which doth quench
their arrogance, and make them fit to obey long.
We plant the vineyard, and you drink the wine ;
by which you beget good spirits, and we get good
money. You keep open houses for all that bring
you in mirth, till your estates run out of doors, and
find new landlords. We shut our gates to all but

such whose conversation brings in profit, and so, by the help of what you call ill-nature and parsimony, have the good luck to keep our inheritances for our issue.

Before I leave you in your houses—where your estates are managed by your servants, and your persons educated by your wives—I will take a short survey of your children; to whom you are so terrible, that you seem to make use of authority whilst they are young, as if you knew it would not continue till their manhood. You begin to them with such rough discipline, as if they were born mad, and you meant to fright them into their wits again before they had any to lose. When they encrease in years, you make them strangers; keeping them at such distance, out of jealousy they should presume to be your companions, that when they reach manhood they use you as if they were none of your acquaintance. But we submit to be familiar with ours, that we may beget their affection before 'tis too late to expect it. If you take pains to teach them anything, 'tis only what they should not learn, bashfulness; which you interpret to be their respect towards you, but it rather shews they are in trouble, and afraid of you; and not only of you, but of all that are elder than themselves; as if youth were a crime, or, as if you had a greater quarrel to nature than to the devil: you seem to teach them to be ashamed of their persons, even then when you are willing to excuse their faults. Methinks when ours are grave. they are but dull; and we are content not to have them demure and tame whilst they are youths, lest restraint—which always inclines to extremes when it is chang'd to liberty—should make them rude and wild when they are men.

This education you give them at home; but

though you have frequently the pride to disdain the behaviour of other nations, yet you have sometimes the discretion to send your sons abroad to learn it. To Paris they come, the school of Europe, where is taught the approaches and demeanours towards power: where they may learn honour, which is the generous honesty, which is the civil boldness of Courts. But there they arrive, not to converse with us, but with themselves; to see the gates of the Court, not to enter and frequent it or to take a hasty survey of greatness as far as envy, but not to study it as far as imitation. At last return home, despising those necessary virtues which they took not pains to acquire; and are only ill altered in their dress and mind, by making that a deformity in seeming over-careful and forced, which we make graceful in being negligent and easy.

I have now left your houses, and am passing through your streets; but not in a coach, for they are uneasily hung, and so narrow, that I took them for sedans upon wheels. Nor is it safe for a stranger to use them till the quarrel be decided whether six of your nobles, sitting together, shall stop, and give place to as many barrels of beer. Your city is the only metropolis of Europe where there is a wonderful dignity belonging to carts. Master Londoner! be not so hot against coaches: take advice from one that eats much sorrel* in his broth. Can you be too civil to such a singular gentry as bravely scorn to be provident? who, when they have no business here to employ them, nor public pleasures to divert them, yet even then kindly invent occasions to bring them hither, that,

---

* Acid austere vegetables contract and strengthen the fibres, as all kinds of sorrel, the virtues of which lie in acid astringent salt, a sovereign antidote against the putrescent bilious alkali. —*Arbuthnot.*

at your own rates, they may change their land for
your wares; and have purposely avoided the coarse
study of arithmetic, lest they should be able to
affront you with examining your accompts.

I wonder at your riches when I see you drink in
the morning; but more at your confidence, when I
see grey beards come out of a tavern and stay at
the door to make the last debate of their business;
and I am yet more amaz'd at your health when I
taste your wine ; but most of all at your politics,
in permitting such a public poisoning under the
style of free mystery to encourage trade and diligence.

I would now make a safe retreat, but that methinks I am stopt by one of your heroic games,
call'd foot-ball, which I conceive—under your
favour—not very conveniently civil in the streets,
especially in such irregular and narrow roads as
Crooked Lane. Yet it argues your courage much
like your military pastime of throwing at cocks.
But your mettle would be more magnified—since
you have long allow'd those two valiant exercises
in the streets—to draw your archers from Finsbury,
and during high market let them shoot at butts in
Cheapside. I have now no more to say but what
refers to a few private notes which I shall give you
in a whisper when we meet in Moorfields, from
whence—because the place was meant for public
pleasure, and to show the munificence of your city
—I shall desire you to banish the laundresses and
bleachers, whose acres of old linen make a shew like
the fields of Carthagena, when the five months'
shifts of the whole fleet are washt and spread : or
else you will give me leave to conclude in behalf
of Luxemberg and the Tuilleries, as no ill accom-
modations for the citizens of Paris.

*After a concert of Music, imitating the* WAITS *of* LONDON, *the* LONDONER *rises and thus answers.*

### THE LONDONER.

Ever noble and most sufficient judges ! I am so little angry with my adversary, that I am ready to entitle him, as a stranger, to protection from you, and civility from my self. You find, in his survey of this renown'd city, he has undertaken to be pleasant, and to make you so too : but men who are pleased themselves cannot when they list disperse their gay humour amongst others : it being much more easy to incite to anger than to mirth. I presume I am so far from needing the advantage, or from growing insolent with the honour, of having you my judges, that I refer my self to him ; whilst I present him Paris in the same glass where he reflected London : and he is not a little obliged in being made capable of reforming his judgment by the helps of comparison.

Give me leave, Monsieur de Paris, to be conducted from Dieppe by one of your messagers,—who are as magisterial on the road as old rangers in a forest,—and on my Norman nag—which, though it has not as many legs as a caterpillar, yet by the advantage of being well spurred, makes shift to travel as fast—I enter your city at Porte St Martin ; and ere I light, would, by leaving a limb to compound for the rest of my body ; so furious are you in your hospitality when you call aloud and take in strangers, spite of their teeth, into your houses, and lodge them for more than enough of their money. But such importunity, and even for mean profit, should rather be interpreted as the vehemence of a witty people, that have hot brains, than as the signs of general poverty : Whilst we, phlegmatic islanders, are too dull to be so troublesome for a little money as may shew we want it.

Before I enter your houses, I cannot chuse but take notice of your streets; by which I discern, though you are now unanimously glorious, yet your ancestors and you had different minds; for though læ Rue St Antoine, St Honoré, and St Denis are large enough for the Vista; yet læ Rue Tirechape, La Tannerie, and la Huchette stand so much in the shade, that there your beautiful wives need neither veils nor fans; you being fain to lay traps at your windows to catch the sun-beams. But this, you will say, was the defect of our ancestors, not of yours; who, in a wandering humour, made bold to cross the Channel, march up to Paris, and build your houses after their own fashion.

As I pass along, I bow before every palace; but 'tis to the giant Switz that stands in carbonaded breeches at the gate; who, coming a long journey, merely to keep your natives in awe, has reason to expect reverence from a stranger. Now methinks you wish the gout in my finger, because I point not with great wonder at the Louvre; which I confess has a very singular way of being wonderful; the fame of the palace consisting more in the vast design of what it was meant to be, than in the largeness of what it is: the structure being likewise a little remarkable for what is old, but more even for the antiquity of what is new; having been begun some ages past, and is to be finished many ages hence; which, I take it, may be a sign of the glory, but not of the wealth of your founders. I will pass into your Fauxbourgs by Pont Rouge; a bridge not built to be useful to you in the strength of it, but rather to shew the strength of your river to strangers, when, maugre

your guards of Switz, it often carries an arch out or
your city.

Already, methinks, passing o'er this bridge, I
stop at a broken arch ; and finding my self a heavy
Londoner, who wants the French vivacity to frisk
o'er so wide a gap to the Fauxbourgs, I am willing
to return, that I may afford you the civility of
taking more notice of the ornaments of your river.
I find your boats much after the pleasant shape of
those at common ferries ; where your bastelier* is
not so turbulently active as our watermen, but
rather, his fare being two brass liards,† stands as
sullen as an old Dutch skipper after shipwreck,
and will have me attend till the rest of the herd
make up his freight ; passing in droves like cattle ;
embroidered and perfumed with carters and crocheteurs ; ‡ all standing during the voyage as if we
were ready to land as soon as we put from shore ;
and with his long pole gives us a tedious waft, as
if we were all the while poching for eels. We
neither descend by stairs when we come in, nor
ascend when we go out, but crawl through the mud
like cray-fish, or anglers in a new plantation. I
could wish you had the adornments of wall'd
banks ; but in this witty region of civility, as well
as in our dull rude town, I perceive there is not a
perfect coherence in all the parts of magnificence.

I will now visit your houses ; which I confess
transcendent as towers compar'd to the stature of
those in our city ; but as they are as high rooft as
our belfries, so have they in them more than the
noise of our bells ; lodging distressed families in a
room ; and where there is no plenty, there is seldom

---

* Boatman.
† Liard, the fourth of a sou ; according to English value,
half a farthing.
‡ Street porters.

quietness. This chorus of clamour from several apartments will be sooner acknowledged when you consider that your nation affects not such brevity of speech as was practis'd by the Spartans, nor that majestical silence which is us'd by the Turks. But I accuse you of that of which you may take occasion to boast ; because the stuffing of rooms with whole families denotes a populous city. But, farewell the happiness of the nation ! when the populousness of the city argues the litigiousness of the country ; where, with a multitude of procez you lose your wits, and afterwards come up to live by them at Paris. Though you are shy to eat at our entertainments, yet I would accept of yours if you were not hinder'd from giving any by the great expense of your habits and superfluous trains. And I would drink with you, if you were as posed * and grave in your wine as we dull traficquers, who use it to sharpen our wits when we conclude bargains. But I have a mind to suppose, under your favour, that your heads are bottles, and your brains the cork ; for the one, being a little stirred, the others fly out, and fill the room with froth. I would lodge with you, but that your large beds are taken up with punezes ; which our skins, being tender and not so much condensed by the cold as you imagine, can ill endure, and worse permit the ubiquitary attacks of those dexterous little persecutors, which suit more with the nimble disposition of men of your climate, than those other slow enemies which were bred in Italy.†

Noise in your habitations of sleep is not so improper as your dead silence in the very regions of noise, your kitchens ; where your cooks, though by education choleric and loud, are ever in profound contemplation ; that is, they are considering

* Stupified.                    † Bugs—

how to reform the mistakes of nature in the original compositions of flesh and fish ; she having
not known, it seems, the sufficient mystery of
hautgouts : and the production of their deep
studies are sometimes so full of delicious fancy,
and witty seasoning, that at your feasts when I
uncover a dish, I think I feed on a very epigram.
Who can comprehend the diversity of your pot-
tages, carbonnades, grillades, ragouts, haches, sau-
piquets, demi-bisques, bisques, capilotades, and
entre-mets ?   But, above all, I admire at the vast
generation of your embroiderers of meat, your
larders ; their larding being likewise diversified
from bacon of Mayence to porpoise of St Malo ;
which, though it may be some cause of obliging
and calling in the Jews, yet your perpetual persecution of that poor fish will so drive away the
species from your coasts, as you will never be able
to foretell a storm.

These are your feasts, which are but fasts to
your servants ; who, being confined within the
narrow bounds of pension, are accomptable for all
the orts * by weight ; for which your sufficient
reason is, because such as are ordained to service,
should be continually allay'd by temperance, lest
they might lose obedience.   Your sons you dignify
betimes with a taste of pleasure and liberty ;
which perhaps breeds in them—that they may
maintain the vast expenses of high pleasure—too
hasty and violent an appetite to such power as
makes them, when they are men, soon turbulent
to supreme authority.   When they provoke a province to rise against the Court, 'tis excus'd as high
gallantry, and in fashion whilst they are young
and strongly attended ; but 'tis call'd treason

* Offal.  See vol. i. p. 171.

when they grow old and deserted. Here I expect your rebuke; for why should I censure the education of your children, since we send ours to learn the honour and deportment of manhood at Paris? Yet I will recommend one consideration to your city as well as to our own; whether the ancient jurisdiction of parents and masters, when it was severe, did not make all degrees of human life more quiet and delightful than we have found it since that privilege hath been ignorantly and negligently lost.

You are disordered with the rudeness in our streets; but have more reason to be terrified with the frequent insurrections in your own. In ours, a few disturb the quiet of coaches; but in yours, whole armies of lackies invade the peace of public justice; whose image—were the tumult drawn by a poetical painter—you would imagine fencing with a broad sword, like an old grave Switz against the tucks* of fantastical pages; who strive to rescue the condemned, as if the nobles were concerned in honour not to suffer malefactors to be affronted by a base executioner on the scaffold for so generous an exercise as killing. But when I observed your twelfth-nights, with the universal shout of *le Roy boit!* I could not but think that the whole vintage of France was in the heads of the servants of Paris.

I will now suppose it late, and that I am retiring to my country-men at the good Hotel de Venise; but shall make haste; for you must needs acknowledge the famous dangers of Pont Neuf; where robbing is as constant and as hereditary a trade as amongst the Arabs; where old grand-

* A long rapier.
"If he by chance escape your venom'd tuck,
Our purpose may hold there."—*Shakspeare.*

fathers-filous,* in beards fit to be reverenced by all
that scape their clutches, set the watch—which
consists wholly of their grand-children—carefully
at nine at night, and take it as want of respect in
such who are so indecent as to pass that way in
their old cloaks.

When I consider both our cities, I conclude
they were built and are inhabited by mortal men ;
therefore am resolv'd to burn some private notes
which I intended to impart in answer of those that
you referred to our next meeting.   If I could reach
your hand, I would endeavour to kiss it ; for I
should account my self worse bred than in a
forest, if I had not learned a little from the
abundant civility of Paris ; where I have heard of
two aged crocheteurs, heavy loaden with billets,
who were so equally concerned in the punctilios of
salutation, and of giving the way, that with the
length of ceremony, " *monsieur c'est a vous, monsieur vous vous moques de vostre serviteur,*" they
both sunk under their burdens, and so died, divid-
ing the eternal honour of genty† education.

*The Curtains are suddenly closed, and the Company
entertain'd by instrumental and vocal music, with
this song.*

SONG.

1.

London is smother'd with sulph'rous fires ;
Still she wears a black hood and cloak,
Of sea-coal smoke,
As if she mourned for brewers and dyers.
*Chorus.*
But she is cool'd and cleans'd by streams
Of flowing and of ebbing Thames.

---

* Aged pickpockets or thieves.
† See vol. ii., p. 23.

2.

Though Paris may boast a clearer sky,
  Yet wanting flows and ebbs of Seine,
    To keep her clean,
She ever seems choakt when she is adry.
                    *Chorus.*
And though a ship her scutcheon be,
Yet Paris hath no ship at sea.           ·

*The Song ended, the curtains are drawn open again,
and the* Epilogue *enters.*

### EPILOGUE.

Too late we told you, some two hours ago,
The ills, which you were sure too soon to know.
Had we fore-warn'd you but the day before,
By half so much, said at our outward door,
We had been civil, but had weakly shown
More care to watch your profit than our own.
We have your money, true ; if you can call
That ours of which we make no use at all.
The poets never mind such toys as these——
                    [*Shews money in his hand.*
But keep them to be sent for when you please.
At worst—if you may credit, in frail times,
Bankers who turn and wind a world of rhymes—
They are but bow'd, laid in a trunk above,
And kept as simple tokens of your love.
If this were raillery it could not please,
After a tedious dull Diogenes :
A poet a mile longer, then two more
To vex you, having had too much before.
Perhaps, some were so cozen'd as to come,
To see us weave in the dramatic loom :
To trace the winding scenes, like subtle spies
Bred in the Muses' camp, safe from surprise :

Where you by art learn joy, and when to mourn ;
To watch the plot's swift change, and counterturn :
When Time moves swifter than by nature taught,
And by a *Chorus* miracles are wrought,
Making an infant instantly a man :
These were your plays, but get them if you can.

*After a flourish of loud music the curtain is clos'd
and the Entertainment ended.*

*The vocal and instrumental music was compos'd by
Doctor Charles Coleman, Captain Henry Cook,
Mr. Henry Lawes, and Mr George Hudson.*

THE SIEGE OF RHODES.

*The Siege of Rhodes. Made a Representation by the Art of Prospective in Scenes, and the Story sung in Recitative Musick. At the back part of Rutland House, in the upper end of Aldersgate Street, London. London, Printed by J. M. for Henry Herringham, and are to be sold at his shop, at the Sign of the Anchor, on the Lower Walk, in the New Exchange. 1656. No dedication.*

*Published 29th September apparently. It seems to have been the custom of some publishers to note the date of issue of plays in pen and ink on the title page.*

*The Siege of Rhodes. The first and second part. As they were lately represented at his Highness the Duke of York's Theatre in Lincoln's-Inn-Fields. The first part being lately enlarged. Written by Sir William D'avenant. London, printed for Henry Herringham, and are to be sold at his shop, at the Sign of the Anchor, on the Lower Walk, in the New Exchange. 1663. The second part has the title repeated.\**

*The Siege of Rhodes. A verbatim reprint. 4to. 1670.*

*The Siege of Rhodes. The first and second part. In the folio edition of Sir W. D'avenant's Works. [Dated] 1672.*

\* This edition is dedicated to the Earl of Clarendon, which dedication is inscribed by D'avenant himself.

IMMEDIATELY after the foregoing "Entertainment" had
been presented, and so had paved the way for the introduction of other entertainments more dramatic in
character, the "Siege of Rhodes" was brought forward.
It was the first attempt at English opera in this country.
The "Siege of Rhodes," as then produced, was merely
an epitome of the first part as now printed from the
later text. The character Roxolana was not introduced, and Haly, although not included in the list
of Dramatis Personæ, is mentioned in the scene of the
Siege. Scenery was now for the first time presented
in England on the stage of a theatre.

On the reproduction of the piece in 1662, at the Duke
of York's Theatre, Lincoln's Inn Fields, the text was
enlarged, and the second part was added. Particulars
of those alterations and additions will be found noted in
the text which follows.

The first edition of the original piece is comprehended
in forty pages, with, further, a Prefatory Address to the
Reader, not subsequently printed, and at the end a cast
of the characters under the title of "The Story Presented."

These are as follows ;—

### TO THE READER.

I may receive disadvantage by this address designed
for excuses; for it will too heartily put you in mind
that errors are not far off when excuses are at hand; this
refers to our Representation: and some may be willing to
be led to find the blemishes of it, but would be left to their
own conduct to discover the beauties, if there be any.
Yet I may forewarn you that the defects which I intend
to excuse are chiefly such, as you cannot reform but only
with your purse ; that is, by building us a larger room ;
a design which we began and shall not be left for you to
finish, because we have observed that many who are

liberal of their understanding when they could issue it
out towards discovery of imperfections, have not always
money to expend in things necessary towards the making
up of perfection.

It has been often wisht that our Scenes (we having
oblig'd ourselves to the variety of five changes according to the Ancient Dramatic distinctions made for time)
had not been confined to eleven foot in height, and about
fifteen in depth, including the places of passage reserv'd
for the Musick. This is so narrow an allowance for the
fleet of Solyman the Magnificent, his army, the Island
of Rhodes, and the varieties attending the Siege of the
City, that I fear you will think we invite you to such a
contracted trifle as that of the Cæsars carved upon a
nut.

As these limits have hinder'd the splendour of our
scene, so we are like to give no great satisfaction in the
quantity of our Argument, which is in Story very copi-
ous ; but shrinks to a small narrative here, because we
could not convey it by more than seven persons ; being
constrain'd to prevent the length of *Recitative* Music, as
well as to conserve, without encumbrance, the narrowness of the place. Therefore you cannot expect the
chief ornaments belonging to a History dramatically
digested into turns and counter-turns, to double walks,
and interweavings of design.

This is exprest to forbid your excess of expectation ;
but we must take care not to deter you from the hope of
some satisfaction ; for that were not only to hang out no
bush, but likewise to shut up our doors. Therefore, as
you have heard what kind of excellencies you should not
expect ; so I will be brief, and hope without vanity, to
give you encouragement by telling you there are some
things at least excusable which you may resolve to meet.

We conceive it will not be unacceptable to you if we
recompense the narrowness of the Room, by containing
in it so much as could be conveniently accomplisht by
Art and Industry : which will not be doubted in the
Scenes by those who can judge that kind of Illustration,
and know the excellency of Mr John Web, who design'd
and order'd it. The music was compos'd, and both the
Vocal and Instrumental is exercis'd by the most trans-

cendent of England in that art, and perhaps not unequal
to the best masters abroad; but being *Recitative*, and
therefore unpractis'd here, though of great reputation
amongst other nations, the very attempt of it is an obligation to our own. The story as represented (which
will not require much apology because it expects but
little praise) is Heroical, and notwithstanding the continual hurry and busy agitations of a hot Siege, is (I
hope) intelligibly convey'd to advance the characters
of Virtue in the shapes of Valour and conjugal Love.
And though the main argument hath but a single walk,
yet perhaps the movings of it will not seem unpleasant.
You may inquire, being a Reader, why in a heroic argument my numbers are so often diversify'd and fall into
short fractions; considering that a continuation of the
usual length of English verse would appear more heroical in reading. But when you are an Auditor you will
find that in this I rather deserve approbation than need
excuse; for frequent alterations of measure (which cannot be so unpleasant to him that reads as troublesome to
him that writes) are necessary to *Recitative* music for
variation of airs. If what I have said be taken for
excuses, I have my intent; because excuses are not
always signs of error, but are often modest explana-
tions of things that might otherwise be mistaken. But
I have said so much to vindicate myself from having
occasion to be excus'd for the Poem, that it brings me at
last to ask pardon for the length of the Epistle.

                                        WILL. D'AVENANT.

*August* 17, 1656.

### THE PERSONS REPRESENTED.

| | |
|---|---|
| *Solyman,* | The Magnificent. |
| *Villerius,* | Grand Master of *Rhodes*. |
| *Alphonso,* | A *Sicilian* Duke. |
| *Admiral,* | Of *Rhodes*. |
| *Pirrhus,* | Bassa. |
| *Mustapha,* | Bassa. |
| *Ianthe,* | Wife to *Alphonso*. |

               *The Scene* :

                  RHODES.

THE STORY PERSONATED.

Solyman by Capt. Henry Cook.
Villerius  ,,  Mr Gregory Thorndall.
Alphonso ,,  Mr Edward Coleman.
Admiral    ,,  Mr Matthew Lock.
Pirrhus   ,,  Mr John Harding.
Mustapha ,,  Mr Henry Persill.
Ianthe     ,,  Mrs Coleman, wife to Mr Coleman.

The Composition of Vocal Music was perform'd,

The First Entry   by Mr Henry Lawes.
  ,,  Second Entry  ,, Capt. Henry Cook.
  ,,  Third Entry   ,, Capt. Henry Cook.
  ,,  Fourth Entry  ,, Mr Matthew Lock.
  ,,  Fifth Entry   ,, Mr Henry Lawes.

The Instrumental Music was composed by Dr Charles
Coleman, and Mr George Hudson.

There is no Prologue to the first or second editions of
the first part, but there is both a Prologue and Epilogue
prefixed to the second part in the second edition.

Although on the authority of Anthony Wood, who
himself played the violin originally by ear, "but not
with the same tuning that others used "—his tuning being
in fourths—and who subsequently, when properly instructed by a competent master at the charge of " two
shillings and sixpence entrance, and so quarterly," obtained a proficiency in music ; it has been asserted that
Oliver Cromwell "loved a good voice and instrumental
music well," yet during the Protectorate no encouragement was afforded either to vocal or instrumental performers for a public display of their talents, and those
who had been employed in the Chapel Royal, cathedrals,
or public exhibitions in the capital, were compelled to
skulk about the country, soliciting an asylum in the
houses of private patrons whose ability to protect them
must have been somewhat precarious.  Henry Lawes,
however, retained his place in the Chapel Royal, and
in a great measure supported himself by teaching ladies
to sing, the cultivation of music being confined to private
families.  He also composed and published his celebrated
" Ayres and Dialogues."  The musical compositions of

Lawes had been long so greatly admired that Fenton, the editor of Waller's works, states that "the best poets of his time were ambitious of having their verses set to music by this admirable artist;" while on the other hand Peck says, "Milton wrote his Masque at the request of Lawes," a notice of whom will be found in the Appendix to the Masque of the Prince D'Amour, in vol. i. p. 350.

The Puritanical mania for the abolition of anything like formality or display in churches, caused not only the destruction of painted glass windows, monuments, ornamental masonry and adornments, but collegiate and parochial churches were stripped of their organs, musical service-books of every kind, being denounced alike superstitious and ungodly, were committed to the flames, and those retainers whose function it had been to assist at "such prophane vanities" were enjoined to betake themselves to some employment "less offensive to the Lord." Nothing in the shape of music, in their new form of Divine worship was permitted, except discordant psalm-singing, such as may still be heard in Presbyterian churches where the congregation is untutored. It was, therefore, exceedingly difficult when, at the Restoration, the heads of the Church proceeded to re-establish Cathedral service, to find either suitable instruments, professors, choral books, or singers. By slow degrees the several choirs throughout the kingdom were supplied with masters; but for a long time, for want of trained boys, the treble parts were either played on cornets, or sung by men in falsetto.

In France the high favour accorded to operas and operatic music, the result of the united talents of Quinault and Lulli, induced managers in this country to turn their attention towards that species of entertainment, so that, from time to time, after the production of the "Siege of Rhodes" had introduced a taste for the mixture of music with poetic declamation, "dramatic operas" were brought forward. Of these were Circe, Psyche, the altered versions of the Tempest, Macbeth, and others, all "set off," says Cibber, "with the most expensive decorations of scenes and habits, and with the best voices and dancers." The music in Macbeth, of which the rude and wild excellence cannot be surpassed, has been attributed by some to Henry Purcell and not to Mathew Lock, whose productions otherwise are far inferior, while to Purcell's peculiar style it bears a closer resemblance. Burgh, in his Anecdotes of Music, mentions that a musical friend of his "assured him that he possessed the original score of the music in Macbeth, in Henry Purcell's own handwriting."

In none of the operas produced on the English stage at that time was the entire dialogue carried on in recitative, neither has recitative ever been used in any English opera since, unless, perhaps, we except the serious opera of Artaxerxes. Downes tells us that "the scenes, machines, dresses, and other necessary decorations of Psyche, cost upwards of eight hundred pounds;" so that, although performed eight successive nights it did not prove so remunerative as the Tempest. Cibber, in dilating on these dramatic operas, says, "the sensual taste for sight and sound was lashed by several good prologues of those days." With the taste for opera a taste for French music was imported into this country, in order to flatter the partiality of the king for everything that came from France, albeit he himself knew little of music.

Dryden, in the preface to his unsuccessful political drama, which he styles an opera, Albion and Albanius, has a brief disquisition upon opera, the argument of which is in favour of the more ready adaptation of the French than of the English language to music, and more in favour of the Italian than either. The preface to "the Fairy Queen, an opera represented at the Queen's Theatre, by their Majesties' Servants," in 1692, an alteration of the Midsummer-Night's Dream,* argues thus in favour of the establishment of an Opera House in this country at private cost.

"'Tis known to all who have been any considerable

---

* "The opera, of which I spoke to you in my former, hath at last appear'd, and continues to be represented daily. It is called *The Fairy Queen*. The Drama is originally Shakespeare's; the Music and Decorations are extraordinary. I have heard the dancers commended, and without doubt the whole is very entertaining."— *Gentlemen's Journal: or Monthly Miscellany, May* 1692.

time in Italy or France, how operas are esteemed among
'em. That France borrowed what she has from Italy is
evident from the Andromede and Toison D'or of Monsieur
Corneille, which are the first in the kind they ever had,
on their publick Theatres; they being not perfect operas,
but Tragedies with singing, dancing, and machines in-
terwoven with 'em, after the manner of an opera. They
gave 'em a taste first to try their palates, that they
might the better judge whether in time they would be
able to digest an entire opera. And Cardinal Richelieu,
that great encourager of arts and learning, introduced
'em first at his own expense, as I have been informed
amongst 'em.

"What encouragement Signor Baptist Lully had from
the present king of France is well known; they being first
set out at his own expense, and all the ornaments given by
the king for the entertainment of the people. In Italy,
especially at Venice, where operas have the greatest reputation, and where they have 'em every Carnival, the
noble Venetians set 'em out at their own cost. And
what a confluence of people the fame of 'em draw from
all parts of Italy, to the great profit of that city, is well
known to every one who has spent a Carnival there.
And many of the English gentry are sensible what advantages Paris receives by the great number of strangers
which frequent the operas three days in a week throughout the year. If therefore an opera were established
here, by the favour of the nobility and gentry of Eng-
lang, I may modestly conclude it would be to some advantage to London, considering what a sum we must
yearly lay out among tradesmen for the fitting out so
great a work.

"That Sir William D'avenant's Siege of Rhodes was
the first opera we ever had in England no man can deny;
and is indeed a perfect opera, there being this difference
only between an opera and a tragedy, that the one is a
story sung with proper action, the other spoken. And
he mu t be a very ignorant player, who knows not there
is a musical cadence in speaking; and that a man may
as well speak out of tune as sing out of tune. And
though few are so nice as to examine this, yet all are
pleased when they hear it justly performed. 'Tis true,

the Siege of Rhodes wanted the ornament of machines,
which they value themselves so much in Italy, and the
dancing which they have in such perfection in France.
That he designed this, if his first attempt met with the
encouragement' it deserved will appear from these lines
in his Prologue :

   " ' But many travellers here as judges come
      From Paris, Florence, Venice, and from Rome,
      Who will describe, when any scene we draw,
      By each of ours all that they ever saw,
      Those praising for extensive breadth and height,
      And inward distance to deceive the sight.'

   " ' Oh money ! money !' if the wits would dress,
      With ornaments, the present face of peace ;
      And to our poet half that treasure spare
      Which faction gets from fools to nourish war ;
      Then his contracted scenes should wider be,
      And move by greater engines, till you see,
      Whilst you securely sit, fierce armies meet,
      And raging seas disperse a fighting fleet.'

   " That a few private persons should venture on so expensive a work as an opera, when none but Princes or
States exhibit 'em abroad, I hope is no dishonour to our
nation, and I dare affirm, if we had half the encouragement in England that they have in other countries, you
might in a short time have as good dancers in England as
they have in France, though I despair of ever having as
good voices among us as they have in Italy.* These are
the two great things which travellers say we are most
deficient in. If this happens to please, we cannot rea-
sonably propose to ourselves any great advantage, considering the mighty change in setting it out, and the
extraordinary expense that attends it every day 'tis
represented. If it deserves their favour—if they are satis-

   * That is questionable. In Scotland, more especially, as in
other mountainous countries, there have been and are excellent
voices, but the absurd pride of the people cannot, except in
humble families, countenance the (imagined) degradation of
any one of their kindred appearing on a public stage, either in
the capacity of actors or singers.

fied, we venture boldly doing all we can to please 'em.
We hope the English are too generous not to encourage
so great an undertaking."

The fashionable predilection for French music began
to die away after the death of Charles, and the taste for
Italian music, which in the time of Elizabeth had been
adopted as a model by our own masters in the composition of madrigals, began towards the end of the seventeenth century gradually to gain ground. Indeed,
during Charles' lifetime the subject of the introduction
of Italian music had been entertained by the manager of
the King's Theatre. Thus:—*Pepys, 9th Sept.* 1667.—
"I fell in talk with Tom Killigrew about musick, and
he tells me that he will bring me to the best musick in
England, of which, indeed, he is master, and that is two
Italians and Mrs Yates, who, he says, is come to sing the
Italian manner as well as ever he heard any; he says
that Knipp won't take pains enough, but that she under-
stands her part so well upon the stage that no man nor
woman in the House do the like."

In November 1702, "a consort" at York buildings was
advertised in the Daily Courant, by performers lately come
from Rome, which was twice repeated, and on the 26th
of the same month another "consort" was advertised
at "Hickford's Dancing-School, by Signor Saggioni of
Venice, in which the famous Signor Gasparini, lately
arrived from Rome, will play singly on the violin." On
the first of June of the year following, the Rival Queens
was performed at Lincoln's Inn Fields, where "Signora
Francesca Margarita L'Epine will sing, being positively
the last time of her singing on the stage during her stay
in England." Notwithstanding this announcement she
continued singing more "last," and "positively last"
times during the rest of the month. This lady came
from Italy to England with a German musician named
Greber, and she seems to have been one of the first
Italian female singers, who appeared on our stage, previous to the establishment of an Italian Opera. In 1718,
she retired from the stage, having become the wife of
Dr Pepusch. Her death took place about the middle of
last century. She had a constant and formidable rival
in Mrs Tofts, an accomplished vocalist.

III                          Q

The first musical drama, which was performed after the Italian manner, was Arsinoe, Queen of Cyprus, translated from the Italian of Stanzani, of Bologna, who had written it for the theatre there in 1677. The music was arranged by Thomas Clayton, one of the Royal band, who had resided sometime in Italy. He thus prefaces the Book of the Opera :—

" The design of this Entertainment being to introduce the Italian manner of musick on the English stage, which has not been before attempted, I was oblig'd to have an Italian opera translated, in which the words, however mean in several places, suited much better with that manner of musick, than others more poetical would do.

" The style of this musick is to express the Passions, which is the soul of musick. And though the voices are not equal to the Italian, yet I have engaged the best that were to be found in England, and I have not been wanting, to the utmost of my diligence, in the instructing of them.

" The musick being in Recitative, may not, at first, meet with that general acceptation, as is to be hoped for from the audiences being better acquainted with it, but if this attempt shall, by pleasing the nobility and gentry, be a means of bringing this manner of musick to be used in my native country, I shall think all my study and pains well employed."

This opera was produced at the Theatre Royal in Drury Lane, on the 16th January 1705. Mrs Tofts played the heroine Arsinoe ; Mrs Cross, Dorisbe, Princess of the blood ; and Mrs Lyndsay, Nerina, an old nurse. The male singers were Messrs Hughs, Leveridge, and " Cook or Good." Within the subsequent four years other operas, after the same style, were produced at Drury Lane and at the Queen's Theatre in the Haymarket. The principal of these were Camilla, Clotilda, Rosamond, Love's Triumph, and Pyrrhus and Demetrius. The two last performed at the Haymarket were sung partly in Italian partly in English, there being a mixture of Italian and English singers, each of whom entertained his own native tongue. The cast of Love's Triumph was this :—

| | |
|---|---|
| Liso, an Italian Shepherd, | Signor Valentino, who sings in Italian. |
| Olinda, a Shepherd, | Signora Margarita de L'Espine. |
| Neralbo, a merry, amorous Shepherd, | Mr Leveridge. |
| Licisca, a fickle Shepherdess, | Mrs Tofts. |
| Eurillo, in love with Liso, | The Baronness. |
| Serpetta, an innocent Shepherdess, | Mrs Lyndsay. |

The Dramatis Personæ of Pyrrhus and Demetrius were—

| | |
|---|---|
| Pyrrhus, King of Epire, | Signor Cavaliero Nicolini Guinaldi. |
| Demetrius, King of Macedon, | Signor Valentino Urbani. |
| Cleartes, a Prince, | Mr Ramondon. |
| Arbantes, Captain of Guard, | Mr Turner. |
| Marius, his Son, | Signora Margarita. |
| Brennus, Servant to Deidamia, | Mr Cooke. |
| Climene, Daughter of Lysimachus, King of Thebes, | Mrs Tofts. |
| Deidamia, Sister to Pyrrhus, | The Baronness. |

The opera of Camilla was "a splendid success; it was, in the course of four years, represented sixty-four times." *Clayton's Queens of Song*, p. 10. Mrs Tofts, "by her grace, her fine voice, and her acting, achieved her greatest triumph as Camilla." The libretto was by Owen Swinney. It is understood that Addison was induced, by its success, to write Rosamond, which, although more lyrical than the others, was unsuccessful, owing, it has been asserted, to the inferior music which was composed by Clayton. On the other hand, the music of Camilla, borrowed from Marc Antonio Bononcini, was excellent. Mrs Tofts was compelled to quit the stage by an affection of the brain, which caused her to be put under restraint for some time. She however ultimately recovered, and, having realized a considerable sum, relinquished her profession, and became the wife of Joseph Smith, Esq., for many years Consul at Venice, well known to Bibliomaniacs for his rare and

valuable collection of books, which were purchased by
King George III. He died about 1771. The period of
his wife's decease, which was anterior to his, has not
been accurately ascertained. She had had a return of
her malady, which excluded her from the world. She was
alive in 1735. It has been conjectured that her un-
paralleled success as Camilla was the cause of her mental
aberration.

The first Italian Opera, sung entirely in that language,
seems to have been Etearco, "performed at y$^e$ Queen's
Theatre," also during the reign of Queen Anne. The
title page of the music in that opera bears no date.

The several writers quoted as authorities on the subject of the drama in the seventeenth century are somewhat at variance respecting the progress of Sir William
D'avenant in the early stage of his dramatic venture—
some having it that his company acted at the Cockpit
up till the time when he took possession of his new
theatre in Lincoln's Inn Fields in the Spring of 1662,
while others say they performed at Salisbury Court.
Now, it seems quite clear that both of these theatres
were occupied by him during the five years he was in
management prior to his entering the theatre at Lincoln's
Inn Fields. He opened first at the Cockpit, where in
1658 he produced his "Cruelty of the Spaniards in
Peru," and in 1659 his "History of Sir Francis Drake."
On 15th Nov. 1660 he removed to the theatre in Salisbury Court. Aubrey asserts that the Siege of Rhodes
was acted at the Cockpit, but this does not appear to
have been the case. It is believed that D'avenant's play
of the Siege was produced there; Aubrey, therefore, may
have confounded the one with the other.

Downes again, who became prompter to the Duke's
company when it went to Lincoln's Inn Fields, and who
does not appear to have known much, if anything, of
previous dramatic history, has this entry in his "Roscius
Anglicanus:"—"His company being now compleat, Sir
William, in order to prepare plays to open his theatre,
it being then a building in Lincoln's Inn Fields, re-
hearsed the first and second part of the Siege of Rhodes,
and the Wits at Apothecaries' Hall; and in Spring 1662,
opened the house with his said Plays having new Scenes

and Decorations, being the first that e'er were introduced in England." Peter Cunningham's "Hand Book of London," 8vo, 1849, informs us that the Apothecaries' Hall, Water Lane, Blackfriars, was not erected until 1670.

The second part of the Siege of Rhodes appears from Pepys to have been acted at Salisbury Court, in July 1661 :—2d, "My father writes that my uncle is by fits stupid, and like a man that is drunk, and sometines speechless. Went to Sir William D'avenant's Opera; this being the fourth day that it hath begun, and the first that I have seen it. To-day was acted the second part of the 'Siege of Rhodes.' We staid a very great while for the king and the queen of Bohemia; and by the breaking of a board over our heads, we had a great deal of dust fell into the ladies' necks and the men's haire, which made good sport. The king being come, the scene opened; which indeed is very fine and magnicent, and well acted, all but the Eunuch, who was so much out that he was hissed off the stage."

It would seem that this second part of the Siege of Rhodes was not successful, and it was accordingly withdrawn. Two days afterwards Pepys has this entry in his Diary:—July 4, "I went to the theatre, and there I saw Claracilla (the first time I ever saw it) well acted. But strange to see this house, that was to be so thronged, now empty since this opera began; and so will continue for a while I believe." Claracilla is a tragi-comedy by Thomas Killigrew, originally produced at the Cockpit.

A different fate awaited the Siege of Rhodes when the two parts were performed together at Lincoln's Inn Fields, illustrated as it was by new and appropriate scenery, dresses, and decorations. Downes gives the caste of characters thus: Betterton performed Solyman the Magnificent; Harris, Alphonso; Lilliston, Villerius (the Grand Master); Blagden, the Admiral; Mrs Davenport, Roxolana; and Mrs Saunderson, Ianthe. He adds, "all the parts were justly and excellently performed, and the play was acted twelve days together without interruption, and with great applause."

Downes himself, being desirous to try his fortune on the stage, was cast for the character of Haly in this piece,

the first day that Lincoln's Inn Fields Theatre was
opened, but the sight of the king, the Duke of York,
and many of the nobility put him into such a tremor
that he was unable to proceed.  Otway and Nat. Lee, who
also subsequently appeared upon the public boards, were
equally abashed, and could not get over the "stage
fright."

Dryden, in his Essay on Heroick Plays, in descanting
on D'avenant's desire " to introduce the examples of
moral virtue, writ in verse, and performed in recitative
music," thus observes : — " At his majesty's return,
growing bolder, as now being owned by publick authority, D'avenant reviewed his Siege of Rhodes, and
caused it to be acted as a just drama.   But, as few
here have the happiness to begin and finish any new pro-
ject, so neither did he live to make his design perfect.
There wanted the fulness of a plot, and the variety of
characters, to form it as it ought ; and, perhaps, somewhat might have been added to the treating of the stile ;
all which he would have performed with more exactness
had he pleased to have given us another work of the
same nature."

Among Flecknoe's Epigrams, 1671, is the following,
more particularly referable to the estimation in which
the play of the Siege of Rhodes was held :—

### ON THE DEATH OF SIR WM. D'AVENANT.

Now D'avenant's dead, the stage will mourn,
And all to barbarism turn,
Since he it was this latter age,
Who chiefly civilized the stage.
Not only Dedalus' arts he knew,
But even Prometheus's too,
And *living machins* made of men,
As well as dead ones for the scene ;
And if the Stage or theatre be
A little world, 'twas chiefly he
Who, Atlas-like, supported it
By force of 's industry and wit.
All this and more he did beside,
Which having perfected, he dy'd ;
If he may properly be sed
To die, whose fame will ne'er be dead.

For of his playes th' Unfortunate Lovers
The depth of tragedy discovers ;
In's Love and Honour you may see
The heighth of tragi-comedy,
And in his Wits the comic fire
In none e'er flamed or sparkled higher ;
But coming to his Siege of Rhodes,
It out-goes all the rest by odds,
And somewhat's in't that does outdo
Both ancients and the moderns too,
And him himself, as far and more
Than he all others did before.

For the story on which the Siege of Rhodes is founded the following authorities may be consulted :—" Boissarde Icones et Vitæ Sultanorum Turcicorum in Vit. Solym. 2. Thomas Artus continuation de la Histoire de Turcs, and our English History of the Turks by Knolles."

Further, the following particulars are recorded in " An Exact Chronology of the several successes of the Christians against the Turks," being the fifteenth chapter of " A New Survey of the Turkish Empire," Lond., 1664. 16mo.

" In 1480 the Turks were beaten off from the Siege of Rhodes with the loss of above 300C men.

In 1522. The Rhodes valiantly defended by the Christians against the siege of the Turks for six months. together, wherein Solyman lost, besides them that were slaine, thirty thousand that died of the Flix."

The siege of 1480 occurred during the reign of Mahomet, who " was a perfect Atheist, of no faith or religion, murdered his brethren, subdued Mentesia, and took Constantinople on the 29th May 1453, and thereby put an end to the Greek empire, and caused himself to be stiled Emperor."

The second siege was during that of Solyman, successor to his father Selymus, who had been seized " by a canker in his back, and breathed out his revengeful soul in the year 1520."

In Solyman's reign " this great empire rose to its highest pinnacle and culmination of glory. He was surnamed the Magnificent for the nobleness of his acts. He first conquered the Isle of Rhodes, defeated King

Lewis of Hungary, and slew him at Mobaez, and besieged Vienna, but in vain.  In fine, this was the potent
monarch that conquered Hungary, took Buda Strigonum,
Alba Regalis, in pretence of the right of King John and
his Orphant elected by the Hungarian nobility against
the due title of Ferdinand.  He likewise threatened
Italy with his fleets, and aided the French king by them
against Charles the Fifth, as he likewise combated the
Persian Kings, Hysmael and Tamas.  He besieged Malta
by his general Mustapha, but was there worsted.
Towards the latter end of his reign he was enjealoused
by his paramour Recotane against the noble Prince
Mustapha, his eldest son by another woman, to make
way for her children, and Mustapha strangled, as Solyman was upon a pretended expedition against the Per-
sians.  In his seventh and last expedition against Hungary he died, at the siege of Zigerb, 1566, having made
Hungary a province of Turkie."  See "A New Survey of
the Turkish Empire, History and Government com-
pleated.  Lond.  Printed by J. B. for Samuel Bolton.
1664."  16mo.  The engravings throughout this book
would seem to have been done on brass, as the title page
bears : "With several *brass pieces* lively expressing the
most eminent *Personages* concerned in this subject."

Pope in his imitation of Horace, Book II. first epistle, *
satirizing the effeminacy of the court of Charles II.,
says —

> Lely on animated Canvas stole
> The sleepy eye, that spoke the melting soul.
> No wonder then, when all was love and sport,
> The willing Muses were debauch'd at Court.
> On each enervate string they taught the note
> To pant, or tremble through an Eunuch's throat.

In explanation, Pope in a note says the last two lines
referred to the "Siege of Rhodes by Sir William
D'avenant, the first opera sung in England."

When the Siege of Rhodes was first presented to the
public at Rutland House in 1656, Mrs Coleman, wife of
Mr Edward Coleman, performed the part of Ianthe,

---

* Pope's Works, by Bowles, Vol. IV., page 185.  London,
1806.  8vo.

which stamps her as the first female who appeared on a
public stage in this country. Mr Edward Coleman was
the representative of Alphonso. In what degree of
relationship he stood to Dr Coleman, the composer of a
portion of the music of the piece, does not appear.
A Mr Charles Coleman represented Hymen in 1617, in
a masque performed in the Ladies' Hall at Deptford,
in Greenwich, 4th May, entitled Cupid's Banishment,
written by Robert White, and printed from original
MS. which formerly belonged to John Evelyn. This
performer, it is highly probable, was the Dr. himself
when a youth.

The character of Ianthe, when the Siege of Rhodes
was reproduced, with alterations and amendments, at
Lincoln's Inn Fields in 1662, was, as formerly observed,
acted by Mrs Saunderson, who afterwards became the
wife of Betterton.

The introduction of females on the stage led the young
bucks and nobles of the day, as is even now the case, to
seek their acquaintance, a course which resulted in
some honourable and many dishonourable proposals.
The most cruel of the latter class was the abduction by
the Earl of Oxford of the lady who performed Roxolana, or Roxana, as the name is frequently called in
the text of the Siege of Rhodes. The case is thus
related in Grammont's Memoirs, translated edition, London, 1809, by Miss Hobart, who had the superintend-
ence of the baths of the Duchess of York, to Miss
Temple, one of the Court ladies:—

" The Earl of Oxford fell in love with a handsome,
graceful actress, and a most excellent performer, belonging to the Duke's theatre. The part of Roxana, in a
very fashionable new play, had brought her so much
into vogue, that she ever after retained that name.
This creature being both very virtuous and very modest,
or, if you please, wonderfully obstinate, proudly rejected
the addresses and presents of the Earl of Oxford. This
resistance inflamed his passion; he had recourse to
invectives, and even to spells, but all in vain. This
disappointment had such effect upon him that he could
neither eat nor drink. This did not signify to him; but
his passion at length became so violent that he could

neither play nor smoke. In this extremity love had
recourse to Hymen.  The Earl of Oxford, one of the
first peers of the realm, is, as you know, a very handsome man : he is of the order of the Garter, the habit of
which greatly adds to an air naturally noble.   In short,
from his outward appearance, you would suppose he was
really possessed of some sense ; but as soon as you hear
him speak, you are perfectly convinced of the contrary.
This passionate lover presented her with a promise of
marriage, in due form, signed with his own hand.  She
would not, however, rely upon this, but the next day
she thought there could be no danger, when the Earl
himself came to her lodgings attended by a clergyman,
and another man for a witness.   The marriage was
accordingly solemnized with all due ceremonies in the
presence of one of her fellow-players, who attended as a
witness on her part.  You will suppose, perhaps, that
the new Countess had nothing to do but to appear at
Court according to her rank, and to display the Earl's
arms upon her carriage.  No such thing.  When examination was made concerning the marriage, it was found
to be a mere deception : it appeared that the pretended
priest was one of my lord's trumpeters, and the witness
his kettle-drummer.   The parson and his companion
never appeared after the ceremony was over, and as for
the other witness, they endeavoured to persuade her that
the Sultana Roxana might have supposed, in some part
or other of a play, that she was really married.   It was
to no purpose that the poor creature claimed the protection of the laws of God and man, both which were so
shamefully violated, as well as herself, by this infamous
imposition ; in vain did she throw herself at the King's
feet to demand justice ; she had only to rise up again
without redress ; and happy might she think herself in
obtaining a pension of a thousand crowns instead of a
dowry, and to resume the name Roxana instead of taking
that of Countess of Oxford."

There is a note upon this by the translator as follows :
—" *The Earl of Oxford.*—This was Aubrey de Vere, the
last Earl of Oxford of that name, and the twentieth and
last Earl of that family.  He was chief justice in Eyre ;
and in the reign of Charles II., lord of the bed-chamber,

privy counsellor, colonel of the royal regiment of horse guards, and lord-lieutenant of the county of Essex; and lieutenant-general of the forces in the reign of William III., and also Knight of the Garter. He died March 12, 1702, aged eighty years and upwards, and was buried in Westminster Abbey. The author of a History of the English Stage, published by Curll, 1741, 8vo, says that Mrs Marshall, a celebrated actress, more known by the name of Roxana, from acting that part, was the person deceived by the Earl of Oxford in this manner. The particulars of the story as there related do not materially vary from the present account of the transaction. A more detailed narrative of this seduction is given in Madam Dunois' Memoirs of the Court of England, part 2, p. 71. Mrs Marshall, who was the original Roxana in Lee's Rival Queens, belonged not to the Duke's but to the King's theatre. Lord Orford, I know not on what authority, has given the name of Miss Barker to this lady, a name totally unknown, I believe, in the annals of the stage."

The particulars of this affair, as given in the History of the English Stage, printed by Curll, from the papers of Thomas Betterton, 1741, shew King Charles' interference in the lady's behalf in a more amiable light, although scarcely in accordance with his general character. The Earl had made an attempt to capture the lady, as she went home one evening in her chair from the theatre, but having been apprised of his intention, she obtained a party of the King's Guards to protect her, who repulsed the assailants. "This adventure was the whole talk of the Court and town. Many parties were found both for and against her. The Fanatics cried out, saying, it was a shame they should bring up girls in the school of Venus, teaching them such airs and tricks to tempt mankind." The King remonstrated with the Earl upon his pursuit of the lady, adding, " it was so heinous, he would not, though a sovereign, indulge the thought of such an action, much more permit it to be done by a subject." This reproof caused the Earl to answer with some reserve. He said he would think no more of her; but soon after he renewed his assault, telling her it was impossible to live without her, that

her exalted virtue had inspired him with other senti-
ments, proposing to marry her in private. This bait
Roxolana greedily swallowed, her vanity inclining her to
believe the Earl sincere. In short, the Earl comes,
brings his coachman dressed like a minister, marries her,
and took her down to one of his country seats, where,
soon growing weary of her, he pulled off the mask, and,
with scorn, bid her return to the stage. Upon this, she
threw herself at the King's feet, who countenanced her
so far, that he made the Earl allow her £500 a-year;
and, as long as her son lived, would not suffer him to
marry any other lady; but, on the child's death, the
concern for so ancient a family's becoming extinct (the
Earl being the last of it), his Majesty, through great
intercession, was prevailed on to permit of the Earl's
re-marriage."

As in the several accounts of this disgraceful transaction the real name of the actress has not been given,
much speculation has arisen as to who the lady called
Roxolana really was; but the question has been so
narrowed as to rest the case between Mrs Davenport and
Mrs Marshall. Mrs Davenport was certainly the representative of Roxolana in the Siege of Rhodes, on the first
introduction of that character into the piece; and
although to connect Mrs Marshall and others with the
story of the abduction, the Roxolana of Lord Orrery's
Mustapha and the Roxana of Lee's Rival Queens have
been dragged into argument as giving the popular title
to the actress in question, Pepys sets these conjectures
at rest. Thus :—

"20th May 1662.—My wife and I by coach to the
opera, and there saw the second part of 'the Siege of
Rhodes,' but it is not so well done as when Roxalana was
there, who, it is said, is now owned by my Lord Oxford."

Besides, both Mustapha and the Rival Queens were
not acted until some time after the abduction had taken
place. Mrs Betterton was the Roxolana in the former, when
produced in April 1665. Mrs Davenport is included, by
Downes, among those ladies who were " by force of love
erept the stage," the others being Mrs Davies and Mrs
Jenning.

Lord Braybrook, the editor of Pepys' Diary, offers no opinion as to the name of the actress, but simply confines himself to a reference to the passage of Grammont. It seems pretty evident, however, that Mrs Davenport was the lady who was so sadly used.

"Hamlet" and "Love and Honour" were revived by D'avenant soon after he opened his theatre in Lincoln's Inn Fields, but the precise date has not been recorded by Downes. Mrs Davenport acted the Queen in the former, and Evandra in the latter, on which occasion it was that the King, the Duke of York, and the Earl of Oxford, presented their coronation suits to Betterton, Harris, and Price, to give greater effect to Sir William D'avenant's production. "The play," says Downes, "had a great run," and as the Earl of Oxford, in all likelihood, was frequently present, and so took the opportunity to gain the affections of Mrs Davenport, who appears to have quitted the stage within two months after the opening of the theatre. Besides the characters just named, she played Lady Ample in the Wits, a character which she had previously acted at Salisbury Court. Evelyn in his Diary has this entry:—"9th Jan. 1661-62.—I saw acted 'the third part of the Siege of Rhodes.' In this acted the fair and famous comedian called Roxalana, from the part she performed; and I think it was the last, she being taken to be the Earl of Oxford's *miss* (as at this time they began to call lewd women). It was in recitative music." Evelyn means of course the second part of the Siege of Rhodes. There never was a third part.

Assuming that Mrs Davenport was the Roxolana, of which there scarcely can be any reasonable doubt, she would seem to have been a superior and very attractive actress. Thus Pepys, 18th Feb. 1661-62, remarks, that having gone to the opera to see D'avenant's "Law against Lovers," the play was "well performed, especially the little girl's (whom I never saw act before) dancing and singing; and were it not for her, the loss of Roxalana would spoil the house."

Whether Mrs Davenport, after the great affliction which had befallen her, ever again appeared on the stage has been questioned.

In January 1663 a Mrs Davenport was among the

company at Lincoln's Inn Fields. Her name appears as Camilla in Tuke's Adventures of five hours.

Again, on 2d March 1667, we have at the King's theatre a Mrs E. Davenport in the character of Sabina, and Mrs F. Davenport in the character of Flavia, in Dryden's Secret Love, or the Maiden Queen. In October in the same year was produced at the same theatre the Earl of Orrery's "Black Prince." These ladies figure among the Dramatis Personæ as: Valeria, *disguised*, F. Damport; Lady, Betty Damport.

There is no evidence, however, to show that either or any of those ladies was the original Mrs Davenport, who acted in D'avenant's company at Salisbury Court, and who, as the first of his principal actresses, resided in his house, the others being Mrs Saunderson, Mrs Davies, and Mrs Long. That her Christian name was Elizabeth it has been understood, but it does not seem at all probable that on her resumption of the calling of an actress, she would have consented to appear in such insignificant parts as Sabina or a Lady-attendant, the more so as the Maiden Queen was frequently patronized by the King, who had given it its title, and so called it "his own" play. Neither could Mrs Frances Davenport, the representative of Flavia, and Valeria (disguised as her own brother)— also, perhaps, of Camilla—have been the original Mrs Davenport, inasmuch as these characters are simply in the line technically called "Walking Lady."

To associate Mrs Ann Marshall's name with the case of the Earl of Oxford is an argument untenable. Mrs Marshall was principal actress for many years in the King's company, where she certainly played Roxana in the Rival Queens. But that was in 1677. She was never a member of Sir William D'avenant's company.

Downes says, "the following came not into the company till after they had begun in the new theatre in 1663." Among these were Mrs Ann and Mrs Rebecca Marshall. That was Killigrew's company, and in all likelihood this was the first appearance of the Marshalls.

"Mrs Ann Marshall was the elder sister, and the great actress. Previously to the publication of Pepys' Diary little was known of Mrs Rebecca Marshall."— *Genneste's English Stage.*

The latter engaged in Court intrigues, as Pepys thus records: "7th April 1668. Mrs Knipp tells me that my Lady Castlemaine is mightly in love with Hart, of their house; and he is much with her in private, and she goes to him, and do give him many presents; and that the thing is most certain, and Bech Meadale only privy to it, and the means of bringing them together, which is a very odd thing; and by this means she is even with the King's love to Mrs Davis."

Sir Peter Leycester states in his History of Cheshire that "the two famous woman-actors in London" were daughters of —— Marshall, chaplain to Lord Gerard of Bromley, by Elizabeth, a natural daughter of John Dutton of Dutton. Sir Peter had married a daughter of Lord Gerard.

Edward Hyde, Earl of Clarendon, to whom the second and later editions of this piece have been dedicated, was, "for his comprehensive knowledge of mankind, styled the chancellor of human nature. His character at this distance of time may, and ought to be impartially considered. His designing or blinded contemporaries heaped the most unjust abuse upon him. The subsequent age, when the partisans of prerogative were at least the loudest, if not the most numerous, smit with a work that deified their martyr, have been unbounded in their encomium."—*Catalogue of Noble Authors*, vol. ii., p. 18. Lord Orford, who professes to steer a middle course, and separate his great virtues as a man from his faults as a historian, acknowledges that he possessed almost every virtue of a minister which could make his character venerable. He died in exile in the year 1674. *See also Introduction to Albovine in our 1st volume.*

The music of the Siege of Rhodes has been lost to us, but that of Clotilda, Camilla, and Etearco, are still extant, and copies are in the library of one of the editors of the present series.

THE PERSONS REPRESENTED,

| | |
|---|---|
| SOLYMAN, | The Magnificent. |
| PIRRHUS, | Visier Bassa. |
| MUSTAPHA, | Bassa. |
| RUSTAN, | Bassa. |
| HALY, | Eunuch Bassa. |
| VILLERIUS, | Grand Master of Rhodes. |
| ALPHONSO, | A Cicilian Duke. |
| ADMIRAL | Of Rhodes. |
| HIGH MARSHAL, | Wife to Solyman. |
| ROXOLANA, | Wife to Alphonso. |
| IANTHE, | Wife to Alphonso. |
| WOMEN, | Attendants to Roxolana. |
| WOMEN, | Attendants to Ianthe. |
| FOUR PAGES, | Attendants to Roxolana. |

*The Scene:* RHODES.

# THE RIGHT HONOURABLE

## THE EARL OF CLARENDON,

### LORD HIGH CHANCELLOR OF ENGLAND, &c.

MY LORD,—Though poems have lost much of their ancient value, yet I will presume to make this a present to your lordship; and the rather, because poems (if they have anything precious in them) do, like jewels, attract a greater esteem when they come into the possession of great persons, than when they are in ordinary hands.

The excuse which men have had for dedication of books, has been to protect them from the malice of readers: but a defence of this nature was fitter for your forces, when you were early known to learned men (and had no other occasion for your abilities but to vindicate authors) than at this season, when you are of extraordinary use to the whole nation.

Yet when I consider how many, and how violent they are who persecute dramatic poetry, I will then rather call this a Dedication than a Present; as not intending by it to pass any kind of obligation, but to receive a great benefit; since I cannot be safe unless I am shelter'd behind your lordship.

Your name is so eminent in the justice which you convey, through all the different members of this great empire, that my Rhodians seem to enjoy a better harbour in the pacific Thames, than they had on the Mediterranean; and I have brought Solyman to be arraign'd at your tribunal, where you are the censor of his civility and magnificence.

Dramatic poetry meets with the same persecution now, from such who esteem themselves the most refin'd and civil, as it ever did from the barbarous. And yet whilst those virtuous enemies deny Heroic Plays to the gentry, they entertain the people with a seditious Farce of their own counterfeit gravity. But I hope you will not be unwilling to receive (in this poetical dress)

neither the besieg'd nor the besiegers, since they come
without their vices: for as others have purg'd the stage
from corruptions of the art of the drama, so I have endeavour'd to cleanse it from the corruption of manners; nor
have I wanted care to render the ideas of greatness and
virtue pleasing and familiar.

In old Rome the magistrates did not only protect but
exhibit plays; and not long since, the two wise Cardi-
nals* did kindly entertain the great images, represented
in tragedy by Monsieur Corneille.  My Lord, it proceeds
from the same mind, not to be pleas'd with Princes on
the stage, and not to affect them in the throne; for those
are ever most inclin'd to break the mirror, who are unwilling to see the images of such as have just authority
over their guilt.

In this poem I have reviv'd the remembrance of that
desolation which was permitted by Christian princes,
when they favour'd the ambition of such as defended
the diversity of religions (begot by the factions of learning) in Germany; whilst those who would never admit
learning into their empire (lest it should meddle with
their religion, and entangle it with controversy) did
make Rhodes defenceless; which was the only fortify'd
academy in Christendom, where divinity and arms were
equally profess'd.  I have likewise, for variety, softened
the martial encounters between Solyman and the Rhodians,
with intermingling the conjugal virtues of Alphonso
and Ianthe.

If I should proceed, and tell your Lordship of what
use theatres have anciently been, and may be now, by
heightening the characters of valour, temperance, natural
justice, and complacency to Government, I should fall
into the ill manners and indiscretion of ordinary Dedi-
cators, who go about to instruct those from whose abilities they expect protection.  The apprehension of this
error makes me hasten to crave pardon for what has
been already said by, MY LORD, Your Lordship's most
humble and most obedient Servant,

                                    *Will. D'avenant.*

* Richelieu and Mazarine.

# THE SIEGE OF RHODES.

*The ornament which encompass'd the scene, consisted of several columns of gross rustic work; which bore up a large freese. In the middle of the freese was a compartiment, wherein was written* RHODES. *The compartiment was supported by divers habili-ments of war; intermix'd with the military ensigns of those several nations who were famous for defence of that island; which were the* French, Germans, *and* Spaniards, *the* Italians, Avergnois, *and* Eng-lish. *The renown of the English valour made the Grand Master Villerius to select their station to be most frequently commanded by himself. The prin-cipal enrichment of the freese was a crimson drapery, whereon several trophies of arms were fixt, those on the right hand representing such as are chiefly in use amongst the western nations; together with the proper cognizance of the order of the* Rhodian *knights; and on the left, such as are most esteem'd in the eastern countries; and on an antique shield the crescent of the* Ottomans.

### The Scene before the First Entry.

*The curtain being drawn up, a lightsome sky appear'd, discovering a maritime coast, full of craggy rocks and high cliffs, with several verdures naturally grow-ing upon such situations; and, afar off, the true prospect of the City of* RHODES, *when it was in prosperous estate; with so much view of the gardens and hills about it, as the narrowness of the room could allow the scene. In that part of the horizon, terminated by the sea, was represented the* Turkish Fleet, *making towards a promontory, some few miles distant from the town.*

*The* ENTRY *is prepared by Instrumental Music.*

The First ENTRY.

*Enter* ADMIRAL.

ADMIR. Arm, arm, Villerius, arm!
　Thou hast no leisure to grow old ;
Those now must feel thy courage warm,
　Who think thy blood is cold.

*Enter* VILLERIUS.

VILL. Our admiral from sea !
What storm transporteth thee ?
Or bringst thou storms that can do more
Than drive an admiral on shore ?
　ADM. Arm, arm ! the Bassa's fleet appears ;
To Rhodes his course from Chios steers ;
Her shady wings to distant sight
Spread like the curtains of the night.
Each squadron thicker and still darker grows ;
The fleet like many floating forests shows.
　VILL. Arm, arm ! Let our drums beat
To all our out-guards, a retreat ;
And to our main-guards add
Files double lin'd from the parade.
Send horse to drive the fields ;
Prevent what rip'ning summer yields.
To all the foe would save
Set fire, or give a secret grave.
　ADM. I'll to our gallies haste,
Untackle ev'ry mast ;
Hale 'em within the pier,
To range and chain 'em there,
And then behind St Nic'las cliffs
Shelter our brigants, land our skiffs.
　VILL. Our field and bulwark-cannon mount
　　with hast !
Fix to their blocks their brazen bodies fast !

Whilst to their foes their iron entrails fly :
Display our colours, raise our standard high !
[Exit Adm.

Enter ALPHONSO.

ALPH. What various noises do mine ears invade,
And have a concert of confusion made ? *
The shriller trumpet, and tempestuous drum :
The deaf'ning clamour from the cannon's womb,
Which through the air like sudden thunder breaks,
Seems calm to soldier's shouts, and women's shrieks.
What danger, Rev'rend Lord, does this portend ?
  VILL. Danger begins what must in honour end.
  ALPH. What Vizards does it wear ?
  VILL. Such, gentle Prince,
As cannot fright, but yet must warn you hence.
What can to Rhodes more fatally appear
Than the bright Crescents which those Ensigns
    wear ?
Wise emblems that encreasing Empire show ;
Which must be still in nonage and still grow.
All these are yet but the fore-running van
Of the prodigious gross† of Solyman.
  ALPH. Pale shew those crescents to our bloody
    cross ;
Sink not the western kingdoms in our loss ?
Will not the Austrian eagle moult her wings ;
That long hath hover'd o'er the Gallic kings ?
Whose lillies too will wither when we fade,
And th' English lion shrink into a shade.
  VILL. Thou seest not, whilst so young and
    guiltless too,
That Kings mean seldom what their statesmen do ;

---

\* " KING ASH. But stay, what sound is this invades our ears ?
KING'S PHYS. Sure 'tis the music of the moving spheres "
Buckingham's Rehearsal, Act 5. Scene 1.
† The main body.

Who measure not the compass of a crown
To fit the head that wears it, but their own ;
Still hind'ring peace, because they stewards are,
Without account, to that wild spender, war.

*Enter* HIGH MARSHAL OF RHODES.*

MAR. Still Christian wars they will pursue, and
  boast
Unjust successes gain'd whilst Rhodes is lost :
Whilst we build monuments of death, to shame
Those who forsook us in the chase of fame.

  ALPH. We will endure the colds of Court-
    delays ;
Honour grows warm in airy vests of praise.
On rocky Rhodes we will like rocks abide.

  VILL. Away, away, and hasten to thy bride !
'Tis scarce a month since from thy nuptial rites
Thou cam'st to honour here our Rhodian knights :
To dignify our sacred annual feast :
We love to lodge, not t'entomb a guest.
Honour must yield, where reason should prevail.
Aboard, aboard ! and hoyse up ev'ry sail
That gathers any wind for Sicily !

  MAR. Men lose their virtue's pattern, losing
    thee.
Thy bride doth yield her sex no less a light,
But, thy life gone, will set in endless night.
Ye must like stars shine long ere ye expire.†

  ALPH. Honour is colder virtue set on fire :
My honour lost, her love would soon decay :
Here for my tomb or triumph I will stay.
My sword against proud Solyman 1 draw,
His cursed prophet, and his sensual law.

  * In the first edition, there being no entrance of the High
Marshal, Villerius speaks the four following lines set down for
that dignitary.
  † These four lines are also spoken by Villerius.

CHORUS.

Our swords against proud Solyman we draw,
His cursed prophet, and his sensual law. [*Exeunt.*

*Enter* IANTHE, MELOSILE, MADINA (*her two women*)
*bearing two open Caskets with Jewels.**

IANTH. To Rhodes this fatal fleet her course does
   bear.
Can I have love, and not discover fear ?
When he, in whom my plighted heart doth live
      (Whom Hymen gave me in reward
      Of vows, which he with favour heard
And is the greatest gift he e'er can give)
Shall in a cruel Siege imprison'd be,
And I, whom love has bound, have liberty ?
Away ! Let's leave our flourishing abodes
In Sicily, and fly to with'ring Rhodes.
   MELO. Will you convert to instruments of war,
To things which to our sex so dreadful are,
Which terror add to death's detested face,
These ornaments which should your beauty grace ?
   MAD. Beauty laments ! and this exchange
      abhors ;
      Shall all these gems in arms be spent
      Which were by bounteous Princes sent
To pay the valour of your ancestors ?
   IANTH. If by their sale my lord may be
      redeem'd,
Why should they more than trifles be esteem'd,
Vainly secur'd with iron bars and locks ?
They are the spawn of shells, and warts of rocks.
   MAD. All, Madam, all ? Will you from all depart ?
   IANTH. Love a consumption learns from chymists'
      art.

* This dialogue, down to "else lost with thee," does not
occur in the first edition, the Chorus by Soldiers immediately
following the exit of Alphonso and Villerius.

Saphires and harder di'monds must be sold ₁
And turn'd to softer and more current gold.
With gold we cursed powder may prepare,
Which must consume in smoke and thinner air.
 MELO. Thou idol-love, I'll worship thee no more,
Since thou dost make us sorrowful and poor.
 IANTH. Go, seek out cradles, and with child-
  hood dwell !
   Where you may still be free
    From love's self-flattery,
And never hear mistaken lovers tell
Of blessings, and of joys in such extremes
As never are possest but in our dreams.
They woo apace, and hasten to be sped ;
And praise the quiet of the marriage-bed :
But mention not the storms of grief and care
   When love does them surprize
    With sudden jealousies,
Or they are sever'd by ambitious war.
 MAD. Love may perhaps the foolish please :
   But he shall quickly leave my heart
    When he persuades me to depart
From such a horde of precious things as these.
 IANTH. Send out to watch the wind ! with the
  first gale
I'll leave thee Sicily, and, hoysing sail,
Steer strait to Rhodes.   For love and I must be
Preserved, Alphonso, or else lost with thee.
          [*Exeunt.*

CHORUS.

*By Soldiers of several Nations.*

 1. Come, ye termagant Turks,
  If your Bassa dares land ye,
  Whilst the wine bravely works
   Which was brought us from Candy.

2. Wealth, the least of our care is,
  For the poor ne'er are undone ;
Avous, Monsieur of Paris,
  To the back-swords of London.

3. Diego, thou, in a trice,
  Shalt advance thy lean belly ;
For their hens and their rice
  Make Pillau like a jelly.

4. Let 'em land fine and free ;
  For my cap though an old one,
Such a turbant shall be,
  Thou wilt think it a gold one.

5. It is seven to one odds
  They had safer sail'd by us :
Whilst our wine lasts in Rhodes
  They shall water at Chios.

*End of the first entry.*

*The* SCENE *is changed, and the* CITY RHODES *appears
beleagur'd at sea and land.*
*The* ENTRY *is again prepar'd by instrumental music.*

The Second ENTRY.

*Enter* VILLERIUS *and* ADMIRAL.

ADM. The blood of Rhodes grows cold : life
  must expire !
VILL. The Duke still warms it with his
  valour's fire !
ADM. If he has much in honour's presence
  done,
Has sav'd our ensigns, or has others won,
Then he but well by your example wrought ;
Who well in honour's school his childhood taught.
VILL. The foe three moons tempestuously has
  spent

Where we will never yield nor he relent ;
Still we but raise what must be beaten down,
Defending walls, yet cannot keep the town ;
Vent'ring last stakes where we can nothing win ;
And, shutting slaughter out, keep famine in.

 ADM. How oft and vainly Rhodes for succour
  waits
From triple diadems, and scarlet hats ?
Rome keeps her gold, cheaply her warriors pays,
At first with blessings, and at last with praise.

 VILL. By armies, stow'd in fleets, exhausted
  Spain
Leaves half her land unplough'd, to plough the
 main ;
And still would more of the old world subdue,
As if unsatisfied with all the new.

 ADM. France strives to have her lillies grow
  as fair
In other realms as where they native are.

 VILL. The English lion ever loves to change
His walks, and in remoter forests range.

CHORUS.

All gaining vainly from each others' loss ;
Whilst still the crescent drives away the cross.

*Enter* ALPHONSO.

ALPH. 1. How bravely fought the fiery French,
   Their bulwark being stormed !
   The colder Almans kept their trench,
   By more than valour warm'd.

  2. The grave Italians paus'd and fought,
   The solemn Spaniards too ;
   Study'ng more deaths than could be
    wrought
   By what the rash could do.

3. Th' Avergnian colours high were rais'd,
    Twice tane, and twice reliev'd.
Our foes, like friends to valour, prais'd
    The mischiefs they receiv'd.

4. The cheerful English got renown;
    Fought merrily and fast:
'Tis time, they cry'd, to mow them down,
    War's harvest cannot last.

5. If death be rest, here let us die,
    Where weariness is all
We daily get by victory,
    Who must by famine fall.

6. Great Solyman is landed now;
    All fate he seems to be;
And brings those tempests in his brow
    Which he deserv'd at sea.

VILL. He can at most but once prevail,
    Though arm'd with nations that were
      brought by more
Gross gallies then would serve to hale
    This island to the Lycian shore.
ADM. Let us apace do worthily, and give
Our story length, though long we cannot live.

### CHORUS.

So greatly do, that being dead,
    Brave wonders may be wrought
By such as shall our story read,
    And study how we fought. [*Exeunt.*

*Enter* SOLYMAN, PIRRHUS.

SOLY. What sudden halt hath stay'd thy swift
    renown,
O'er-running kingdoms, stopping at a town?
He that will win the prize in honour's race,
Must nearer to the goal still mend his pace.

If age thou feel'st the active camp forbear ;
In sleepy cities rest, the caves of fear.
Thy mind was never valiant, if, when old,
Thy courage cools because thy blood is cold,
   PIR. How can ambitious manhood be exprest
More than by marks of our disdain of rest?
What less than toils incessant can, despite
Of cannon, raise these mounts to castle-height ?
Or less than utmost or unwearied strength
Can draw these lines of batt'ry to that length ?
   SOLY. The toils of ants, and mole-hills rais'd in
     scorn
Of labour, to be levell'd with a spurn.
These are the Pyramids that shew your pains ;
But of your armies' valour, where remains
One trophy to excuse a Bassa's boast ?
   PIR. Valour may reckon what she bravely lost ;
Not from successes all her count does raise :
By life well lost we gain a share of praise.
If we in danger's glass all valour see,
And death the farthest step of danger be,
Behold our mount of bodies made a grave ;
And prise our loss by what we scorn'd to save.
   SOLY. Away ! range all the camp for an assault ;
Tell them they tread in graves who make a halt.
Fat slaves, who have been lull'd to a disease,
Cramm'd out of breath, and crippled by their
     ease !
Whose active fathers leapt o'er walls too high
For them to climb : Hence from my anger fly !
Which is too worthy for thee, being mine,
And must be quench'd by Rhodian blood or thine.
                [*Exit Pirrhus, bowing.*
In honour's orb the Christians shine ;
   Their light in war does still increase ;
Though oft misled by mists of wine,
   Or blinder love, the crime of peace.

Bold in adult'ries frequent change ;
　And ev'ry loud expensive vice ;
Ebbing out wealth by ways as strange
　As it flow'd in by avarice.
Thus vilely they dare live, and yet dare die.
　If courage be a virtue, 'tis allow'd
But to those few on whom our crowns rely,
　And is condemn'd as madness in the crowd.

*Enter* MUSTAPHA, IANTHE *veil'd.*

MUSTA. Great Sultan, hail ! though here at land
Lost fools in opposition stand ;
Yet thou at sea dost all command.
　SOLY. What is it thou wouldst shew, and yet
　　dost shroud ?
　MUSTA. I bring the morning pictur'd in a cloud ;*
A wealth more worth than all the sea does hide,
Or courts display in their triumphant pride.
　SOLY. Thou seem'st to bring the daughter of the
　　night ;
And giv'st her many stars to make her bright.
Dispatch my wonder and relate her story.
　MUSTA. 'Tis full of fate, and yet has much of glory.
A squadron of our gallies that did ply
West from this coast met two of Sicily,
Both fraught to furnish Rhodes, we gave 'em chase,
And had, but for our number, met disgrace.
For, grappling, they maintain'd a bloody fight,
Which did begin with day and end with night.
And though this bashful lady then did wear
Her face still veil'd, her valour did appear :
She urg'd their courage when they boldly fought,
And many shun'd the dangers, which she sought.

* " VOLCIUS. Can vulgar vestments high-born beauty shroud ?
　　　　　Thou bring'st the morning pictur'd in a cloud.
BAYES. The morning pictur'd in a cloud ! A gadzookers, what
　a conceit is there.″
　　　　　*Buckingham's Rehearsal, Act 3, Scene 5.*

SOLY. Where are the limits thou would'st set for
    praise ?
Or to what height wilt thou thy wonder raise ?
  MUSTA. This is Ianthe, the Sicilian flower,
Sweeter than buds unfolded in a shower,
Bride to Alphonso, who in Rhodes so long
The theme has been of each heroic song ;
And she for his relief those gallies fraught ;
Both stow'd with what her dow'r and jewels
    bought.
  SOLY. O wond'rous virtue of a Christian wife !
Advent'ring life's support, and then her life
To save her ruin'd Lord.   Bid her unveil !
                          [*Ianthe steps back.*
  IANTH. It were more honour, Sultan, to assail
A public strength against thy forces bent,
Then to unwall this private tenement,
To which no monarch, but my lord, has right ;
Nor will it yield to treaty or to might :
Where heaven's great law defends him from surprise :
This curtain only opens to his eyes.
  SOLY. If beauty veil'd so virtuous be,
'Tis more than Christian husbands know ;
Whose ladies wear their faces free,
  Which they to more than husbands show.
  IANTH. Your Bassa swore, and by his dreadful
    law,
None but my lord's dear hand this veil should
    draw ;
And that to Rhodes I should conducted be,
To take my share of all his destiny
      Else I had quickly found
      Sure means to get some wound,
Which would, in death's cold arms,
  My honour instant safety give
From all those rude alarms,
  Which keep it waking whilst I live.

SOLY. Hast thou engag'd our prophet's plight,
To keep her beauty from my sight,
And to conduct her person free,
To harbour with mine enemy ?
MUSTA. Virtue constrain'd the privilege I gave :
Shall I for sacred virtue pardon crave ?
SOLY. I envy not the conquests of thy sword :
    Thrive still in wicked war ;
    But, slave, how did'st thou dare
In virtuous love thus to transcend thy lord ?
Thou did'st thy utmost virtue show :
    Yet somewhat more does rest,
    Not yet by thee exprest ;
Which virtue left for me to do.
Thou great example of a Christian wife,
Enjoy thy lord, and give him happy life.
    Thy gallies with their freight,
    For which the hungry wait,
Shall strait to Rhodes conducted be ;
And as thy passage to him shall be free,
So both may safe return to Sicily.
IANTH. May Solyman be ever far
From impious honours of the war ;
Since worthy to receive renown
From things repair'd not overthrown,
And when in peace his virtue thrives,
Let all the race of loyal wives
Sing this his bounty to his glory,
And teach their princes by his story.
Of which, if any victors be,
Let them, because he conquer'd me,
Strip cheerfully each others' brow,
And at his feet their laurel throw.
SOLY. Strait to the port her gallies steer !
Then hale the sentry at the pier.
And though our flags ne'er used to bow,
They shall do virtue homage now.

Give fire still as she passes by,
And let our streamers lower fly !
                    [*Exeunt several ways.*

### CHORUS OF WOMEN.

1. Let us live, live ! for being dead,
            The pretty spots,
            Ribbands and knots,
And the fine French dress for the head,
            No lady wears upon her
            In the cold, cold, bed of honour.
Beat down our grottos, and hew down our bowers,
Dig up our arbours, and root up our flowers !
Our gardens are bulwarks and bastions become :
Then hang up our lutes, we must sing to the drum.
            3. Our patches and our curls,
                    So exact in each station,
            Our powders and our purls*
                    Are now out of fashion.
Hence with our needles, and give us your spades ;
We, that were ladies, grow coarse as our maids.
Our coaches have drove us to balls at the Court,
We now must drive barrows to earth up the port.
            *The End of the Second Entry.*

*The further part of the Scene is open'd and a Royal
    pavilion appears display'd, representing Solyman's
    Imperial throne ; and about it are discern'd the
    quarters of his Bassas and inferior officers.*

    *The* ENTRY *is prepared by Instrumental Music.*

### The Third ENTRY.

*Enter* SOLYMAN, PIRRHUS, MUSTAPHA.

SOLY. Pirrhus, draw up our army wide !
        Then from the gross two strong reserves
            divide :
        * Embroidered and puckered borders of lace.

And spread the wings
As if we were to fight,
In the lost Rhodians' sight,
With all the western Kings!
Each wing with Janizaries line;
The right and left to Haly's sons assign;
The gross to Zangiban.
The main artillery
With Mustapha shall be:
Bring thou the rear, we lead the van!
PIR. It shall be done as early as the dawn,
As if the figure by thy hand were drawn.
MUSTA. We wish that we, to ease thee, could prevent
All thy commands, by guessing thy intent.
SOLY. These Rhodians, who of honour boast,
A loss excuse, when bravely lost:
Now they may bravely lose their Rhodes,
Which never play'd against such odds.
To-morrow let them see our strength and weep
Whilst they their want of losing blame;
Their valiant folly strives too long to keep
What might be render'd without shame.
PIR. 'Tis well our valiant prophet did
In us not only loss forbid,
But has conjoin'd us still to get.
Empire must move apace,
When she begins the race,
And apter is for wings than feet.
MUSTA. They vainly interrupt our speed,
And civil reason lack,
To know they should go back
When we determine to proceed.
PIR. When to all Rhodes our army does appear
Shall we then make a sudden halt,
And give a general assault?

SOLY. Pirrhus not yet, Ianthe being there :
Let them our valour by our mercy prize.
　The respite of this day
　To virtuous love shall pay
A debt long due for all my victories.
MUSTA. If virtuous beauty can attain such grace
　　Whilst she a captive was, and hid,
　　What wisdom can his love forbid
　　When virtue's free, and beauty shews her
　　　face ?
SOLY. 　Dispatch a trumpet to the town ;
　　Summon Ianthe to be gone
　Safe with her lord !　When both are free
　And in their course to Sicily,
　　　Then　Rhodes　shall　for　that　valour
　　　mourn
　　Which stops the haste of our return.
PIR. Those that in Grecian quarries wrought,
And Pioneers from Lycia brought,
Who like a nation in a throng appear,
So great their number is, are landed here :
Where shall they work ?
　SOLY. Upon Philermus' hill.
There, ere this moon her circle fills with days,
They shall, by punisht sloth and cherish'd skill,
　A spacious palace in a castle raise :
A neighbourhood within the Rhodians' view ;
Where, if my anger cannot them subdue,
My patience shall out-wait them, whilst they long
Attend to see weak Princes make them strong :
There I'll grow old, and die too, if they have
The secret art to fast me to my grave.
　　　　　　　　　　　　　　[Exeunt.

*The Scene is chang'd to that of the Town besieg'd.*

*Enter* VILLERIUS, ADMIRAL, ALPHONSO, IANTHE.

VILL. When we, Ianthe, would this act commend,
   We know no more how to begin
   ·Than we should do, if we were in,
How suddenly to make an end.
 ADM. What love was yours which these strong
    bars of fate
   Were all to weak to separate?
   Which seas and storms could not divide,
   Nor all the dreadful Turkish pride?
   Which pass'd secure, though not unseen,
Even double guards of death that lay between.
 VILL. What more could honour for fair virtue do?
What could Alphonso venture more for you?
 ADM. With wonder and with shame we must
    confess
All we ourselves can do for Rhodes, is less.
 VILL. Nor did your love and courage act alone.
Your bounty too has no less wonders done.
And for our guard you have brought wisely down
A troop of virtues to defend the town :
The only troop that can a town defend,
Which heav'n before for ruin did intend.
 ADM. Look here, ye western monarchs, look with
    shame,
   Who fear not a remote, though common foe !
  The cabinet of one illustrious dame
   Does more than your exchequers join'd
    did do.
 ALPH. Indeed I think, Ianthe, few
    So young and flourishing as you,
    Whose beauties might so well adorn
    The jewels which by them are worn,
    Did ever muskets for them take,
    Nor of their pearls did bullets make.

IANTH. When you, my Lord, are shut up
          here,
       Expence of treasure must appear
       So far from bounty, that, alas!
       It covetous advantage was:
       For with small cost I sought to save
       Even all the treasure that I have.
Who would not all her trifling jewels give,
Which but from number can their worth derive,
If she could purchase or redeem with them
          One great inestimable gem?
  ADM.  O ripe perfection in a breast so young!
  VILL. Virtue has tun'd her heart and wit
          her tongue.
  ADM.  Though Rhodes no pleasure can allow,
       I dare secure the safety of it now;
       All will so labour to save you,
       As that will save the city too.
IANTH. Alas! the utmost I have done
       More than a just reward has won,
If by my lord and you it be but thought,
I had the care to serve him as I ought.
  VILL. Brave duke, farewell! the scouts for
          orders wait,
       And the parade does fill,
  ALPH. Great Master, I'll attend your pleasure
          strait,
       And strive to serve your will.
                    [*Exeunt Vill., Adm.*
       Ianthe, after all this praise
       Which fame so fully to you pays,
       For that which all the world beside
       Admires you, I alone must chide.
       Are you that kind and virtuous wife,
       Who thus expose your husband's life?
       The hazards, both at land and sea,
         Through which so boldly thou hast run,

Did more assault and threaten me,
  · Than all the Sultan could have done.
Thy dangers, could I them have seen,
Would not to me have dangers been,
But certain death.   Now thou art here
A danger worse than death I fear.
Thou hast, Ianthe, honour won,
But mine, alas, will be undone :
For as thou valiant wer't for me,
I shall a coward grow for thee.

    IANTH. Take heed, Alphonso, for this care of me,
        Will to my fame injurious be ;
Your love will brighter by it shine,
        But it eclipses mine.
Since I would here before, or with you fall,
Death needs but beckon when he means to call.

    ALPH. Ianthe, even in this you shall command
        And this my strongest passion guide ;
        Your virtue will not be denied :
It could even Solyman himself withstand ;
        To whom it did so beauteous show :
        It seem'd to civilize a barb'rous foe.
        Of this your strange escape, Ianthe say,
        Briefly the motive and the way.

    IANTH. Did I not tell thee how we fought
        How I was taken and how brought
        Before great Solyman ? but there
        I think we interrupted were.

    ALPH. Yes, but we will not be so here,
        Should Solyman himself appear.

    IANTH. It seems that what the Bassa of me said,
Had some respect and admiration bred
In Solyman ; and this to me encreast
The jealousies which honour did suggest.
All that of Turks and Tyrants I had heard,
But that I fear'd not death, I should have fear'd.
I, to excuse my voyage, urg'd my love

To your high worth ; which did such pity move,
That straight his usage did reclaim my fear.
He seem'd in civil France ; and monarch there :
For soon my person, gallies, freight, were free
By his command.
    ALPH. O wondrous enemy !
    IANTH. These are the smallest gifts his bounty
        knew.
    ALPH. What could he give you more ?
    IANTH. He gave me you ;
And you may homeward now securely go
Through all his Fleet.
    ALPH. But honour says not so. *
    IANTH. If that forbid it, you shall never see
        That 1 and that will disagree.
        Honour will speak the same to me.
    ALPH. This generous Turk amazes me, my dear!
        How long, Ianthe, stay'd you there ?
    IANTH. Two days with Mustapha.
    ALPH. How do you say ?
        Two days, and two whole nights ? alas !
    IANTH. That it, my Lord, no longer was,
        Is such a mercy, as too long I stay,
        Ere at the altar thanks to Heav'n I pay.
    ALPH. To Heav'n, confession should prepare the
    way.                 [*Exit Ianthe.*
She is all harmony, and fair as light,
But brings me discord, and the clouds of night.
And Solyman does think Heaven's joys to be
In women not so fair as she.
'Tis strange ! Dismiss so fair an enemy !
She was his own by right of war,
We are his dogs, and such as she, his angels are.

    * VOLS. " Shall I to honour or to love give way ?
       Go on, cries honour ; tender love says nay."
           *Buckingham's Rehearsal, Act 3, Scene 5.*

O wondrous Turkish chastity!
Her gallies, freight, and those to send
　　　Into a town which he would take!
Are we besieg'd then by a friend?
　　　Could honour such a present make,
　　　Then when his honour is at stake?
Against itself, does honour booty play?
　　　We have the liberty to go away!
Strange above miracle! But who can say
　　　If in his hands we once should be
What would become of her? For what of me,
　　　Though love is blind, ev'n love may see.
　　　Come back my thoughts, you must not
　　　　　rove!
　　　For sure Ianthe does Alphonso love!
Oh Solyman, this mystic act of thine,
　　　Does all my quiet undermine:
　　　But on thy troops, if not on thee,
This sword my cure, and my revenge shall be.
　　　　　　　　　　　　　　[*Exit.*

　　　*The Scene Changes to Solyman's Camp.*

　　　*Enter* ROXOLANA, PIRRHUS, RUSTAN.*

RUST. You come from sea as Venus came before;
And seem that goddess, but mistake her shore.

PIR. Her temple did in fruitful Cyprus stand;
The Sultan wonders why in Rhodes you land.

RUST. And by your sudden voyage he doth fear
The tempest of your passion drove you here.

ROX. Rustan, I bring more wonder than I find;
And it is more than humour bred that wind
　　　Which with a forward gale
　　　Did make me hither sail.

RUST. He does your forward jealousy reprove.

* There is no change of scene in the first edition, nor is this
entrance, and dialogue ending " himself dares say," but the
previous scene terminates the Third Entry with the " Chorus
of Men and Women."

Rox. Yet jealousy does spring from too much
  love ;
  If mine be guilty of excess,
  I dare pronounce it shall grow less.
. Pir. You boldly threaten more than we dare hear.
Rox. That which you call your duty is your fear.
Rust. We have some valour or our wounds are
  feign'd.
Rox. What has your valour from the Rhodians
  gain'd ?
Unless, Ianthe, as a prize, you boast ;
Who now has got that heart which I have lost.
Brave conquest, where the taker's self is taken !
  And, as a present, I
  Bring vainly, ere I die,
That heart to him which he has now forsaken.
Rust. Whispers of Eunuchs, and by Pages
  brought
To Lycia, you have up to story wrought.
Rox. Lead to the Sultan's tent. Pirrhus, away !
For I dare hear what he himself dares say.

   Chorus *of Men and Women.*

Men. Ye wives all that are, and wives would be,
  Unlearn all ye learnt here, of one another,
  And all you have learnt of an aunt or a
   mother :
Then straight hither come, a new pattern to see,
Which in a good humour kind fortune did send ;
  A glass for your minds, as well as your faces :
  Make haste then and break your own looking-
   glasses ;
If you see but yourselves, you'll never amend.
Women. You that will* teach us what your
  wives ought to do,
Take heed ! there's a pattern in town too for you.

   * " Would," 1st Ed.

   Be you but Alphonsos, and we
   Perhaps Ianthes will be.
MEN. Be you but Ianthes, and we
   Alphonsos a while will be.
BOTH. Let both sides begin then, rather then
   neither;
Let's both join our hands, and both mend together.

*End of the Third Entry.*

-- - - ------

*The Scene is varied to the prospect of Mount Philermus:
 Artificers appearing at work about that castle
 which was there, with wonderful expedition,
 erected by Solyman. His great army is discovered
 in the plain below, drawn up in battalia, as if it
 were prepar'd for a general assault.*

*The Entry is again prepared by instrumental music.*

### The Fourth ENTRY.

*Enter* SOLYMAN, PIRRHUS, MUSTAPHA.

SOLY. Refuse my pass-port, and resolve to die,
Only for fashion's sake, for company?
Oh costly scruples! But I'll try to be,
Thou stubborn honour, obstinate as thee.
My pow'r thou shalt not vanquish by thy will,
I will enforce to live whom thou would'st kill.
 PIR. They in to-morrow's storm will change
  their mind,
Then, though too late instructed, they shall find
That those who your protection dare reject,
No human power dares venture to protect.
They are not foes, but rebels, who withstand
The pow'r that does their fate command.
 SOLY. Oh Mustapha, our strength we measure ill,
  We want the half of what we think we have;

For we enjoy the beast-like pow'r to kill,
   But not the God-like power to save.
Who laughs at death, laughs at our highest pow'r;
The valiant man is his own emperour.
   Musta. Your pow'r to save, you have to them
     made known,
      Who scorn'd it with ingrateful pride ;
Now, how you can destroy, must next be shown ;
      And that the Christian world has tried.
   Soly.      'Tis such a single pair
      As only equal are
Unto themselves ; but many steps above
All others who attempt to make up love.
Their lives will noble History afford,
And must adorn my sceptre, not my sword.
My strength in vain has with their virtue strove ;
In vain their hate would overcome my love,
My favours I'll compell them to receive :
Go, Mustapha, and strictest orders give
Through all the camp, that in assault they spare,
      And in the sack of this presumptuous town,
The lives of these two strangers with a care
      Above the preservation of their own.
Alphonso has so oft his courage shown,
That he to all but cowards must be known.
Ianthe is so fair that none can be
Mistaken among thousands which is she.


*The Scene returns to that of the town besieg'd.*


*Enter* ALPHONSO, IANTHE.


Ianth. Alphonso, now the danger grows so near,
    Give her that loves you leave to fear.
    Nor do I blush this passion to confess,
    Since it for object has no less

Than even your liberty, or life ;
I fear not as a woman, but a wife.
We were too proud no use to make
  Of Solyman's obliging proffer ;
For why should honour scorn to take
  What honour's self does to it offer ?

ALPH. To be o'ercome by his victorious sword,
  Will comfort to our fall afford ;
Our strength may yield to his ; but 'tis not fit
  Our virtue should to his submit ;
In that, Ianthe, I must be
  Advanc'd, and greater far than he.

IANTH. Fighting with him who strives to be
  your friend,
You not with virtue, but with power contend.

ALPH. Forbid it heav'n, our friends should think
  that we
Did merit friendship from an enemy.

IANTH. He is a foe to Rhodes and not to you.

ALPH. In Rhodes besieg'd we must be Rhodians
too.

IANTH. 'Twas fortune that engag'd you in this
war.

ALPH. 'Twas Providence ! heaven's pris'ners here
we are.

IANTH. That Providence our freedom does
restore ;
The hand that shut now opens us the door.

ALPH. Had heav'n that pass-port for our freedom
sent,
It would have chose some better instrument
Than faithless Solyman.

IANTH. O say not so !
To strike and wound the virtue of your foe
Is cruelty, which war does not allow :
Sure he has better words deserv'd from you.

ALPH. From me, Ianthe, no ;

What he deserves from you, you best must know.

IANTHE. What means my Lord?

ALPH. For I confess, I must
The poison'd bounties of a foe mistrust:
    And when upon the bait I look,
    Though all seem fair, suspect the hook.

IANTH. He, though a foe, is generous and true;
What he hath done declares what he will do.

ALPH. He in two days your high esteem has
   won:
What he would do, I know; who knows what he
   has done?
Done? wicked tongue, what hast thou said?
                           [*Aside.*
What horrid falsehood from thee fled?
Oh jealousy, if jealousy it be
Would I had here an asp instead of thee!

IANT. Sure you are sick: your words, alas!
    Gestures, and looks, distempers shew.

ALPH. Ianthe, you may safely pass;
    The pass, no doubt, was meant to you.

IANT. He's jealous, sure; Oh, virtue! can
   it be?
Have I for this serv'd virtue faithfully?
Alphonso——

ALPH. Speak, Ianthe, and be free.

IANT. Have I deserv'd this change?

ALPH. Thou do'st deserve
So much, that Emperours are proud to serve
The fair Ianthe; and not dare
To hurt a land whilst she is there.
Return, renown'd Ianthe, safely home,
    And force thy passage with thine eyes;
    To conquer Rhodes will be a prize
Less glorious than by thee to be o'ercome.
But since he longs, it seems, so much to see,
    And be possest of me,

Tell him, I shall not fly beyond his reach :
Would he could dare to meet me in the breach.

[Exit.

IANT. Tell him! tell him? Oh no, Alphonso, no.
  Let never man thy weakness know ;
   Thy sudden fall will be a shame
   To man's and virtue's name.
Alphonso's false! for what can falser be
Than to suspect that falsehood dwells in me ?
Could Solyman both life and honour give ?
And can Alphonso me of both deprive ?
   Of both, Alphonso; for believe
   Ianthe will disdain to live
   So long as to let others see
Thy true, and her imputed, infamy.
No more let lovers think they can possess
  More than a month of happiness.
   We thought our hold of it was strong ;
   We thought our lease of it was long :
But now, that all may ever happy prove,
   Let never any love.
And yet these troubles of my love to me
  Shall shorter than the pleasures be.
I'll till to-morrow last ; then the assault
Shall finish my misfortune and his fault.
I to my enemies shall doubly owe,
For saving me before, for killing now.  [Exit.

Enter VILLERIUS, ADMIRAL.

 ADM. From out the camp, a valiant Christian
  slave
Escap'd, and to our knights assurance gave
   That at the break of day
   Their mine will play.
 VILL. Oft Martiningus struck and tried the
 . ground,

And counter-digg'd, and has the hollows found :
　　　　We shall prevent
　　　　Their dire intent.
Where is the Duke, whose valour strives to keep
Rhodes still awake, which else would dully sleep ?
　　Adm. His courage and his reason is o'erthrown.
　　Vill. Thou sing'st the sad destruction of our
　　town.
　　Adm. I·met him wild as all the winds,
　　　　When in the ocean they contest :
　　　And diligent suspicion finds
　　　　He is with jealousy possest.
　　Vill. That arrow, once misdrawn, must ever
　　rove.
O weakness, sprung from mightiness of love !
　　　　O pitied crime !
　　Alphonso will be overthrown
　　Unless we take this ladder down,
Where, though the rounds are broke,
　　　He does himself provoke
　　　　Too hastily to climb.
　　Adm. Invisibly as dreams, fame's wings
　　　　Fly every where ;
Hov'ring all day o'er palaces of kings ;
　　　At night she lodges in the people's ear :
Already they perceive Alphonso wild,
　　　And the beloved Ianthe griev'd.
　　Vill. Let us no more by honour be beguil'd ;
　　　This town can never be relieved ;
　　　Alphonso and Ianthe being lost,
Rhodes, thou dost cherish life with too much cost !

### Chorus.

Away, unchain the streets, unearth the ports.
　　Pull down each barricade
　　Which women's fears have made,
And bravely sally out from all the forts !

Drive back the crescents, and advance the cross!
Or sink all human empires in our loss.

*Enter* ROXOLANA, PIRRHUS, RUSTAN, *and two*
*of her Women.**

ROX. Not come to see me ere th' assault be
past?

PIR. He spoke it not in anger, but in haste.

RUST. If mighty Solyman be angry grown,
It is not with his Empress, but the town.

ROX. When stubborn Rhodes does him to anger
move,
'Tis by detaining there what he does love.

PIR. He is resolv'd the city to destroy.

ROX. But more resolv'd Ianthe to enjoy.

RUST. T'avoid your danger cease your jealousy.

ROX. Tell them of danger who do fear to die.

PIR. None but your self dares threaten you with
death.

1. WOM. Do not your beauty blast with your own
breath.

2. WOM. You lessen't in your own esteem
When of his love you jealous seem.

1. WOM. And but a faded beauty make it
When you suspect he can forsake it.

2. WOM. Believe not, Empress, that you are
decay'd,
For so you'll seem by jealous passion sway'd.

ROX. He follows passion, I pursue my reason:
He loves the traitor, and I hate the treason.

*Enter* HALY.

HALY. Our foes appear! Th' assault will strait
begin.

[*Pirrhus, Rustan, in chorus.*

* This entrance, subsequent dialogue and Haly's entrance,
down to "whom he forsakes," not in first edition," the "Chorus
of Wives" following up the previous scene, and so ending the
fourth entry.

They sally out where we must enter in.

Rox. Let Solyman forget his way to glory,
Increase in conquest and grow less in story.
    That honour which in vain
    His valour shrinks to gain,
When from the Rhodians he Ianthe takes,
Is lost in losing me whom he forsakes.

                  *[Exeunt several ways.*

CHORUS *of Wives.*

1.

1. This cursed jealousy, what is't ?
2. 'Tis love that has lost it self in a mist.
3. 'Tis love being frighted out of his wits.
4. 'Tis love that has a fever got ;
Love that is violently hot ;
But troubled with cold and trembling fits.
'Tis yet a more unnatural evil :

CHORUS.

'Tis the God of Love, 'tis the love of God,
   possest with a devil.

2.

1. 'Tis rich corrupted wine of love,
Which sharpest vinegar does prove.
2. From all the sweet flowers which might honey
   make,
It does a deadly poison bring.
3. Strange serpent which it self doth sting !
4. It never can sleep, and dreams still awake.
5. It stuffs up the marriage bed with thorns.

CHORUS.

It gores it self, it gores it self, with imagin'd
   horns.

*The end of the Fourth Entry.*

*The Scene is chang'd into a representation of a general
    assault given to the Town ; the greatest fury of the
    army being discerned at the English station.*

*The ENTRY is again prepar'd by instrumental music.*

The Fifth ENTRY.

*Enter* PIRRHUS.

PIR. Traverse the cannon! mount the batt'ries
            higher !
        More gabions, and renew the blinds ;
        Like dust they powder spend,
        And to our faces send
The heat of all the element of fire ;
        And to their backs have all the winds.
                    *Enter* MUSTAPHA.
MUSTA. More ladders and reliefs to scale !
The fire-crooks are too short ! Help, help to hale !
That battlement is loose, and strait will down !
        Point well the cannons and play fast !
        Their fury is too hot to last.
That rampire shakes, they fly into the town.
    PIR. March up with those reserves to that
            redoubt !
        Faint slaves ! the Janizaries reel !
        They bend, they bend ! and seem to feel
        The terrors of a rout.
    MUSTA.  Old Zanger halts, and re-inforcement
            lacks !
    PIR. March on !
    MUSTA. Advance those pikes, and charge their
            backs ! *

_____

* The witty Villiers, Duke of Buckingham, in his Rehearsal,
Act 5, Scene 1, satirizes this battle chiefly on account of its
having been performed in recitative music " by seven persons
only."

*Enter* SOLYMAN.

SOLY. Those platforms are too low to reach !
Haste, haste ! call Haly to the breach !
Can my domestic Janizaries fly,
And not adventure life for victory ?
Whose childhood with my palace milk I fed :
Their youth, as if I were their parent bred.
What is this monster Death, that our poor slaves,
Still vext with toil, are loth to rest in graves ?
   MUSTA. If life so precious be, why do not they,
Who in war's trade can only live by prey, .
      Their own afflicted lives expose
      To take the happier from their foes ?
PIR. Our troops renew the fight !
      And those that sally'd out
        To give the rout,
     Are now return'd in flight !
SOLY. Follow, follow, follow! make good the line !
In, Pirrhus, in ! Look, we have sprung the mine !
                     [*Exit Pirrhus.*
   MUSTA. Those desp'rate English ne'er will fly !
     Their firmness still does hinder others' flight,
     As if their mistresses were by
      To see and praise them whilst they fight.
SOLY. That flame of valour in Alphonso's eyes
Outshines the light of all my victories !
Those who were slain when they his bulwark
    storm'd,
          Contented fell,
          As vanquish'd well ;
      Those who were left alive may now,
Because their valour is by his reform'd,
         Hope to make others bow.
   MUSTA. Erewhile I in the English station saw
Beauty that did my wonder forward draw,
Whose valour did my forces back disperse ;

Fairer than woman, and than man more fierce :
It shew'd such courage as disdain'd to yield,
And yet seem'd willing to be kill'd.
　SOLY. This vision did to me appear :
Which mov'd my pity and my fear :
It had a dress much like the imag'rie
For heroes drawn, and may Ianthe be.

### Enter PIRRHUS.

　PIR. Fall on ! the English stoop when they give
　　　fire !
They seem to furl their colours and retire !
　SOLY. Advance ! I only would the honour have
To conquer two, whom I by force would save.

### Enter ALPHONSO *with his sword drawn.*

　ALPH. My reason by my courage is misled !
　Why chase I those who would from dying fly,
Enforcing them to sleep amongst the dead,
　Yet keep myself unslain that fain would die ?
Do not the pris'ners whom we take declare
　How Solyman proclaim'd through all his host,
That they Ianthe's life and mine should spare ?
　Life ill preserv'd is worse than basely lost.
Mine by dispatch of war he will not take,
But means to leave it ling'ring on the rack ;
That in his palace I might live, and know
Her shame, and be afraid to call it so.
Tyrants and devils think all pleasures vain,
But what are still deriv'd from others' pain.

### Enter ADMIRAL.

　ADM. Renown'd Alphonso, thou hast fought to-
　　　day,
As if all Asia were thy valour's prey.
　　　But now thou must do more
　　　Than thou hast done before ;

Else the important life of Rhodes is gone.
 ALPH. Why from the peaceful grave
  Should I still strive to save
The lives of others, that would lose mine òwn !
 ADM. The soldiers call, Alphonso! thou hast
 taught
The way to all the wonders they have wrought
  Who now refuse to fight
  But in thy valour's sight.
 ALPH. I would to none example be to fly ;
But fain would teach all human kind to die.
 ADM. Haste, haste ! Ianthe in disguise
At the English bulwark wounded lies ;
And in the French, our old great master strives
From many hands to rescue many lives.
 ALPH. Ianthe wounded ? where, alas !
  Has mourning pity hid her face ?
Let pity fly, fly far from the opprest,
Since she removes her lodging from my breast.
 ADM. You have but two great cruelties to chuse
By staying here ; you must Ianthe lose,
  Who ventur'd life and fame for you ;
  Or your great master quite forsake,
  Who to your childhood first did shew
  The ways you did to honour take.
 ALPH. Ianthe cannot be
  In safer company :
For what will not the valiant English do
When beauty is distress'd and virtue too ?
 ADM. Dispatch your choice, if you will either
 save,
  Occasion bids you run ;
  You must redeem the one
And I the other from a common grave.
  Alphonso, haste !
 ALPH. Thou urgest me too fast.
This riddle is too sad and intricate ;

The hardest that was e'er propos'd by fate
  Honour and pity have
 Of both too short a time to chuse ;
  Honour the one would save,
 Pity would not the other lose.
ADM. Away, brave Duke, away !
  Both perish by our stay.
ALPH. I to my noble master owe
  All that my youth did nobly do :
 He in war's school my master was,
  The ruler of my life ;
 She my lov'd mistress but, alas !
  My now suspected wife.
ADM. By this delay we both of them forsake.
Which of their rescues wilt thou undertake ?
 ALPH. Hence, Admiral, and to thy master hie !
I will as swiftly to my mistress fly,
Through ambush, fire, and all impediments
The witty cruelty of war invents :
For there does yet some taste of kindness last,
Still relishing the virtue that is past.
But how, Ianthe, can my sword successful prove,
Where honour stops, and only pity leads my love ?
      *[Exeunt several ways.*

    *Enter* PIRRHUS.

 PIR. O sudden change ! repulst in all the heat
Of victory, and forc'd to lose retreat !
Seven crescents, fixt on their redoubts, are gone !
  Horse, horse ! we fly
  From victory !
Wheel, wheel from their reserves, and charge our
 own !
  Divide that wing !
  More succour bring !
  Rally the fled,
  And quit our dead !

Rescue that ensign and that drum !
Bold slaves ! they to our trenches come :
Though still our army does in posture stay
Drawn up to judge, not act, the business of the
    day ;
As Rome, in theatres, saw fencers play.

*Enter* MUSTAPHA.

MUSTA. Who can be loud enough to give
    command ?
    Stand, Haly, make a stand !
Those horses to that carriage span ! Drive, drive !
    Zanger is shot again, yet still alive !
    Coyns for the culv'rin, then give fire
To clear the turn-pikes, and let Zanger in !
    Look, Pirrhus, look, they all begin
To alter their bold count'nance, and retire !

*The Scene returns to that of the Castle on*
*Mount Philermus.*

*Enter* SOLYMAN.

SOLY. How cowardly my num'rous slaves fall
    back !
Slow to assault, but dext'rous when they sack !
    Wild wolves in times of peace they are ;
    Tame sheep and harmless in the war.
Crowds fit to stop up breaches ; and prevail
But so as shoals of herrings choke a whale.
This dragon-duke so nimbly fought to day,
As if he wings had got to stoop at prey,
Ianthe is triumphant, but not gone ;
And sees Rhodes still beleaguer'd, though not won.
Audacious town ! thou keep'st thy station still ;
And so my castle tarries on that hill,
Where I will dwell till famine enter thee ;
And prove more fatal than my sword could be.

Nor shall Ianthe from my favours run,
But stay to meet and praise what she did shun.

*The Scene is changed to that of the Town besieg'd.*

*Enter* VILLERIUS, ADMIRAL, IANTHE.

*She in a night-gown and a chair is brought in.*

VILL. Fair virtue, we have found
Nor danger in your wound.
   Securely live,
   And credit give
   To us and to the surgeon's art.
IANTH. Alas! my wound is in the heart;
   Or else, where e'er it be,
   Imprison'd life it comes to free,
By seconding a worser wound that hid doth lie :
   What practice can assure
   That patient of a cure,
Whose kind of grief still makes her doubt the
  remedy ?
  ADM. The wounded that would soon be eas'd
   Should keep their spirits tun'd and pleas'd ;
   No discords* should their mind subdue :
   And who, in such distress
   As this, ought to express
   More joyful harmony than you ?
   'Tis not alone that we assure
   Your certain cure ;
   But pray remember that your blood's expence
   Was in defence
Of Rhodes, which gain'd to-day a most important
  victory :
   For our success, repelling this assault,
   Has taught the Ottomans to halt ;
Who may, wasting their heavy body, learn to fly.

   * " Discord " in first edition.

VILL. Not only this should hasten your content,
But you shall joy to know the instrument
   That wrought the triumph of this day ;
   Alphonso did the sally sway ;
To whom our Rhodes, all that she is does owe,
And all that from her root of hope can grow.
 IANTH. Has he so greatly done ?
   Indeed, he us'd to run .
As swift in honour's race as any he
Who thinks he merits wreaths for victory.
This is to all a comfort, and should be,
If he were kind, the greatest joy to me.
Where is my alter'd Lord ? I cannot tell
If I may ask, if he be safe and well ?
For whilst all strangers may his actions boast,
   Who in their songs repeat
   The triumphs he does get,
1 only must lament his favours lost.
 VILL. Some wounds he has ; none desperate* but
  yours ;
Ianthe cur'd, his own he quickly cures.
 IANTH. If his be little, mine will soon grow less.
   Ay me !  What sword
   Durst give my Lord
Those wounds, which now Ianthe cannot dress ?
 ADM. Ianthe will rejoice when she did hear
How greater than himself he does appear
In rescue of her life ; all acts were slight,
And cold, even in our hottest fight,
   Compar'd to what he did,
When with death's vizard she her beauty hid.
 VILL. Love urg'd his anger, till it made such
  haste
   And rusht so swiftly in,
   That scarce he did begin
Ere we could say, the mighty work was past.

   * " Dangerous " in first edition.

IANTH. All this for me? something he did for
you :
      But when his sword begun,
      Much more it would have done
If he, alas! had thought Ianthe true.
  ADM. Be kind, Ianthe, and be well?
      It is too pitiful to tell
      What way of dying is exprest
      When he that letter read
You wrote before your wounds were drest;
When you and we despair'd you could recover :
      Then he was more than dead,
And much out-wept a husband and a lover.

*Enter* ALPHONSO *wounded, led in by two Mutes.*

  ALPH. Tear up my wounds! I had a passion
coarse
And rude enough to strengthen jealousy ;
But want that more refin'd and quicker force
Which does out-wrestle nature when we die.
Turn to a tempest all my inward strife :
      Let it not last,
      But in a blast
Spend this infectious vapour, life!
  IANTH. It is, my Lord! enough of strength I feel
To bear me to him, or but let me kneel.
He bled for me when he achiev'd for you
This day's success ; and much from me is due.
Let me but bless him for his victory,
And hasten to forgive him ere I die.
  ALPH. Be not too rash, Ianthe, to forgive,*
      Who knows but I ill use may make
      Of pardons which I could not take ;
For they may move me to desire to live.

  * From here down to "tedious councils meet" not in first
edition.

IANTH. If ought can make Ianthe worthy grow
   Of having pow'r of pard'ning you,
It is, because she perfectly doth know
   That no such pow'r to her is due.
Who never can forget herself, since she
Unkindly did resent your jealousie.
A passion against which you nobly strove :
I know it was but over-cautious love.
  ALPH. Accursed crime! Oh, let it have no name
Till I recover blood to shew my shame.
  IANTH. Why stay we at such distance when we
  treat?
    As monarch's children, making love
    By proxy, to each other move,
    And by advice of tedious councils meet.
  ALPH. Keep back, Ianthe, for my strength does*
  fail
When on thy cheeks I see thy roses pale.
Draw all your curtains, and then lead her in!
Let me in darkness mourn away my sin.  [*Exeunt.*

  *Enter* ROXOLANA, *and Women Attendants.†*

  SOLY. Your looks express a triumph at our loss.
  ROX. Can I forsake the crescent for the cross?
  SOLY. You wish my spreading crescent shrunk
  no less.
  ROX. Sultan, I would not lose by your success,
  SOLY. You are a friend to the besiegers grown!
  ROX. I wish your sword may thrive
    Yet would not have you strive
To take Ianthe rather than the town.
  SOLY. Too much on wand'ring rumour you rely;
Your foolish women teach you jealousy.

 * " Will " in first edition.
 † This entrance and subsequent dialogue down to " learn to
wink " not in first edition, Chorus of Soldiers following up the
exit of Alphonso and others.

1. WOM. We should too blindly confident
    appear,
If, when the Empress fears, we should not fear.
    2. WOM. The camp does breed that loud report
            Which wakens echo in the Court.
    1. WOM. The world our duty will approve,
            If for our mistress' sake,
            We ever are awake
To watch the wand'rings of your love.
    SOLY. My war with Rhodes will never have
    success,
Till I at home, Roxana, make my peace.
            I will be kind, if you'll grow wise;
            Go, chide your whisp'rers and your spies !
Be satisfied with liberty to think ;
And, when you should not see me, learn to wink.

### CHORUS of Soldiers.

#### 1.

With a fine merry gale,
Fit to fill ev'ry sail,
They did cut the smooth sea
That our skins they might flea :
Still as they landed, we firkt them with sallies ;
    We did bang their silk sashes,
    Through sands and through plashes
Till amain they did run to their gallies.

#### 2.

They first were so mad
As they jealousies had
That our Isle durst not stay,
But would float strait away ;
For they landed still faster and faster,
    And their old Bassa, Pirrhus.
    Did think he could fear us ;
But himself sooner fear'd our Grand-Master.

### 3.

Then the hug'ous great Turk
Came to make us more work ;
With enow men to eat
All he meant to defeat ;
Whose wonderful worship did confirm us
     In the fear he would bide here
     So long till he died here,
By the Castle he built on Philermus.

### 4.

You began the assault
With a very long halt ;
And, as halting ye came,
So ye went off as lame ;
And have left our Alphonso to scoff ye.
     To himself, as a dainty,
     He keeps his Ianthe,
Whilst we drink good Wine, and you drink but
  coffee.

*The end of the fifth Entry.*

*The Curtain is let fall.*

FINIS.

# SIEGE OF RHODES.

---

## THE SECOND PART.

---

## PROLOGUE.

What if we serve you now a trick, and do
Like him who pasted Bills that he would shew
So many active feats, and those so high,
That Court and City came to see him fly ?
But he, good man, careful to empty still
The money-boxes, as the house did fill,
Of all his tricks had time to shew but one :
He lin'd his purse, and, presto ! he was gone !
Many were then as fond, as you are now,
Of seeing stranger things than art can shew.
We may perform as much as he did do ;
We have your money, and a back-door too.
Go, and be cozen'd thus, rather than stay
And wait to be worse cozen'd with our play.
For you shall hear such coarse complaints of Love,
Such silly sighing, as no more will move
Your passion than Dutch madrigals can do,
When skippers, with wit beards,* at Wapping woo.
Hope little from our Poet's wither'd wit ;
From infant-players, scarce grown puppets yet.
Hope from our women less, whose bashful fear
Wond'red to see me dare to enter here :
Each took her leave, and wisht my danger past ;
And though I come back safe and undisgrac'd,
Yet when they spy the WITS here, then I doubt
No Amazon can make 'em venture out.
Though I advis'd 'em not to fear you much ;

* Wet beards.—*Folio.*

For I presume not half of you are such.
But many trav'lers here as judges come
From Paris, Florence, Venice, and from Rome,
Who will describe, when any scene we draw,
By each of ours all that they ever saw.
Those praising for extensive breadth and height,
And inward distance to deceive the sight.
When greater objects, moving in broad space,
You rank with lesser in this narrow place,
Then we like chess-men on a chess board are,
And seem to play like pawns the Rhodian war.
Oh money ! money ! if the WITS would dress,
With ornaments, the present face of peace ;
And to our poet half that treasure spare,
Which faction gets from fools to nourish war ;
Then his contracted scenes should wider be,
And move by greater engines, till you see,
Whilst you'securely sit, fierce armies meet,
And raging seas disperse a fighting fleet.
Thus much he bade me say ; and I confess,
I think he would, if rich, mean nothing less ;
But, leaving you your selves to entertain,
Like an old rat retire to parmazan.

ACT THE FIRST, SCENE THE FIRST.

*The scene is a prospect of Rhodes beleagur'd at sea
and Land by the Fleet and Army of Solyman.*

*Enter* ALPHONSO, ADMIRAL, MARSHAL *of Rhodes.*

ALPH. When shall we 'scape from the delays of
   Rome ?
   And when, slow Venice, will thy succours
   come ?
MAR. How often too have we in vain
   Sought aid from long consulting Spain ?
ADM. The German eagle does no more
   About our barren island soar.
Thy region, famisht Rhodes, she does forsake ;
And cruelly at home her quarry make.
ALPH. The furious French, and fiercer English
   fail.
ADM.    We watch from steeples and the pier
   What flags remoter vessels bear ;
But no glad voice cries out, a sail ! a sail !
MAR. Brave Duke ! I find we are to blame
   In playing slowly honour's game,
   Whilst ling'ring famine wastes our
   strength,
   And tires afflicted life with length.
ALPH. The Council does it rashness call,
   When we propose to hazard all
The parcels we have left in one bold cast :
But their discretion makes our torments last.
ADM. When less'ning hope flies from our ken,
   And still despair shews great and near,
   Discretion seems to valour then
   A formal shape to cover fear.
ALPH. Courage, when it at once adventures all,
   And dares with human aids dispense,
   Resembles that high confidence

III       U

Which priests may faith and heav'nly valour call.

ADM. Those who in latter dangers of fierce war
      To distant hope and long consults are
      given,
Depend too proudly on their own wise care;
      And seem to trust themselves much more
      than Heav'n.

ALPH. Let then the Elder of our Rhodian knights
Discourse of slow designs in ancient fights;
Let them sit long in council to contrive
How they may longest keep lean fools alive:
Whilst, Marshal, thou, the Admiral and I,
      Grown weary of this tedious strife
      Which but prolongs imprison'd life
Since we are freely born will freely die.

ADM. From sev'ral ports we'll sally out
      With all the bolder youth our seas have bred.

MAR. And we at land through storms of war
      have led,
Then meet at Mustapha's redoubt.

ALPH. And this last race of honour being run,
We'll meet again, far, far above the sun.

ADM. Already Fame her trumpet sounds:
      Which more provokes and warms ·
      Our courage than the smart of wounds.
      Away! to arms! to arms!

*Enter* VILLERIUS.

VILL. What from the camp, when no assault is
      near,
      Fierce Duke does thee to slaughter call?
Or what bold fleet does now at sea appear,
      To hale and board our Admiral?

ADM. We give, great master, this alarm
      Not to forewarn your chiefs of harm:
      To whom assaults from land or sea
      Would now but too much welcome be.

ALPH.  We want great dangers, and of mischiefs
       know
No greater ill but that they come too slow.
    ADM.    Why should we thus, with art's great care
             Of Empire, against nature war?
Nature, with sleep and food, would make life last ;
But artful Empire makes us watch and fast.
    ALPH.  If valour virtue be, why should we lack
             The means to make it move ?
             Which progress would improve ;
But cannot march when famine keeps it back.
    ADM.    When gen'ral dearth
             Afflicts the earth,
Then even our loudest warriors calmly pine.
             High courage, though with sourness still
             It yields to yokes of human will,
Yet gracefully does bow to pow'r divine.
    ALPH.  But when but mortal foes
             Imperiously impose
             A martial Lent
             Where strength is spent ;
That famine, doubly horrid, wears the face
Both of a ling'ring death, and of disgrace.
    MAR.   For those, whose valour makes them
             quickly die,
Prevent the Fast to shun the infamy.
    VILL.  Whom have I heard ? 'Tis time all pow'r
             should cease
             When men high born, and higher bred,
             Who have out-done what most have read,
Grow like the gowd,* impatient of distress.
Is there no room for hope in any breast ?
    ADM.   Not since she does appear
             Boldly a dweller where
The first was entertain'd but as a guest.

* Goud : Woad—A plant cultivated for dyers, who use it as
the foundation of many colours.

ALPH. She may in sieges be receiv'd,
  Be courted too and much believ'd ;
And thus continue after wants begin ;
But is thrust out when famine enters in.
 VILL. You have been tir'd in vain with passive-
     ness ;
But where, when active, can you meet success ?
 ALPH. With all the strength of all our forts
  We'll sally out from all the ports ;
  And with a hot and hot alarm
  Still keep the Turkish tents so warm
That Solyman shall in a fever lye.
 MAR. His Bassas, marking what we do,
  Shall find that we were taught by you
To manage life, and teach them how to die.
 VILL. Valour's designs are many heights above
All pleasures fancied in the dreams of Love.
But whilst, voluptuously, you thus devise
Delightful ways to end those miseries
Which over-charge your own impatient mind ;
Where shall the softer sex their safety find ?
When you with num'rous foes lye dead,
(I mean asleep in honour's bed)
  They then may subject be
To all the wild and fouler force
  Of rudest victory ;
Where noise shall deafen all remorse.
 ALPH. If still concern'd to watch and arm,
  That we may keep from harm
  All who defenceless are
  And seldom safe in war,
  When, Admiral, shall we
  From weariness be free ?
 VILL. The Rhodians by your gen'ral sally may
  Get high renown ;
Though you at last must bravely lose the day,
  And they their town.

Then when by anger'd Solyman 'tis sway'd,
On whom shall climbing infants smile for aid ?
Or who shall lift and rescue falling age,
When it can only frown at Turkish rage ?
The living thus advise you to esteem
And keep your life that it may succour them :
But though you are inclin'd to hear death plead
As strongly to invite you to the dead,
Whilst glory does beyond compassion move,
Yet stay till your Ianthe speaks for love !

ALPH. Ianthe's name is such a double charm,
As strait does arm me, and as soon unarm.
Valour as far as ever valour went
Dares go, not stopping at the Sultan's tent,
To free Ianthe when to Rhodes confin'd :
       But halts, when it considers I
       Amidst ten thousand Turks may die,
Yet leave her then to many more behind.

ADM. Since life is to be kept, what must be
      done ?

VILL. All those attempts of valour we must shun
Which may the Sultan vex ; and, since bereft
Of food, there is no help but treaty left.

ADM. Rhodes, when the world shall thy submis-
      sion know,
Honour, thy ancient friend, will court thy foe.

MAR. Honour begins to blush, and hide his face :
      For those who treat sheath all their swords,
      To try by length of fencing words
How far they may consent to meet disgrace.

ALPH. As noble minds with shame their wants
      confess ;
So Rhodes will bashfully declare distress.

      [*A shout within, and a noise of forcing of doors.*

VILL. Our guards will turn confed'rates with the
      crowd,
Whose mis'ries now insult and make them loud.

Their leaders strive with praises to appease,
And soften the misled with promises.

[*Exit Admiral.*

ALPH. These us'd with awe to wait
Far from your palace gate ;
But, like lean birds in frosts, their hunger now
Makes them approach us and familiar grow.

VILL. They have so long been dying, that 'tis fit
They death's great privilege should have ;
Which does in all a parity admit :
No rooms of state are in the grave.

*Enter* ADMIRAL.

ADM. The people's various minds
(Which are like sudden winds,
Such as from hilly-coasts still changing blow)
Were lately as a secret kept
In many whispers of so soft a breath,
And in a calm so deeply low,
As if all life had soundly slept ;
But now, as if they meant to waken death,
They rashly rise, and loud in tumults grow.

MAR. They see our strength is hourly less,
Whilst Solyman's does still increase.

ADM. Thus, being to their last expectance driven,
Ianthe, now they cry !
Whose name they raise so high
And often, that it fills the vault of Heaven.

ALPH. If Solyman does much her looks esteem,
Looks captive him, and may enfranchise them.

ADM. By many pris'ners, since our siege began,
They have been told, how potent Solyman,
In all assaults, severely did command
That you and she
Should still be free
From all attempts of every Turkish hand.

ALPH. It rudeness were in me not to confess

That Solyman has civil been,
And did much Christian honour win
When he Ianthe rescu'd from distress.

ADM. They were from many more advertis'd too,
That he hath pass-ports sent for her and you :
Which makes them hope the pow'r divine
Does by some blessed cause design
Ianthe to procure their liberty :
.Or if by Heav'n 'tis not entirely meant
That powerful beauty's force should set them free,
Yet they would have her strait in treaty sent
To gain some rest for those,
Who of their restless foes
Continual wounds and fasts are weary grown.

MAR. Whose mighty hearts conceiv'd before,
That they were built to suffer more
Assaults and batt'ries then our rocky town.

VILL. Those who, with giant-stature, shocks
receiv'd,
Now down to dwarfish size and weakness fall.

MAR. Who once no more of harm from shot
believ'd
Than that an arrow hurts a wounded wall.

ALPH. She treat ? what pleasant but what
frantic dreams
Rise from the people's fever of extremes !
I will allay their rage, or try
How far Ianthe will comply. [Exit.

*Enter* IANTHE *and her two Women at the other door.*

IANTH. Why, wise Villerius, had you power to
sway
That Rhodian valour, which did yours obey ?
Was not that pow'r deriv'd from awful Heav'n
Which to your valour hath your wisdom given ?
And that directs you to the seasons meet
For deeds of war, and when 'tis fit to treat.

VILL.    Ere we to Solyman can sue,
   Ianthe, we must treat with you.
The people find that they have no defence
But in your beauty and your eloquence.
  MAR. To your requests great Solyman may
   yield.
  IANTH. Can hope on such a weak foundation
   build ?
  MAR. In you the famish't people's hopes are fed.
  IANTH.    Can your discerning eyes
    (Which may inform the wise)
Be by vain hope, their blind conductor, led ?
  VILL.    When winds in tempests rise
    Pilots may shut their eyes.
  MAR. And though their practice knows their way,
Must be content a while to stray.
  IANTH.    Though Solyman should softer grow,
    And to my tears compassion shew ;
What shape of comfort can appear to me,
   When all your outward war shall cease,
If then my lord renew his jealousy
   And straight destroy my inward peace ?
  VILL. The Rhodian knights shall all in council sit ;
And with persuasions, by the public voice,
Your lord shall woo till you to that submit
Which is the people's will and not your choice.
No arguments, by forms of senate made,
Can magisterial jealousy persuade ;
It takes no counsel, nor will be in awe
Of reason's force, necessity, or law.
    [*Exit with the Marshal and her women.*
  VILL.    Call thy experience back,
    Which safely coasted ev'ry shore ;
    And let thy reason lack
    No wings to make it higher soar ;
For all those aids will much too weak appear,
With all that gath'ring fancy can supply,

When she hath travell'd round about the sphere,
To give us strength to govern jealousy.
ADM. Will you believe that fair Ianthe can
Consent to go, and treat with Solyman,
Vainly in hope to move him to remorse ?
VILL. 'Twill not be said by me
　　　　That she consents, when she
Does yield to what the people would inforce.
Their strength they now will in our weakness find,
　　　　Whom in their plenty we can sway,
　　　　But in their wants must them obey,
And wink when they the cords of pow'r unbind.
　ADM. 'Tis likely then that she must yield to go.
　VILL. Who can resist, if they will have it so ?
　ADM. Where'er she moves she will last innocent.
　VILL. Heaven's spotless lights are not by motion
　　　spent.
　ADM. Alphonso's love cannot so sickly be
As to express relapse of jealousy.
　VILL. Examine jealousy and it will prove
To be the careful tenderness of love.
It can no sooner than celestial fire
Be either quench't, or of it self expire.
　ADM. No signs are seen of embers that remain
　　　　For windy passion to provoke.
　VILL. Talk not of signs ; celestial fires contain
　　　　No matter which appears in smoke.
Be heedful, Admiral ! the private peace
　　　　Of lovers so renown'd requires your care :
Their league, renew'd of late, will if it cease
　　　　As much perplex us as the Rhodian war. [Exit.
　ADM. How vainly must I keep mine eyes awake,
Who now, Alphonso, am enjoin'd to take,
For public good, a private care of thee ;
When I shall rather need thy care of me ?
Love, in Ianthe's shape, pass't through my eyes
And tarries in my breast. But if the wise

Villerius does high jealousy approve
As virtue, and, because it springs from love,
My love, I hope, will so much virtue be
As shall, at least, take place of jealousy.
    For all will more respect
    The cause than the effect.
What I discern of love seems virtue yet,
And whilst that face appears I'll cherish it.

                    [*Exit.*

## THE SECOND ACT.

*The same Scene continues.*

*A great noise is heard of the people within.*

*Enter* VILLERIUS, ADMIRAL, MARSHAL.

ADM. Their murmurs with their hunger will in-
    crease :
Their noises are effects of emptiness.
    Murmurs, like winds, will louder prove
    When they with larger freedom move.
VILL. Winds which in hollow caverns dwell,
    Do first their force in murmurs waste ;
    Then soon, in many a sighing blast,
Get out, and up in tempests swell.
    ADM. Your practis'd strength no public burden
    fears ;
Nor stoops when it the weight of Empire bears.
    VILL. Pow'r is an arch which ev'ry common hand
    Does help to raise to a magnific height,
And it requires their aid when it does stand
        With firmer strength beneath increasing
        weight.
    ADM. 'Tis noble to endure and not resent
    The bruises of affliction's heavy hand.
But can we not this Embassy prevent ?

VILL. Ianthe needs must go. Those who with-
 stand
The tide of flood, which is the people's will,
 Fall back when they in vain would onward row :
We strength and way preserve by lying still.
 And sure, since tides ebb longer than they flow,
  Patience, which waits their ebbs, regains
  Lost time, and does prevent our pains.
 ADM. Can we of saving and of gaining boast
In that by which Ianthe may be lost ?
She wholly honour is ; and, when bereft
Of any part of that, has nothing left.
For honour is the soul, which by the art
Of schools is all contain'd in ev'ry part.
 VILL. The guiltless cannot honour lose, and she
Can never more than virtue guilty be.
 ADM. The talking world may persecute her name.
 VILL. Her honour bleeds not, when they wound
  her fame.
Honour's the soul which nought but guilt can
 wound ;
Fame is the trumpet which the people sound.
 ADM. Can no expedient stop their will ?
 VILL. The practice grows above our skill.
Last night, in secret, I a pris'ner sent
To Mustapha, with deep acknowledgment
For fair Ianthe's former liberty,
And pass-ports, offer'd since, to set her free.
My letters have no ill acceptance met ;
But his reply forbids all means to treat,
Unless Ianthe, who has oft refus'd
That pass, which honour might have safely us'd,.
Appear before great Solyman, and sue
To save those lives which famine must subdue.
 ADM. Sad fate ! were all those drowsy syrups
  here          [*Aside.*
Which art prescribes to madness or to fear,

To jealousy or careful States-men's eyes
To waking tyrants, or their watchful spies,
They could not make me sleep when she is sent
To lie love's lieger in the Sultan's tent.

[*A great noise within.*

MAR. What sudden pleasure makes the crowd
  rejoice ?
What comfort can thus raise the public voice ?

VILL. 'Tis fit that with the people's insolence,
When in their sorrows rude, we should dispense ;
Since they are seldom civil in their joys,
Their gladness is but an uncivil noise.

ADM. They seldom are in tune, and their tunes
  last
But, like their loves, rash sparkles struck in haste.

VILL. Still brief, as the concordance of a shout.

ADM. What is so short as music of the rout ?

VILL. Though short, yet 'tis as hearty as 'tis
  loud.

ADM. Dissembling is an art above the crowd.

VILL. Whom do they dignify with this applause?

*Enter* ALPHONSO, IANTHE.

ALPH. Of this, grave Prince, Ianthe is the cause,
  I from the temple lead her now :
  Where she for Rhodes paid many a vow ;
  And did for ev'ry Rhodian mourn
   With sorrows gracefully devout :
  But they paid back at our return
   More vows to her than she laid out.

VIL. If they such gratitude express
  For your kind pray'rs in their distress,
  Ianthe, think, what the besieg'd will do
  When the besieger is o'ercome by you.
Though Rhodes by Kings has quite forsaken been
Without, whilst all forsake their chiefs within ;
Yet who can tell but Heav'n has now design'd

Your shining beauty and your brighter mind
To lead us from the darkness of this war,
Where the besieg'd forgotten pris'ners are:
Where glorious minds have been so much obscur'd
    That fame has hardly known
    What they have boldly done,
And with a greater boldness have endur'd.

ALPH. If Heaven of innocence unmindful were,
Ianthe then might many dangers fear.
Your hazards, and what Rhodes does hazard too,
Are less than mine when I adventure you ;
    Who doubtful perils run
    That we may try to shun
Such certain loss as nought can else prevent.

ADM. Revolted jealousy! can he consent?
                            [*Aside.*

IANTH. If Rhodes were not concern'd at all
In what I am desired to undertake
    I should it less than duty call
To seek the Sultan for Alphonso's sake.

ALPH.     The Sultan has with forward haste
        Climb'd to the top of high renown,
      And sure, he cannot now as fast,
        By breaking trust, run backward
        down.

IANTH. We should not any with suspicion wound
        Whom none detect, much less believe
        that those,
In whom by trial we much virtue found,
        Can quickly all their stock of virtue lose.

ADM. How sweetly she, like infant-innocence,
                            [*Aside.*
        Runs harmlessly to harm?
        High honour will unarm
Itself to furnish others with defence.

MAR. Her mind, ascending still o'er human
    heights,

Has all the valour of our Rhodian knights.

    VILL. What more remains but pray'rs to recommend
        Your safety to the Heav'nly pow'rs,
        You being theirs much more than ours.
I'll to the Sultan for your pass-port send.

    IANTH. That may disgrace the trust which we should give,
And lessen the effects we should receive.
        Let such use forms so low
        As not by trial know
How high the honour is of Solyman :
        Who never will descend
        Till he in valleys end
That race which he on lofty hills began.
        His pow'r does every day increase,
        And can his honour then grow less ?
        Bright power does like the sun
        Tow'rds chief perfection run,
When it does high and higher rise.
    From both the best effects proceed,
    When they from heights their glories spread,
And when they dazzle gazing eyes.

    ALPH. How far, Ianthe, will these thoughts extend ?
Vain question, honour has no journey's end !

    ADM. Her honour's such, as he who limits it
Must draw a line to bound an infinite.

    VILL. Since fate has long resolv'd that you must go,
And you a pass decline, what can we do ?

    IANTH. The great example which the Sultan gave
Of virtue, when he did my honour save,
        And yours, Alphonso, too in me,
        When I was then his enemy,
Shall bring me now a suppliant to his tent,
Without his plighted word or pass-port sent.

So great a test of our entire belief
Of clemency, in so renown'd a chief,
Is now the greatest present we can make :
His pass-port is the least that we can take.
    ALPH. Ianthe, I am learning not to prize
Those dangers, which your virtue can despise.
    ADM. My love is better taught ;
          For with the pangs of thought,
I must that safety much suspect,
Which she too nobly does neglect. [*A shout within.*
    VILL. You hear them, Admiral !
    ADM. Again the people call,
Our haste provoking by a shout.
    VILL. Go hang a flag of treaty out,
        High on Saint Nic'las fort !
        Then clear the western port
To make renown'd Ianthe way !     [*Shout again.*
    ADM. Hark ! they grow loud !
That tide, the crowd,
Will not for lovers' leisure stay.
    MAR. That storm by suddenness prevails,
And makes us lower all our sails.
    VILL. To Mustapha I'll straight a herald send,
      That Solyman may melt when he shall know,
How much we on his mighty mind depend
      By trusting more than Rhodes to such a foe.
          [*Exeunt Villerius, Admiral, Marshal.*
    ALPH. How long, Ianthe, should I grieve
If I perceiv'd you could believe
That I the Rhodians can so much esteem,
As to adventure you to rescue them ?
Yet I for Rhodes would frankly hazard all
That I could mine, and not Ianthe's call.
        But now I yield to let you go
        A pledge of treaty to the foe,
        In hope that saving Rhodes you may
        Prepare to Sicily your way.

Were Rhodes subdu'd, Ianthe being there,
Ianthe should the only loss appear.

IANTH. Much from us both is to the Rhodians due,
But when I sue for Rhodes, it is for you.

ALPH. Ianthe, we must part! you shall rely
On hope, whilst I in parting learn to die.

IANTH. Take back that hope! your dealing is
not fair,
To give me hope, and leave your self despair.

ALPH.    I will but dream of death, and then
    As virtuously as dying men
Let me to scape from future punishment
Come to a clear confession, and repent.

IANTH.    I cannot any story fear
    Which of Alphonso I shall hear,
Unless his foes in malice tell it wrong.

ALPH. Ianthe, my confession is not long,
For since it tells what folly did commit
Against your honour, shame will shorten it.

IANTH.    Lend me a little of that shame;
    For I perceive I grow to blame
In practising to guess what it can be.

ALPH. It is my late ignoble jealousy.
Though parting now seems death, yet but forgive
That crime, and after parting I may live.
And as I now again great sorrow shew,
    Though I repented well for it before,
So let your pardon with my sorrows grow;
    You much forgive me, but forgive me more.

IANTH. Away! away! How soon will this augment
    The troubled people's fears,
When they shall see me by Alphonso sent
    To treat for Rhodes in tears?

ALPH.    What in your absence shall I do
    Worthy of fame, though not of you?

IANTH.    By patience, not by action now,
    Your virtue must successful grow.
    [*A shout within.*

ALPH. In throngs the longing people wait
   Your coming at the palace gate.
   Let me attend you to the pier.
IANTH. But we must leave our sorrows here.
   Let not a Rhodian witness be
   Of any grief in you or me ;
For Rhodes, by seeing us at parting mourn,
Will look for weeping clouds at my return.

          [*Exeunt.*

*The Scene is chang'd to the camp of Solyman, the tents
and guards seem near, and part of Rhodes at a distance.*

  *Enter* SOLYMAN, PIRRHUS, RUSTAN.

PIR. None, glorious Sultan, can your conquest
  doubt
When Rhodes has hung a flag of treaty out ?
 SOLY.   Thy courage haughty Rhodes,
     When I account the odds
Thou hast oppos'd, by long and vain defence,
Is but a braver kind of impudence.
Thou knew'st my strength, but thou didst better
  know
How much I priz'd the brav'ries of a foe.
 PIR. Their sallies were by stealth, and faint
  of late.
 SOLY. Can flowing valour stay at standing
  flood ?
 PIR. No, it will quickly from the mark abate.
 RUST. And then soon shew the dead low ebb
  of blood.
 SOLY. When those who did such mighty deeds
  before,
    Shall less, but by a little, do,
     It shews to me and you,
Old Pirrhus, that they mean to do no more.
By treaty they but boldly beg a peace.

III        X

PIR. Shall I command that all our batt'ries
cease ?

SOLY. You may ! then draw our out-guards to
the line.

PIR. And I'll prevent the springing of the
mine.                                      [*Exit.*

*Enter* MUSTAPHA.

MUSTA. Villerius sends his homage to your feet:
And, to declare how low
The pride of Rhodes can bow,
Ianthe will be here to kneel and treat.

RUST. What more can fortune in your favour
do ?
Beauty, which conquers victors, yields to you.

SOLY. What wand'ring star does lead her forth ?
Can she,
Who scorn'd a pass-port for her liberty,
Vouchsafe to come, and treat without it now ?
The first did glory, this respect may shew.
Pow'rs best religion she,
Perhaps does civilly believe
To be establish'd, and reform'd in me,
Which councils monarchs to forgive.

*Enter* PIRRHUS.

PIR. A second morn begins to break from
Rhodes ;
And now that threat'ning sky grows clear,
Which was o'ercast with smoke of cannon-clouds,
The fair Ianthe does appear.

SOLY. Pirrhus, our forces from the trenches lead,
And open as our flying ensigns spread.
And Mustapha, let her reception be
As great as is the faith she has in me.
I keep high int'rest hid in this command ;

Which you with safety may
　　Implicitly obey,
But not without your danger understand.
Your tried obedience I shall much engage,
Join'd to the prudence of your practis'd age.
　MUSTA. We are content with age, because we live
　　So long beneath your sway.
　PIR.　　Age makes us fit t' obey
Commands which none but Solyman can give.
　　　　　　*[Exeunt Pirrhus, Mustapha, Rustan.*
　SOLY. Of spacious Empire what can I enjoy ?
Gaining at last but what I first destroy.
　　　'Tis fatal, Rhodes, to thee,
　　　And troublesome to me
That I was born to govern swarms
Of vassals boldly bred to arms :
For whose accurs'd diversion, I must still
Provide new towns to sack, new foes to kill.
Excuse that pow'r, which by my slaves is aw'd :
　　　For I shall find my peace
　　　Destroy'd at home, unless
I seek for them destructive war abroad.　　*[Exit.*

*Enter* ROXOLANA, HALY, PIRRHUS, MUSTAPHA,
　　RUSTAN, *Pages, Women.*

　ROX. Th' ambassadors of Persia, are they
　come ?
　HALY. They seek your favour and attend their
　doom.
　ROX. The Vizier Bashaw, did you bid him wait ?
　HALY. Sultana, he does here expect his fate.
　ROX. You take up all our Sultan's bosom now ;
Have we no place but that which you allow ?
　RUST. Your beauteous greatness does your ear
　incline
To rumours of those crimes which are not mine.

My foes are prosp'rous in their diligence,
And turn e'en my submission to offence.

   Rox. Rustan, your glories rise, and swell too
     fast.
You must shrink back and shall repent your haste.

   Musta. Th' Egyptian presents which you pleas'd
     t' assign,
As a reward to th' eunuch Saladine,
Are part of those allotments Haly had.

   Rox. Let a division be to Haly made.

   Pir. Th' Armenian cities have their tribute
     paid,
And all the Georgian princes sue for aid.

   Rox. Those cities, Mustapha, deserve our
     care.
Pirrhus, send succours to the Georgian war.

   Musta. Th' ambassador which did the jewels
     bring
From the Hungarian queen, does audience crave.

   Rox. Pirrhus, be tender of her infant King.
Who dares destroy that throne which I would
     save ?

   Rust. Sultana, humbly at your feet I fall,
Do not your Sultan's will, my counsel call.

   Rox. Rustan ! Go, mourn ! but you may long
     repent :
My busy pow'r wants leisure to relent.

   Rust. Think me not wicked, till I doubt to find
Some small compassion in so great a mind.

   Rox. These are Court-monsters, corm'rants of
     the crown :
They feed on favour till th' are over-grown ;
Then saucily believe, we monarch's wives
      Were made but to be dress't
       For a continu'd feast ;
To hear soft sounds, and play away our lives.
They think our fulness is to wane so soon

As if our sex's governess, the moon,
Had plac'd us but for sport on fortune's lap ;
They with bold pencils, by the changing shape
Of our frail beauty, have our fortune drawn ;
And judge our breasts transparent as our lawn ;
  Our hearts as loose, and soft, and slight
  As are our summer vests of silk ;
  Our brains, like to our feathers light ;
  Our blood as sweet as is our milk :
And think, when fav'rites rise, we are to fall
Meekly as doves, whose livers have no gall.
But they shall find, I'm no European Queen,
Who in a throne does sit but to be seen ;
And lives in peace with such State-thieves as these
Who rob us of our business for our ease.
        *[Exeunt omnes.*

---

## THE THIRD ACT.

*The Scene continues.*

*Enter* SOLYMAN, MUSTAPHA, PIRRHUS, RUSTAN.

MUSTA. Majestic Sultan ! at your feet we fall :
  Our duty 'tis and just
   To say, you have encompass'd us with all
   That we can private trust
   Or public honours call.
PIR. In fields our weak retiring age you grace
   With forward action ; and in Court,
   Where all your mighty chiefs resort,
Even they to us, as Kings to them, give place.
RUST. The cords by which we are oblig'd are
 strong.
SOLY. You all have loyal been and loyal long.
  To shew I this retain in full belief,

I'll doubly trust you, with my shame and grief.
      A grief which takes up all my breast :
      Yet finds the room so narrow too
      That being straightened there it takes no
        rest,
      But must get out to trouble you.
That grief begets a shame which would disgrace
My pow'r if it were publisht in my face,
   MUSTA.  Your outward calm does well
        Your inward storm disguise.
   RUST.    But long dead calms fore-tell
        That tempests are to rise.
   SOLY. My Roxolana, by ambitious strife,
To get unjust succession for her son,
      Has put in doubt
      Or blotted out
All the heroic story of my life ;
And will lose back the battles I have won.
   PIR. Ere ill advice shall lead her far, she'll
    scorn
Her guide, and, faster than she went, return.
   MUSTA. Those who advis'd her ill, in that did do
Much more than we dare hear except from you.
   SOLY. O Mustapha ! is it too much for me,
To think, I justly may possessor be
Of one soft bosom, where releas'd from care,
I should securely rest from toils of war ?
But now, when daily tir'd with watchful life,
     (With various turns in doubtful fight,
     And length of talking councils) I at night
In vain seek sleep with a tempestuous wife.
Wink at my shame, that I, whose banners brave
The world, should thus to beauty be a slave.
   PIR.    This cloud will quickly pass
      From Roxolana's face.
   MUSTA. The weather then will change from foul
    to fair.

Rust. Tempests are short, and serve to clear the
    air.
Soly. Since I have told my sickness, it is fit
You hear what cure I have prescrib'd to it.
Those lovers' knots I cannot strait untwine,
  Which, sure, were made to last
  Since they were once tied fast
With strings of Roxolana's heart and mine.
Musta. How can she vast possession more
    improve?
Has she not all in having all your love?
Soly. I have design'd a way to check her pride.
  It is not yet forgot,
  That even the Gordian knot
At last was cut, which could not be untied.
  Does not the fair Ianthe wait
  Without in hope to mitigate,
  By soft'ning looks, the Rhodians' fate?
  Let that new moon appear,
  And try her influence here.
         [*Exit Mustapha.*
Pir. What lab'rynth does our Sultan mean to
    tread?
Shall straying love the world's great leader lead?

    *Enter* Mustapha, Ianthe.

Soly. When warlike cities, fair Embassadress,
Begin to treat they cover their distress.
In showing you, the artful Rhodians know
They hide distress and all their triumphs show.
From with'ring Rhodes you fresher beauty bring,
And sweeter than the bosom of the Spring.
 Ianth. Cities, propitious Sultan, when they treat,
Conceal their wants, and strength may counterfeit:
But sure the Rhodians would not get esteem,
By ought pretended in my self or them.
  If I could any beauty wear

Where Roxolana fills the sphere,
   Yet I bring griefs to cloud it here.
SOLY. Your Rhodes has hung a flag of treaty out.
IANTH. You can as little then my sorrows doubt
As I can fear that any humble grief
May sue to Solyman and want relief.
   SOLY. You oft the proffer'd freedom did refuse,
Which now you seek, and would have others use.
   IANTH. I then did make my want of merit known;
And thought that gift too much for me alone;
      And as 'twas fit
      To reckon it
More favour than Ianthe should receive;
      So it did then appear
      That single favours were
Too little for great Solyman to give.
   SOLY. Much is to every beauty due:
      Then how much more to all
      Those divers forms we beauty call;
      And all are reconcil'd in you?
But those who here for peace by treaty look,
Must meet with that which beauty least can brook;
Delay of Court, which makes the blood so cold
That youngest Agents here look pale and old.
Here you must tedious forms of pow'r obey:
Your business will all night require your stay.
   IANTH. Bus'ness, abroad at night? sure bus'ness
   then
Only becomes the confidence of men.
      Those who the greatest wand'rers are,
      Wild birds, that in the day
      Frequent no certain way,
      And know no limits in the air,
      Will still at night discreetly come
      And take their civil rest at home.
   SOLY. Is the protection of my pow'r so slight,
That in my camp you are afraid of night?

IANTH. Stay in the camp at night, and Rhodes so
   near,
Honour my guide and griev'd Alphonso there ?
   SOLY. Treaties are long, my Bassas old and
   slow :
With whom you must debate before you go.
Let not your cause by any absence fail.
Your beauteous presence may on age prevail.
   IANTH. Alas, I came not to capitulate,
And shew a love of speech by long debate :
                       [*She kneels.*
But to implore from Solyman what he
     To Rhodes may quickly grant,
     And never feel a want
Of that which by dispatch would doubled be.
   SOLY. Ianthe rise ! your grief may pity move ;
     But graceful grief,
     Whilst it does seek relief
May pity lead to dang'rous ways of love.
   IANTH. Why Heav'n, was I mistaken when I
   thought
     That I the coarsest shape had brought
And the most wither'd too that sorrow wears ?
   SOLY. If you would wither'd seem, restrain your
   tears.
     The morning dew makes roses blow
     And sweeter smell and fresher shew.
Take heed, Ianthe, you may be to blame.
Did you not trust me when you hither came ?
Will you my honour now too late suspect,
     When only that can yours protect ?
   IANTH. If of your virtue my extreme belief
     May virtuous favour gain,
     My tears I will restrain.
It is my faith shall save me, not my grief.
   SOLY. Conduct her strait to Roxolana's tent
And tell my haughty Empress I have sent

Such a mysterious present as will prove
A riddle both to honour and to love.

[*Exeunt sev'ral ways.*

*The Scene returns to that of the town besieg'd.*

*Enter* ADMIRAL.

ADM. Dwells not Alphonso in Ianthe's breast ;
As prince of that fair palace, not a guest ?
Can it be virtue in a Rhodian knight
To seek possession of another's right ?
Yet how can I his title there destroy
By loving that which he may still enjoy ?
My passion will no less than virtue prove
Whilst it does much Ianthe's virtue love.
If in her absence I her safety fear,
'Tis virtuous kindness then to wish her here.
  But of her dangers I in vain
  Shall with my watchful fears complain
Till he grows fearful too, whose fears must be
Rais'd to the husband's virtue, jealousy.

*Enter* VILLERIUS, MARSHAL.

VILL.   Does he not seem
   As if in dream,
His course by storm were on the ocean lost ?
 MAR. He now draws cards to shun a rocky
 coast.
 ADM. The foolish world does jealousy mistake :
  'Tis civil care which kindness does
 improve.
Perhaps the jealous are too much awake ;
  But others dully sleep o'er those they love.
He must be jealous made, for that kind fear,
When known, will quickly bring and stay her here.
 VILL.   What can thy silence now portend,
  When the assembled people send

Their thankfulness to Heav'n in one loud voice ?
The hungry, wounded, and the sick rejoice.
  VILL.   Our quires in long procession sing,
    The bells of all our temples ring,
     Our enemies
     Begin to rise,
And from our walls are to their camp retir'd
  To see Ianthe there in triumph shewn.
Their cannon in a loud salute are fir'd,
  And echo'd too by louder of our own.
ADM.   Who is so dully bred,
    Or rather who so dead
Whom fair Ianthe's triumph cannot move ?
From th' ocean's bosom it will call
  A sinking Admiral,
Who flies to stormy seas from storms of love.

*Enter* ALPHONSO.

 ALPH.  Our foes, great master, wear the looks
 of friends.
    A Zanjack from the camp attends
    Behind the out-let of the pier;
    And he demands your private ear.
       [*Ex. Vil. and Mar.*
ADM.   Would you had met Ianthe there.
 ALPH.  Since well receiv'd, you wish her here
 too soon.
    The morning led her out
    And we may doubt
How her dispatch could bring her back ere noon.
 ADM.  Her high reception was but justly due ;
   Who with such noble confidence,
   Could with her sexes fears dispense
And trusting Solyman could part from you.
 ALPH.  By that we may discern her rising mind
O'er all the pinnacles of female kind.

ADM. Strangely she shun'd what custom does
        afford,
The pledges of his pass and plighted word.
    ALPH. Not knowing guilt, she knows no fear,
And still must strange in all appear,
As well as singular in this ;
            The crowd of common gazers fill
            Their eyes with objects low and ill,
But she a high and good example is.

### Enter VILLERIUS, MARSHAL.

    MAR. Ianthe's laurels hourly will increase!
    VILL. I have receiv'd some secret signs of peace
From Mustapha, whose trusted messenger
Has brought me counsel how to counsel her.
She must a while make such appliances
As may the haughty Roxolana please,
To whom she now by Solyman is sent,
And does remain our lieger in her tent.
    ADM. In Turkish dialect, that word, remain,
May many sums of tedious hours contain :
And in a Rhodian lover's swift account,
To what a debt will that sad reck'ning mount.
    VILL. To-night, Alphonso, you must sleep alone.
But time is swift, a night is quickly gone :
For lovers' nights are like their slumbers short.——
I must dispatch this Zanjack to the Court.
    ALPH.  The quiet bed of lovers is the grave ;
For we in death no sense of absence have.
                    [*Exeunt Villerius, Marshal.*
    ADM. Rhodes  in  her  view,  her  tent  within
        your sight !
And yet to be divided a whole night !
    ALPH.  A single night would many ages seem,
Were I not sure that we shall meet in dream.
    ADM.  She must no more such dang'rous visits
        make.

Methinks I grow malicious for your sake,
And rather wish Rhodes should of freedom fail,
Than that Ianthe's power should now prevail.
    ALPH. Your words mysterious grow.
    ADM.              Alphonso, no !
For if whilst thus you for her absence mourn
    Her pow'r should much appear,
        She'll want excuse,
        Unless she use
A little of that power for her return
    To-day, and nightly resting here.
    ALPH. The hardened steel of Solyman is such,
    As with the edge does all the world command,
And yet that edge is softened with the touch
    Of Roxolana's gentle hand.
And as his hardness yields, when she is near,
So may Ianthe's softness govern her.
    ADM. The day sufficient seems for all address,
And is at Court the season of access ;
Deprive not Roxolana of her right ;
Let th' Empress lye with Solyman at night.
And as that privilege to her is due,
So should Ianthe sleep at Rhodes with you.
    ALPH. I'll write ! The Zanjack for my letter stays ;
Love walks his round, and leads me in a maze.
                         [*Exit.*
    ADM. Love does Alphonso in a circle lead ;
And none can trace the ways which I must tread.
Lovers, in searching love's records, will find
    But very few like me
    That still would virtuous be,
Whilst to another's wife I still am kind.
And whilst that wife I like a lover woo,
    I use all art
    That from her husband she may never part,
And yet even then would make him jealous too.
                         [*Exit.*

*The Scene returns to that of the Camp.*

*Enter* ROXOLANA, HALY.

Rox. Think, Haly, think, what I should swiftly
   do ?
A Rhodian lady, and a beauty too,
In my pavilion lodg'd ! It serves to prove
His settled hatred and his wandering love.
Who did he send to plant this canker here ?
   HALY. Old Bassa Mustapha.
   Rox. Bid him appear !               [*Exit Haly.*
Hope thou grow'st weak, and thou hast been too
   strong.
Like night thou com'st too soon, and stay'st too
   long.
Hence ! smiling hope ! with growing infants play :
      If I dismiss thee not, I know
         Thou of thy self wilt go,
And canst no longer than my beauty stay.
I'll open all the doors to let thee out :
And then call in thy next successor, doubt.
Come doubt, and bring thy lean companion, care,
And, when you both are lodg'd, bring in despair.

*Enter* MUSTAPHA, HALY.

MUSTA. Our op'ning buds, and falling blossoms, all
      That we can fresh and fragrant call,
That spring can promise and the summer pay,
      Be strew'd in Roxolana's way.
On nature's fairest carpets let her tread ;
And there, through calms of peace, long may she
   lead
      That pow'r which we have follow'd far,
         And painfully, through storms of war.
   Rox. Blessings are cheap, and those you can
   afford :

Yet you are kinder than your frowning lord.
I dare accuse him ; but it is too late.——— [*Weeps.*
What means that pretty property of State,
Which is from Rhodes for midnight treaties sent ?
Private cabals of lovers in my tent !
Your valour, Mustapha, serv'd to convey
Love's fresh supplies.  You soldiers can make way.
Was it not greatly done to bring her here ?
   MUSTA. Duty in that did over-rule my fear.
It was the mighty Solyman's command.
   ROX. Thou fatal fool ! how canst thou think
To find a basis where thou firm mayst stand
      On those rough waters where I sink ?
   MUSTA. If Roxolana were not ranked above
      Mankind, she strait would fall
      Before that pow'r which all
The valiant follow, and the virtuous love.
   ROX.  I grow immortal, for I life disdain :
      Which ill with thy dislike of dying suits.
Yet thou, for safety, fear'st great pow'r in vain ;
      Who here art but a subject to my mutes.
          [*Mustapha draws a Parchment.*
   MUSTA. Peruse the dreaded will of anger'd power ;
Toucht with the signet of the Emperour :
It does enjoin Ianthe's safety here :
She must be sought with love, and serv'd with fear.
This disobey'd ; your mutes who still make haste
      To cruelty, may rest for want of breath.
'Tis order'd they shall suddenly be past
      Their making signs, and shall be dumb with
         death.
This dreadful doom from Solyman I give,
      But if his will, which is our law,
      Be met with an obedient awe,
The Empress then may long in triumph live.
             [*She weeps.*
   ROX. Be gone ! thy duty is officious fear.

If I am soft enough to grieve,
It is to see the Sultan leave
The warring world, and end his conquests here.
Crawl to my Sultan, still officious grow !
Ebb with his love, and with his anger flow.
                          [*Exit Mustapha.*
HALY. Preserve with temper your Imperial
   mind ;
      And till you can express
      Your wrath with good success,
By ang'ring others to your self be kind.——
   Rox. If thou canst weep, thou canst endure
   to bleed :
      Men who compassion feel have valour too :
I shall thy courage more than pity need :
      Dar'st thou contrive as much as I dare do ?
HALY. I'll on, as far as weary life can go.
Rox. Then I shall want no aid to my design :
We'll dig below them, and blow up their mine.
                          [*Exeunt.*


### THE FOURTH ACT.

*The Scene returns to that of the town beleaguer'd.*

*Enter* SOLYMAN, MUSTAPHA, RUSTAN.

SOLY.   Can Roxalana such a rival bear ?
MUST.   She has her fits of courage and of fear.
As she does high against your anger grow,
So, trusting strait your love, she stoops as low.
   SOLY.   Her chamber-tempests I have known too
   well :
She quickly can with winds of passion swell ;
And then as quickly has the woman's pow'r
Of laying tempests with a weeping show'r.
What looks does the detain'd Ianthe shew ?
   MUSTA.      She still is calm in all her fears.

Rust.           And seems so lovely in her tears,
As when the morning's face is washt in dew.
                *Enter* Pirrhus.
Pir.   The world salutes you Sultan ! ev'ry pow'r
Does shrink before your throne ; and ev'ry hour
A flying packet or an agent brings
From Asia, Africa, and European kings.
  Soly.   With packets to old Zanger go !
           Who, freed from action, can with sleep
           dispense ;
And having little now to do,
           May read dull volumes of intelligence.
These Writing-Princes covet to seem wise
In packets, and by formal Embassies :
They would with symphonies of civil words,
Sweet sounds of Court, charm rudeness from our
           swords :
           Teach us to lay our gauntlets by,
           That they unarm'd, and harmlessly,
From farthest realms, by proxy, might shake hands,
And, off'ring useless friendship, save their lands.
                               [*Exeunt.*

*Enter* Villerius, Alphonso, Admiral, Marshal.

  Adm.   He came disguis'd, who brought your
           letter here,
And sought such privacy as argu'd fear.
  Mar.   But, Sov'reign master, yours did seem to be
Convey'd by one less pain'd with secresy ;
           Who does for answer stay.
  Vill.       Mine came from Mustapha.
It would import a promising increase
Of our conditions by approaching peace.
           But does request us to consent
That fair Ianthe may yet longer stay
           In pow'rful Roxolana's tent ;
    III.                    y

And that request we understand
    As a command
Which, though we would not grant, we must obey.
  ALPH. Mine by a Christian slave was brought,
Who from the Eunuch Bassa, Haly, came;
    And was by Roxolana wrote :
See the Sultana's signet and her name.
She writes—but oh ! why have I breath
To tell, how much 'tis worse than death
      Not to be dead
    Ere I again this letter read ?
  ADM. Oh, my prophetic fear !
  ALPH. She writes, that if I hold my honour dear;
Or if Ianthe does that honour prize,
    I should with all the art
     Of love confirm her heart,
And straight from Solyman divert her eyes.
  ADM. Who knows what end this dire beginning
    bodes ?
  ALPH.    And here she likewise says,
      He to Ianthe lays
A closer siege than e'er he did to Rhodes.
  ADM. Ianthe, I will still my love pursue ;
                     [*Aside.*
Be kind to thee, and to Alphonso true :
But love's small policies great honour now
Will hardly to my rivalship allow :
Those little arts, bold Duke, I must lay by
And urge thy courage more than jealousy.
  VILL. Where is thy honour now, fam'd Eastern
    lord ?
  ADM. Why sought we not his pass-port or his
    word ?
  ALPH. How durst Ianthe have so little fear
      As to believe
      That in the camp she should receive
Freedom from him who did besiege her here ?

ADM. Whilst in her own dispose she here
   remain'd
I of the brav'ry of her trust complain'd:
Her gen'rous faith too meanly was deceiv'd,
And must not be upbraided but reliev'd.
   VILL. To rescue Rhodes she did her self forsake;
And Rhodes shall nobly pay that virtue back.
   ALPH. Great master! what shall poor Alphonso
   do?
        Since all he has Ianthe's is;
        And now in this
Must owe Ianthe and her fame to you.
   VILL. If any virtue can in valour be:
   ADM. Or any valour in a Rhodian knight:
   ALPH. Or any lover can have loyalty:
   VILL. Or any warrior can in love delight.
   MAR. If absence makes not mighty love grow less.
   ADM. Or gentle lovers can compassion feel.
   ALPH. If loyal beauty, when in deep distress,
Can melt our hearts, and harden all our steel.
   VILL. Then let us here in sacred vows combine!
My vow is seal'd ——      *[They join their swords.*
   ADM. And mine.——
   MAR. And mine.——
   ALPH. And trebly mine.——
   VILL. Behold us, fame, then stay thy flight,
And hover o'er our towers to night;
Fresh wings together with the morning take
As early as afflicted lovers wake.
Then tell the world that we have join'd our swords;
But 'tis for griev'd Ianthe, not for Rhodes.
   ALPH. Now we shall prosper, who were weary
   grown
   In Rhodes, and never could successful prove
When Empire led us forth to seek renown,
   For honour should no leader have but love.
              *[Exeunt omnes.*

*The Scene is chang'd.*

*Being wholly fill'd with Roxolana's Rich Pavilion,*
*wherein is discern'd, at distance, Ianthe sleeping on*
*a Couch ; Roxolana at one End of it, and Haly at*
*the other ; Guards of Eunuchs are discover'd at the*
*wings of the Pavilion ; Roxolana having a Turkish*
*embroidered handkerchief in her left hand, and a*
*ponyard in her right.*

Rox.   Thou dost from beauty, Solyman,
   As much refrain as nature can ;
Who making beauty, meant it should be lov'd.
   But how can I my station keep
Till thou, Ianthe, art by death remov'd ?
    To die, when thou art young,
    Is but too soon to fall asleep
    And lye asleep too long.
 Haly.   Your dreadful will what power can here
   command
But pity ? oh, let pity stay your hand !——
 Rox.   Sultan, I will not weep, because my tears
Cannot suffice to quench thy love's false flame :
   Nor will I to a paleness bleed,
   To show my love's true fears.
   Because I rather need
More blood to help to blush away thy shame.
 Haly.   How far are all his former virtues gone ?
Turn back the progress of forgetful time :
   The many favours by your Sultan done
Should now excuse him for one purpos'd crime.
 Rox   Haly, consult ! can I do ill
   If many foul adult'ries I prevent,
When I but one fair mistress kill ?
 Haly.   Be not too early here with punishment.
   Your Sultan now
   Does only shew
The grudgings of a lover's feverish fit.

You find his inclinations strange,
But, being new, they soon may change :
And they have reacht but to intention yet.
Rox.　Long before deeds Heav'n calls intention
　　sin.
'Tis good to end what he would ill begin.
Haly.　Do not relinquish yet your first design.
　　　　Before you darken all her light
　　　　Examine, by your judging sight,
If in your sphere she can unblemisht shine.
You meant to prove her virtue and first try
　　　　How well she here could as a rival live,
Ere as a judg'd adultress she should die :
　　　　In pard'ning her you Solyman forgive.
And can you add to your lov'd greatness more,
When able to forgive the greatest pow'r ?
Rox.　Tell me again Alphonso's short reply
When I by letter wak'd his jealousy ;
And counsell'd him to write and to advise
His wife to lock her breast, and shut her eyes.
Haly.　With silence first he did his sorrows bear ;
Then anger rais'd him, till he fell with fear :
At last said, she was now past counsel grown ;
Or else could take no better than her own.
Rox.　His thoughts a double vizard wear,
　　　　And only lead me to suspense,
It seems he does her dangers fear,
　　　　And fain would trust her innocence.
Wake her ! I will pursue my first design.
Haly.　I go to draw the curtain of a shrine.
Awake ! Behold the pow'rful Empress here.
　　[*Ianthe rises and walks at distance from Roxolana.*
Ianth.　　　　Heav'n has the greatest pow'r ;
Heav'n seeks our love, and kindly comforts fear.
　　　　　　This is my fatal hour.
　　Rox.　　　　Though beauteous when she slept,
　　　　　　Yet now would I had kept

Her safely sleeping still.
She, waking, turns my envy into shame ;
And does it so reclaim,
That I am conquer'd who came here to kill.

IANTH.     What dangers should I fear ?
Her brow grows smooth and clear:
Yet so much greatness cannot want disguise.
The great live all within ;
And are but seldom seen
Looking abroad through casements of their eyes.

ROX.   Have courage, fair Sicilian, and come
near.

IANTH.   My distance shews my duty more than
fear.

ROX.   I have a present for you, and 'tis such
As comes from one who does believe
It is for you too little to receive ;
And I, perhaps, may think it is too much.

IANTH.  Who dares be bountiful to low distress ?
Who to Ianthe can I present make
When Rhodes besieg'd has all she would possess ;
And all the world does ruin'd Rhodes
forsake ?

ROX.   The present will not make the giver poor ;
And, though 'tis single now, it quickly can
Be multiplied ; you shall have many more.
It is this kiss——It comes from Solyman.

IANTH.     You did your creature courage give;
And made me hope that I had leave
to live
When you from duteous distance call'd me near :
But now I soon shall courage lack :
I am amaz'd, and must go back.
Amazement is the ugli'st shape of fear.

ROX.   Are Christian ladies so reserv'd and shy ?

IANTH.     Our sacred law does give
Them precepts how to live,

And nature tells them they must die.

Rox. 'Tis well they to their husbands are so
    true.

But speak, Ianthe, are they all like you?

    IANTH.        I hope they are, and better too,
          Or, if they are not, will be so.

    Rox.   They have been strangely injur'd then.
          But rumour does mistake.
          Some say they visits make;

And they are visited by men.

    IANTH.        What custom does avow
          Our laws in time allow;

And those who never guilty be
Suspect not others' liberty.

    Rox.   This would in Asia wonderful appear:

But time may introduce that fashion here.
Come nearer! Is your husband kind and true?

    IANTH.        If good to good I may compare,
          Excepting greatness, I would dare

To say, he is as Solyman to you.

    Rox.   As he to me? How strong is innocence!

Prevailing till 'tis free to give offence.
Indeed, Alphonso, has a large renown:
          Which does so daily spread,
          As it the world may lead;

And should not be contracted in a town.

    IANTH.        As we in all agree,
          So he will prove like me

A lowly servant to your rising fame.

    Rox.   But is he kind to you, and free from blame?

Civil by day, and loyal too at night?

    IANTH.      By nature, not by skill,
          He is as cheerful still,

And as unblemisht as unshaded light.

    Rox.   These Christian turtles live too happily.

I wish, for breed, they would to Asia fly.——
          You must not at such distance stand;

Draw near, and give me your fair
        hand.——
I have another present for you now ;
        And such a present as I know
You will much better than the first allow,
        Though Solyman will not esteem it so.
'Tis from my self——of friendship such a seal——
                                    [*Kisses her.*
As you to Solyman must ne'er reveal.
        And that I may be more assur'd,
        By this again you are conjur'd.
IANTH.        Presents so good and great as these
        I should receive upon my knees.
ROX. I will not, lest I may revive your fear,
Relate the cause of your confinement here.
        But know, I must
        Your virtue trust ;
Which, proving loyal, you are safe in mine.
IANTH. The light of angels still about you shine !
HALY. The dang'rous secrets of th' Imperial bed
                        [*Haly takes Ianthe aside.*
        Are darker than the riddles of the throne.
The glass, in which their characters are read,
        We Eunuchs grind, and 'tis but seldom
        shewn.
IANTH.        I shall with close and weary eyes
        Retire from all your mysteries ;
And, when occasion shall my honour trust,
You'll find I have some courage, and am just.
ROX. Perhaps, Ianthe, you may shortly hear
Of clouds, which threat'ning me, may urge your fear.
Be virtuous still ! 'tis true my Sultan frowns.
                                    [*She weeps.*
But let him win more battles, take more towns,
And be all day the foremost in the fight ;
Yet he shall find that I will rule at night.
                                    [*Haly looks in.*

HALY. The guards increase, and many mutes
    appear,
Lifting their lights to shew the Sultan near.
    ROX. My new seal'd friendship I must now
    lay by
A while, and seem your jealous enemy.
Be to your self, and to Alphonso, true.
    IANTH. As he to me, and virtue is to you.
                  *[Ianthe steps at distance.*

*Enter* SOLYMAN.

    SOLY. Has night lost all her dark dominion here?
        High hopes disturb your sleep ;
        But I suspect you keep
Ianthe waking, not with hope but fear.
    ROX. Too well, and much too soon I know
        Whom you are pleas'd to grace :
However, since it must be so,
        You'll find I can give place.
    SOLY. You had a place too near me, and too high.
        If but a little you remove
        From place of Empire or of love
You soon become but as a stander-by.
One step descending from a shining throne,
You to the darkest depth fall swiftly down.
    ROX. If I sat nearer to you than 'twas fit,
        For Empires, heralds to admit ;
(I being born below, and you above)
Pray call in death, and I'll, even then, bring love.
        To these all places equal be ;
        For love and death know no degree.
    SOLY. I cannot passion's riddles understand.
    ROX. You still have present death at your
    command ;
        But former love you have laid by :
Which, being gone you know that I can die.
                  *[Weeps.*

SOLY.  I better know that you have cause to weep.
                              [*Turns to Ianthe.*
Ianthe, all is calm within your breast,
Retire into the quiet shade of sleep,
    And let not watchful fear divert your rest.
Let all the nations of my camp suffice,
As guards, to keep you from my enemies ;
                (For of your own
                You can have none)
Whilst I but as love's sent'nel on you wait,
Arm'd with his bow, at your pavilion gate.
    IANTH.  Heaven put it in your mighty mind
                Quickly to be,
                More than to me,
To all the valiant Rhodians kind.
And may you grieve to think how many mourn
Till you shall end their griefs at my return.
    SOLY.  You shall not languish with delay.
                But this is business for the day.
'Tis now so late at night that all love's spies,
                Parents and husbands too,
The watchful, and the watch, seal up their eyes,
                And lovers cease to woo.
                              [*Exeunt Haly, Ianthe.*
    ROX.  You alter ev'ry year the world's known
                face ;
Whilst cities you remove, and nations chase.
These great mutations (which, with shrill
And ceaseless sounds, Fame's trumpet fill,
And shall seem wonders in her brazen books)
Much less amaze me than your alter'd looks ;
Where I can read your love's more fatal change.
    SOLY.  You make my frowns, yet seem to think
                them strange.
    ROX.  You seek a stranger and abandon me.
    SOLY.  Strange coasts are welcome after storms
                at sea.

Rox. That various mind will wander very far,
   Which, more than home, a foreign land prefers.
Soly. The wise, for quietness, when civil war
   Does rage at home, turn private travellers.
Rox. Your love's long frost has made my bosom
   cold.
Soly. Let not the cause be in your story told.
Rox. A colder heart death's hand has never felt;
But 'tis such ice as you may break, or melt.

                        [*She Weeps.*

   Soly. I never shall complain
      When you are wet with rain,
Which softer passion does thus gently pour.
What more in season is than such a shower?
You still, through little clouds, would lovely shew,
Were all your April-weather calm as now.
But March resembles more your haughty mind ;
Froward and loud oft'ner than calmly kind.
Weather which may not inconvenient prove
To country lovers, born but to make love:
   Who grieve not when they mutual kindness
      doubt,
But with indiff'rence meet a frown or smile ;
   As having frequent leisure to fall out,
And their divided breasts to reconcile.
   Rox. The world had less sad bus'ness known if
     you
Had been ordain'd for so much leisure too.
   Soly. Monarchs, who onward still with conquest
     move,
Can only for their short diversion love.
When a black cloud in beauty's sky appears,
They cannot wait till time the tempests clears.
Whilst they to save a sullen mistress, stay,
The world's dominion may be cast away.
   Rox. Why is dominion priz'd above
      Wise nature's great concernment, love ?

SOLY. Of Heav'n what have we found, which we
 do more,
And sooner, than exceeding pow'r adore ?
The wond'rous things which that chief pow'r has
 done,
Are to those early spies, our senses, shewn :
And must at length to reason be assur'd:
Yet how, or what, Heav'n loves is much obscur'd,
  And our uncertain love
  (Perhaps not bred above,
But in low regions, like the wand'ring winds)
Shews diff'rent sexes more than equal minds.
 ROX. Your love, indeed, is prone to change,
  And like the wand'ring wind does range.
  The gale awhile tow'rd Cyprus blew ;
  It turn'd to Crete and stronger grew ;
Then on the Lycian shore it favour'd me :
But now, Ianthe seeks in Sicily.
 SOLY. In progresses of war and love
  Victors with equal haste must move,
And in attempts of either make no stay :
They can but visit, conquer, and away.
 ROX. Love's most victorious and most cruel foe !
Forsake me and to meaner conquests go !
To wars, where you may sack and over-run,
Till your success has all the world undone.
Advance those trophies which you ought to hide ;
  For wherefore are they rais'd
  But to have slaughter prais'd,
And courage which is but applauded pride ?
 SOLY. In so much rain I knew a gust would
 come :
I'll shun the rising storm and give it room.
 ROX. Love's foes are ever hasty in retreat ;
  You can march off ; but 'tis for fear
  Lest you should hear
Those mournings which your cruelties beget.

SOLY. The fear is wise which you upbraid :
   For, whilst thus terrible you grow,
  I must confess, I am afraid,
   And not asham'd of being so.
ROX. Go where you cover greater fear
   Than that which you dissemble here :
Where you breed ill your mis-begotten fame,
  When charging armies and assaulting towns,
You ravish nations with as little shame
   As now you shew in your injurious frowns.
SOLY. If we grow fearful at the face of war,
   You, justly, may our terror blame,
Since, by your darings, we might learn to dare.
   Would you as well could teach us shame.
ROX. Your fears appear, even in your darings,
    great ;
   You would not else sound cheerful
    trumpets when
The charge begins, whilst drums with clamour beat,
   To raise the courage of your mighty men.
With war's loud music shouts are mingled too ;
   Which boastingly such cruel deeds
    proclaim
As beasts, through thickest furs, would blush to do.
   Your wives may breed up wolves to
    teach you shame.
SOLY. 'Tis not still dang'rous when you angry
    grow :
   For, Roxolana, you can anger show.
To those whom you, perhaps, can never hate.
This passion is ; but you have crimes of State.
ROX. Call nature to be judge ! what have I
    done ?
SOLY. You have a husband lost to save a son.
ROX. Sultan, that son is yours as much as mine.
SOLY.    He has some lustre got in fight ;
    But yet beyond the dawning light

Of his new glory, Mustapha does shine;
Who is the pledge of my Circassian wife;
And from my blood as great a share of life
May challenge as your son. Has he not worn
A victor's wreath? He is my eldest born.

Rox. Because her son the Empire shall enjoy,
Must therefore strangling mutes my sons destroy?
Since eldest born you may him Empire give:
But mine, as well as he, were born to live.
They may, as yours, though by a second wife,
Inherit that which nature gave them, life.

Soly. Whilst any life I shew, by any breath,
Who dares approach them in the shape of death?

Rox. When you to Heav'n's high palace shall
　　　remove,
　　To meet much more compassion there
Than you have ever felt, and far more love
　　Than e'er your heart requited here;
Will not your Bassas then presume to do
What custom warrants and our priesthood too?

Soly. Those are the secret nerves of Empire's
　　　force.
　　　　Empire grows often high
　　　　By rules of cruelty,
But seldom prospers when it feels remorse.

Rox. Accursed Empire! got and bred by art!
　　　Let nature govern or at least
　　　Divide our mutual interest:
Yield yours to death, and keep alive my part.

Soly. Beauty, retire! Thou dost my pity move!
Believe my pity, and then trust my love!
　　　　　　　　　　　　[Exit Roxol.
At first I thought her by our prophet sent
　　　As a reward for valour's toils;
　　　More worth than all my father's spoils:
And now she is become my punishment.
　　　But thou art just, O pow'r divine!

With new and painful arts
Of study'd war I break the hearts
Of half the world, and she breaks mine.
[*Exit.*

### THE FIFTH ACT.

*The Scene is chang'd to a Prospect of Rhodes by night,
and the Grand Master's Palace on Fire.*

*Enter* SOLYMAN, PIRRHUS, RUSTAN.

SOLY  Look, Pirrhus, look! what means that
sudden light,
Which casts a paleness o'er the face of night?
The flame shews dreadful, and ascends still
higher!

PIR. The Rhodian master's palace is on fire!

RUST. A greater from Saint George's tower does
shine!

SOLY. Chance it would seem, but does import
design!

*Enter* MUSTAPHA.

MUSTA. Their flag of treaty they have taken in!

SOLY. Dare they this ending war again begin?

PIR. They feed their flames to light their
forces out!

RUST, And now, seem sallying from the French
redoubt!

MUSTA. Old Orchan takes already the alarm!

SOLY. Need they make fires to keep their
courage warm?

PIR. The English now advance!

SOLY. Let them proceed!
Their cross is bloody, and they come to bleed.
Set all the turn-pikes open, let them in!
.         Those island gamesters may,
          (Who desperately for honour play)
Behold fair stakes, and try what they can win.
[*Exeunt omnes.*

*Enter* VILLERIUS, ALPHONSO, ADMIRAL, MARSHAL.

VILL, Burn palace, burn! Thy flame more
beauteous grows
      Whilst higher it ascends.
That now must serve to light us to our foes
      Which long has lodg'd our friends.
    ALPH.      It serves not only as a light
          To guide us in so black a night ;
But to our enemies will terror give.
    MAR.      Who (seeing we so much destroy,
          What we in triumph did enjoy,
That now we know not where to live)
      Will strait conclude that boldly we dare die.
    VILL. And those who to themselves lov'd life
          deny,
      Want seldom pow'r to aid their will
      When they would others kill.
    ADM. Speak both of killing and of saving too.
The utmost that our valour now can do
Is when, by many Bassas pris'ners ta'ne,
We freedom for distress Ianthe gain.
    ALPH. A jewel too sufficient to redeem
Great Solyman were he in chains with them.
    VILL. Here spread our front! our rear is all
          come forth.
We lead two thousand Rhodian knights ;
      All skill'd in various fights :
Fame's roll contains no names of higher worth.
      In whispers give command
      To make a stand !
    ADM. Stand !
    WITHIN. 1. Stand ! 2. Stand ! 3. Stand !
    VILL. Divide our knights, and all their martial
      train !
    ALPH. Let me by storm the Sultan's quarter gain.
    ADM. My lot directs my wing to Mustapha.

MAR. To Pirrhus, o'er his trench, I'll force my
way.

VILL. Our honour bids us give a brave defeat ;
Whilst prudence leaves reserves for a retreat.
All lovers are concern'd in what we do.
Love's crown depends on you, on you, on you,
Love's bow is not so fatal as my sword.

ALPH. As mine.

ADM. And mine.

TOGETHER. Ianthe is the word !          [*Exeunt.*

*A Symphony expressing a Battle is play'd a while.*

### *Enter* SOLYMAN.

SOLY. More horse ! more horse, to shake their
ranks !
Bid Orchan haste to gall their flanks.
Few Rhodian knights making their several stands,
Out-strike assemblies of our many hands.

### *Enter* MUSTAPHA, RUSTAN.

MUSTA. Morat, and valiant Zangiban are slain.

RUST. But Orchan does their yielded ground
regain.

SOLY. Our crescents shine not in the shade of
night.
But now the crescent of the sky appears ;
Our valour rises with her lucky light ;
And all our fighters blush away their fears.

### *Enter* PIRRHUS.

PIR. More pikes ! and pass the trench ! fall in !
fall in !
That we may gain the field ere day begin.

SOLY. Advance with all our guards ! This doubtful strife

III                          Z

Less grieves me than our odds
Of number against Rhodes ;
By which we honour lose to rescue life.. [*Exeunt.*

*A Symphony sounds a battle again.*

*The Scene returns to the town besieg'd.*

*Enter* VILLERIUS, MARSHAL.

VILL. Send back ! send back ! to quench our
fatal fire !
Ere morning does advance we must retire ;
Justly asham'd to let the day's great light
Shew what a little we have done to-night.

*Enter* ADMIRAL.

ADM. We have been shipwreckt in a midnight
storm ;
Who hither came, great master, to perform
Such deeds as might have given us cause to boast.
MAR.    We found the night too black,
        And now no use can make
Of day, but to discern that we are lost.
VILL. Can thy great courage mention our defeat
Whilst any life is left to make retreat ?
ADM.    It is a just rebuke.
VILL.    Where is the Duke ?
ADM. Long tir'd with valour's toils, and in his
breast,
O'ercharg'd with lovers' griefs, he sought for rest.
To Fame's eternal temple he is gone.
        And I may fear
        Is enter'd there,
Where death does keep the narrow gate,
        And lets in none
    But those whom painful honour brings.
Many, without in vain for entrance wait,
        With warrants seal'd by mighty kings.

VILL. Villerius never yet by Turkish swords
Was cut so deep as by thy wounding words.
Is that great youth, the prince of lovers, slain?
 ADM. Who knows how much of life he does
  retain?
Twice I reliev'd him from the double force
Of Zangiban's old foot, and Orchan's horse.
My strength was over-pow'r'd; and he still bent
To follow honour to the Sultan's tent.
 MAR. Alphonso's story has this sudden end:
Ianthe may a longer fate attend.
 VILL. Of life's chief hope we are bereft.
  Go rally all whom death has left!
Let our remaining knights make good the pier!
  Our hearts will serve to beat,
  Unheard, a stol'n retreat.
 ADM. But shall we leave Ianthe captive here?
 VILL. I'll to our temple force our way;
  And there for her redemption pray:
Her freedom now depends on our return.
  In temples we shall nothing gain
  From Heav'n, whilst we of loss complain:
We'll for our crimes, not for our losses, mourn.
        [Exeunt.


*Enter* SOLYMAN, PIRRHUS.

 SOLY. Let us no more the Rhodians' flight
  pursue;
  Who, since below our anger, need our
  care.
Compassion is to vanquish valour due
  Which was not cruel in successful war.
 PIR. Our sultan does his pow'r from heav'n
  derive,
  'Tis raised above the reach of human
  force:

It could not else with soft compassion thrive :
  For few are gain'd or mended by remorse.
The world is wicked grown, and wicked men
  (Since jealous still of those whom they
   have harm'd)
Are but enabl'd to offend again
  When they are pardon'd and left arm'd.

   *Enter* MUSTAPHA, RUSTAN.

MUSTA. The Rhodians will no more in arms
  appear :
   They now are lost before they loss
   their town.
RUST. They may their standards hide and
  ensigns tear :
   For what's the body when the soul
   is gone ?
MUSTA. The pris'ner whom in doubtful fight
  we took
   (Who long maintain'd the strife,
   For freedom more than life)
Is young Alphonso, the Sicilian Duke.
SOLY. Fortune could never find, if she had eyes,
A present for me which I more would prize.

   *Enter* HALY.

HALY. Your bosom-slave, the creature which
  your pow'r
   Has made in all the world the greatest wife
Did all this dang'rous night kneel and implore
   That heav'n would give you length of
   happy life,
In measure to your breadth of spreading fame,
And to the height of Ottoman's high name.
SOLY. Tell Roxolana I esteem her love

So much that I her anger fear
And whilst with passion I the one approve,
The other I with temper bear.

HALY.  She charg'd me not to undertake t'
express
With how much grief her eyes did melt
When she this night your dangers felt;
Nor how much joy she shew'd at your success.
She hears that you have pris'ner took
The bold Sicilian Duke:
And begs he may be straight at her dispose;
That you may try how she can use your foes.

SOLY.  This furious Rhodian sally could not be
Provokt but by his jealousy of me.

MUSTA. He wanted honour who could yours
suspect.

PIR.  The rash, by jealousy, themselves detect.

SOLY.  His jealousy shall meet with punish-
ment.
Convey him straight to Roxolana's tent.
                              [Exit Pirrhus.
But, Haly, know, the fair Ianthe must
Be safe, and free, who did my honour trust.
You want no mutes, nor can they want good skill
To torture or dispatch those whom they kill.
But since this Duke's renown did spread and rise
(Who in attempt at night
Has often scap'd my sight)
Take care that I may see him ere he dies.
                        [Exeunt several ways.

*The Scene returns to Roxolana's Pavilion.*

*Enter* IANTHE *in her night dress.*

IANT.  In this pavilion all have been alarm'd.
The eunuchs, mutes, and very dwarfs
were arm'd.

The Rhodians have a fatal sally made ;
    And many now, to shun
    The griefs of love, are run
Through night's dark walks to death's detested
    shade.
An eunuch lately cry'd Alphonso's slain !
    Now others change my grief,
    And give some small relief,
By new report that he's but pris'ner ta'ne.
    Where, my afflicted lord,
    Is thy victorious sword ?
For now (though 'twas too weak to rescue thee)
    It might successful grow
    If thy triumphant foe
Would make an end of love by ending me.
        *Enter* ROXOLANA.
  ROX. How fares my rival, the Sicilian flow'r ?
  IANTH. As wet with tears as roses in a show'r.
  ROX. I brought you presents when I saw you last.
  IANTH.     Presents ? If you have more,
      Like those you brought before,
They come too late, unless they make great haste.
  ROX. Are you departing without taking leave ?
  IANTH. I would not you, nor can your guards,
    deceive.
  ROX. You'll pay a farewell to a civil Court ?
  IANTH. Souls make their parting ceremonies short.
  ROX. The present which the Sultan sent before
(Who means to vex your bashfulness no more)
Was to your lips, and that you did refuse :
But this is to your ear.  I bring you news.
  IANTH. I hear, my lord and Rhodes have been to
    blame.
  ROX. It seems you keep intelligence with Fame,
Or with some frighted eunuch, her swift post ;
    Who often has from camps to cities
    brought

The dreadful news of battles lost
      Before the field was fought.

IANTH. Then I may hope this is a false alarm ;
And Rhodes has neither done nor taken harm.

ROX. You may believe Alphonso is not slain.

IANTH. Blest angel, speak ! Nor is he pris'ner
      ta'ne ?

ROX. He is a pris'ner, and is given to me.

IANTH. Angels are kind, I know you'll set him free.

ROX. He has some wounds, plac'd nobly in his
      breast.

IANTH. You soon take back the comfort you have
      given.

ROX. They are not deep, and are securely drest.

IANTH. Now you are good again ! O heal them,
      Heav'n !

ROX. In Heav'n, Ianthe, he may mercy find,
He must go thither, and leave you behind.

IANTH. I hope I shall discern your looks less
      strange ;
And your expressions not so full of change——

ROX. Weep'st thou for him, whose saucy
      jealousy
Durst think the Sultan could be false to me ?

IANTH. Though his offence makes him unfit to live,
I hope it is no crime in me to grieve.

ROX. Soft fool ! bred up in narrow western
      Courts ;
Which are by subjects storm'd like paper-forts :
Italian Courts, fair inns for foreign posts,
Where little Princes are but civil hosts.
Think'st thou that she, who does wide Empire sway,
Can breed such storms as lovers show'rs allay ?
Can half the world be govern'd by a mind
That shews domestic pity, and grows kind ?

IANTH. Where are those virtuous vows you
      lately seal'd ?

Rox. I did enjoin they should not be reveal'd.
Ianth. But could you mean they should be
        broken too ?
Rox. Those seals were counterfeit, and pass
        For nothing, since my sealing was
But to a Christian when I seal'd to you.
Ianth. Seal'd by your precious lips ! what is so
        sure
As that which makes the Sultan's heart secure ?
You to religion many temples rear ;
        Justice may find one lodging in your breast.
Rox. Religion is but public fashion here ;
        And justice is but private interest.
Nature our sex does to revenge incite ;
        And int'rest counsels us to keep our own.
Were you not sent to rule with me at night ?
        Love is as shy of partners as the throne.
Haly prepare the pris'ner ; he must die.

*Enter* Haly.

Ianth. If any has offended it is I !——
O think ! think upward on the thrones above.
Disdain not mercy, since they mercy love.
If mercy were not mingled with their pow'r,
This wretched world could not subsist an hour.
Excuse his innocence ; and seize my life !
Can you mistake the husband for the wife ?
    Rox. Are Christian wives so true, and wondrous
        kind ?
Ianthe, you can never change my mind :
For I did ever mean to keep my vow,
Which I renew, and seal it faster now.
                                    [*Kisses her.*
The Sultan frankly gave thy lord to me ;
And I as freely render him to thee.
    Ianth. To all the world be all your virtues known
More than the triumphs of your Sultan's throne.

Rox. Send in her lord, to calm her troubled
breast.
[*Exeunt Roxolana, Haly, several ways.*

IANTH. Now his departing life may stay ;
 But he has wounds. Yet she did say
They were not deep, and are securely drest.

*Enter* HALY, ALPHONSO, *his arms bound.*

HALY. Fate holds your dice ; and here expect
 the cast,
Your chance, if it be bad, will soon be past.
          [*Exit.*

ALPH. My doom contains not much diversity.
To live, to die, to be a slave, or free ?
Death sums up all ! by dying we remove
From all the frowns of pow'r, and griefs of love.
 Ianthe, are you here ?
 I will dismiss my fear.
 Death's dreaded journey I
 Have ended ere I die.
Death does to Heav'n the virtuous lead ;
Which I enjoy ere I am dead.
For it is Heav'n to me where e'er thou art,
And those who meet in Heav'n shall never part.

IANTH. Stay, stay, Alphonso! you proceed too fast ;
For I am chang'd since you beheld me last.
In Rhodes I wholly did myself resign
To serve your pow'r, but you are now in mine.
And that you may perceive how soon I can
Melt the obdurate heart of Solyman ;
Let this confirm your restless jealousy :
You came in bound and thus I make you free.—
         [*Unbinds him.*

ALPH. By this, Ianthe, you express no more
Dominion o'er me than you had before.
In Rhodes I was a subject to your will :
Your smiles preserv'd me, and your frowns did kill.

IANTH. I know your tongue too well; which
   should deceive
One who had study'd all the art
Of love rather than her whose heart
Too simply would your very looks believe.
But now you know, that though you are unbound,
Yet still your walk is on the Sultan's ground.
   ALPH. Ianthe, you are chang'd indeed
      If cruelly you thus proceed,
   IANTH. In tracing human story we shall find
The cruel more successful than the kind.
Whilst you are here submitted to my sway,
It safe discretion were to make you pay
For all those sighs and tears my heart and eyes
Have lost to make you lose your jealousies.
But I was bred in nature's simple school ;
      And am but love's great fool,
      With whom you rudely play,
And strike me hard, then stroke the pain away.
How are your wounds? I hope you find them
      slight?
   ALPH. They scarce will need the rip'ning of a
   night :
      Unless, severe Ianthe, you
      By chiding me, their pains renew.
   IANTH. Was it not jealousy which brought you
   here?
   ALPH. It was my love conducted by my fear.
Fear of your safety, not of virtue, made
The Rhodians, by surprize, this camp invade.
In hope, by bringing home great pris'ners, we
Might set the Rhodians' greater mistress free.
   IANTH. The safety of Ianthe was not worth
That courage which mis-led the Rhodians forth.
The world's contagion, vice, could ne'er infect
The Sultan's heart : but when you did suspect
His favours were too great for me to take,

You then, Alphonso, did unkindly make
    My merit small ; as if you knew
    There was to that but little due.
      Or if he wicked were,
      What danger could you fear ?
Since virtue's force all vicious pow'r controls.
Lucrece a ponyard found, and Porcia coals.
    ALPH. How low to your high virtue shall I fall ?
    IANTH. What chance attended in this fatal night
      The Master, Marshal, and the Admiral ?
    ALPH. I lost them in the thickest mist of fight,
Yet did from Haly this short comfort get
That they to Rhodes have made a brave retreat.
As love's great champions we must them adore.
    IANTH. Be well, Alphonso ! I will chide no more.

*Enter* SOLYMAN, ROXOLANA, MUSTAPHA, PIRRHUS,
    HALY, RUSTAN.

    SOLY. Haly, I did declare that I would see
      The jealous pris'ner ere he died.
    ROX. Look there ! you are obey'd. Yet pardon
      me
Who, ere you pardon'd him, did make him free.
    SOLY. In this I have your virtue tried.
If Roxolana thus revengeless proves
To him whom such a beauteous rival loves,
It does denote she rivals can endure,
Yet thinks she still is of my heart secure.
Duke, this example of her trust may be
A cure for your distrustful thoughts of me.
You may embark for the Sicilian coast ;
And there possess your wife when Rhodes is lost.
    ALPH. Since freedom, which is more than life
      you give
To him, who durst not ask you leave to live :
I cannot doubt your bounty when I crave
That, granting freedom, you will honour save.

My honour I shall lose, unless I share  
In Rhodes, the Rhodians' worst effects of war.  
To Sicily let chaste Ianthe steer :  
And sing long stories of your virtue there :  
Whilst, by your mercy sent, to Rhodes I go,  
To be in Rhodes your suppliant, not your foe.  
    IANTH.   Alphonso, I have honour too ;  
        Which calls me back to Rhodes with you.  
Were this, through tenderness, by you denied  
        For soft concerns of life,  
Yet gracious Solyman will ne'er divide  
        The husband from the wife.  
    SOLY.   Both may to Rhodes return! but it is just  
That you, who nobly did my honour trust,  
        (Without my pass, or plighted word)  
Should more by your advent'rous visit get  
        Than Empires' int'rest would afford,  
Or you expected when you came to treat.  
        Go back, Ianthe ! make your own  
        Conditions boldly for the town.  
I am content it should recorded be,  
That, when I vanquished Rhodes, you conquer'd me.  
    IANTH.   Not Fame's free voice, nor lasting num-  
    bers can  
Disperse, or keep, enough of Solyman.  
    SOLY.   From lovers' beds, and thrones of mon-  
    archs, fly  
Thou ever waking madness, jealousy.  
        And still, to nature's darling, love  
        (That all the world may happy prove)  
Let giant-virtue be the watchful guard,  
Honour, the cautious guide, and sure reward :  
Honour, adorn'd in such a poet's song  
        As may prescribe to fame  
        With loyal lovers' name  
Shall far be spread, and shall continue long.  
                    [*Exeunt omnes.*

## EPILOGUE.

Though, bashfully, we fear to give offence,
Yet, pray allow our poet confidence.
He has the priv'lege of old servants got,
Who are conniv'd at, and have leave to doat ;
To boast past service, and be chol'rick too,
Till they believe at last that all they do
Does far above their master's judgments grow :
Much like to theirs, is his presumption now.
For free, assur'd, and bold his brow appears,
Because, he serv'd your fathers many years.
He says he pleas'd them too, but he may find
You wits, not of your duller fathers' mind.
Which, well consider'd mistress-muse will then
Wish for her old gallants at Fri'rs again :
Rather than be by those neglected here,
Whose fathers civilly did court her there.
But as old mistresses, who meet disdain,
Forbear through pride, or prudence, to complain :
And satisfy their hearts, when they are sad,
With thoughts of former lovers they have had :
Even so poor madame-muse this night must bear,
With equal pulse, the fits of hope and fear ;
And never will against your passion strive :
But, being old, and therefore narrative,
Comfort her self with telling tales, too long,
Of many plaudits had when she was young.

FINIS.

END OF THE THIRD VOLUME.

TURNBULL AND SPEARS, PRINTERS, EDINBURGH